Indirect Taxation
in Developing
Economies

John F. Due

Indirect Taxation in Developing Economies

The Role and Structure of Customs Duties, Excises, and Sales Taxes

The Johns Hopkins Press
Baltimore and London

The Johns Hopkins Press, Baltimore, Maryland 21218
The Johns Hopkins Press Ltd., London

Library of Congress Catalog Card Number 70-119108
ISBN 0-8018-1167-8

Contents

Tables

Preface

Numerous studies and proposals for reform of indirect tax structures have been made in various developing economies. Many of these, however, have not been published, and others are not readily accessible. The general studies have viewed indirect taxation in the context of tax policy generally and have frequently not examined the subject in depth. This study is designed to provide a more intensive analysis of the question than has heretofore appeared, utilizing the growing recent experience with sales taxes in developing economies and drawing where relevant on the experience of more developed countries as well.

No attempt is made here to develop and employ a detailed econometric model, given the limitations of both development theory and empirical data. Instead I indicate some of the conditions that appear to influence economic development, consider the potential effects of indirect taxation upon them, and review experience with various approaches. Nor is an attempt made to use sophisticated statistical techniques to analyze the data available, in part because there are serious questions about the usefulness of such studies on a cross-sectional basis. A more fruitful approach would require time series analyses for a number of countries, a major project in itself that is beyond the scope of this work.

The volume draws upon special studies that I have made in a variety of countries over the last decade, including Venezuela (1958), Honduras (1966), Chile (1968 and 1969), El Salvador (1967), Zambia (1968), the other British Commonwealth countries in Africa in 1962 and 1968, and the Philippines (1969), as well as work in the United States and Canada over a number of years and study of the European sales taxes in 1954. The study has been facilitated by the large volume of literature on value-added taxation that has appeared in recent years in Europe, by the work of Harley

Hinrichs, by a number of World Bank reports, and by other published work. Material for India has been drawn in part from Ph.D. dissertations on sales taxation in that country, particularly those by J. K. Godha (University of Poona) and W. R. Mahler (Syracuse University). Donald Baer provided information from his forthcoming dissertation (University of Illinois) on taxation in Costa Rica and Honduras.

I am indebted to the revenue and finance officials of a number of countries for assistance, particularly those of Honduras, Chile, Zambia, Ghana, Kenya, Uganda, the East African Community, and Canada, and to individuals in a number of countries who supplied current information. The Fiscal Library of the International Monetary Fund allowed the compilation of current data on revenue sources that would otherwise have been impossible. I am indebted to the University of Illinois for providing sabbatical leave in 1968 for the study, to the Department of Economics for assistance, to Mrs. Dorothy Sullivan and Mrs. Wendy Alguero for typing, and to my wife, Jean, for discussion on many aspects of economic development.

                                                                        J. F. D.

Urbana, Illinois

*Indirect Taxation
in Developing
Economies*

1.

The Role of Indirect Taxation
in Developing Economies

Customs duties, excise taxes, and, to a growing extent, sales taxes play a dominant role in the tax structures of the developing economies, as shown in table 1–1. The evolution of the role and structure of indirect taxes as economies develop has been analyzed by Harley H. Hinrichs as a part of his broad study of tax structure change,[1] and the question of the appropriate forms has been reviewed in many studies of taxation and tax reform in specific countries. This study seeks to expand on the work of Hinrichs and others and generalize from the special studies, to present a more complete and synthesized analysis of the changing role and structure of these taxes, and to evaluate various alternative structures and approaches in the light of environmental factors significant for tax policy.

DEFINITIONS AND ASSUMPTIONS

The term *indirect tax* will be used to refer to three categories of taxes: customs duties, excise taxes, and sales taxes.[2] The term is not ideal, since it is used in so many different ways, but it is employed in preference to coining a new one. The term *commodity tax* is sometimes applied to the three categories, but such taxes may apply to services as well as tangible commodities, and this term emphasizes the objects rather than the transactions and the persons involved in them.

The assumption will be made that the taxes are primarily "borne by consumers" in the sense that the reduction in private sector real income that results from the use of resources by government is related to consumption expenditures on the taxed goods. It is further assumed that the result is at-

---

1. *A General Theory of Tax Structure Change during Economic Development* (Cambridge: Harvard Law School, International Tax Program, 1966).

2. A few miscellaneous items such as stamp taxes and motor vehicle licenses are also included.

1

TABLE 1–1. RELIANCE ON INDIRECT TAXES BY PER CAPITA GNP CLASS

Estimated Per Capita GNP, U.S. $[1]	No. of Countries Included	Indirect Taxes[2] as % of Total Tax Revenue (Average)
Developing countries:		
$100 or less	20	68
101–200	11	64
201–500	19	64
501–850	9	50
Highly developed countries:		
Over 850	15	32

Source: See table A–1, appendix. Data given are for latest year available in 1966–69 period.

Note: Information by country is given in table A–1 in the appendix.

[1] "World Bank Atlas," *Finance and Development*, 6 (March 1969), 30–42.

[2] Customs duties, excises, sales taxes, and miscellaneous (primarily vehicle licenses, stamp duties). Export taxes are not included.

tained through increases in prices of consumption goods relative to factor prices (factor incomes), with necessary monetary adjustments made to allow the change in the price level. The same distributional pattern could result if factor incomes fell relative to prices of goods, but typical institutional considerations dictate upward price adjustments for consumer goods. In Richard Musgrave's terminology, a differential approach to incidence is employed, distributional effects of indirect taxes being compared with those of a proportional income tax.

It is recognized that there are exceptions to complete forward shifting of the taxes and thus that a portion of the reduction in real income is distributed in other patterns, specifically through reduction in disposable incomes of certain groups through declines in factor prices. First, firms making more than average profit may find it disadvantageous to raise prices by the amount of the tax. The real incomes of the owners of the firm are therefore reduced. With quantitative controls over imports, domestic sales and excise taxes may be absorbed by domestic producers out of economic rents. The existence of excess profits or economic rents does not ensure absorption of the tax, however. Second, the prices of factors specialized to the taxed industries may fall as less of the commodities are purchased and the factor units cannot find employment in other fields at equal remuneration.[3] Third, the reduced purchases of imported goods may lower the prices at which the commodities are available from abroad if they are produced with specialized factors whose prices decline or if the foreign firms reduce prices net of tax to be able to continue to sell within the country. To the extent that this occurs, no one within the country experiences a reduction

3. This is the traditional increasing-cost industry case. It is assumed that the decline in demand for the factor is not offset by governmental use of the factor.

in real income. But the tax does not curtail aggregate demand, and inflationary consequences will determine the pattern of income redistribution. Fourth, to the extent that purchases from abroad fall as a result of the tax, the ability of foreign countries to purchase the exports of the taxing country falls; export sales then decline and the owners of factors specialized to the export industry experience a reduction in real incomes. Finally, long-run supply schedules of various factors may be altered differently by indirect taxes than by other taxes. For example, a higher cost of subsistence may reduce the birth rate or increase infant mortality and thus ultimately reduce the supply of labor.

The significance of these exceptions will vary with the circumstances of the country and are impossible to ascertain even for a particular country. For lack of better information and on the basis of casual common sense evidence, the assumption is employed that typically the exceptions are not important and therefore that the taxes are distributed primarily on the basis of consumption spending.

THE GOALS OF DEVELOPING ECONOMIES

The goals to be pursued by the government in a developing economy are specified by the dominant political group in the society—the persons responsible for governmental decision-making. The decisions may be made on a democratic basis, reflecting a consensus of the population as a whole. They may be made by a small elite group that, as in many African countries, is genuinely concerned with the welfare of the people. Or they may be made by a dictatorship primarily motivated by concern for the personal welfare of the dictator and his associates; but even such persons rarely ignore entirely the desires of large segments of the population. Regardless of the location of political power, there is a remarkable similarity of goals in the various developing countries. Differences relate primarily to the relative emphasis given various goals, the means of attaining them, and the intensity with which they are pursued.

Four goals are dominant in most developing economies:

1. Acceleration of Growth

In the last two decades, virtually all developing economies have placed great stress on acceleration of economic development, more specifically on raising per capita real income to the level of the developed countries as quickly as possible.

2. Pattern of Income Distribution

Maintenance or attainment of an acceptable pattern of distribution of the gains from development is given major importance. The nature of acceptable patterns varies widely. Some governments, such as those of Tanzania and Zambia, stress the importance of minimizing inequality in income and are willing to sacrifice some growth in national income to ensure the desired pattern. Other countries, such as Kenya, place relatively greater stress on growth. In ones dominated by small groups of wealthy persons, such as some Latin American countries, maintenance of existing patterns of inequality may be a major, although rarely explicitly stated, objective.

3. Resource Allocation

Developing economies are concerned with the utilization of resources so as to best satisfy the wants of the community (or the dominant group in the community). Waste of resources is a more serious matter in a developing economy than in ones with high incomes. The precise resource allocation objectives vary. In some countries national prestige or personal whims of the dominant group take precedence over consumer preference. As a consequence, resources are allocated to prestigious but uneconomic steel mills or jet airlines.

4. Price Stability

Although regarded as secondary to other goals, maintenance of a relatively stable price level is an objective in most economies.

Both governmental expenditure programs and revenue structures can influence the attainment of these goals. In most developing economies today, the government is regarded as the primary instrument for achieving them. But the exact roles assigned to government and to private enterprise vary widely, from the predominantly governmental economies such as Burma and mixed economies such as Zambia and Tanzania, with strong emphasis on the role of the government in production, to the more strictly free enterprise economies of the Philippines, Honduras, and Nicaragua. This study is concerned only with the tax aspects and specifically with the role of a major class of tax under the assumption that expenditure levels and patterns are likewise directed in optimal fashion toward the attainment of the objectives of the economy.[4]

4. With this assumption, an analysis of actual expenditure programs is, in the author's estimation, not necessary for a definition of optimal tax structures except insofar as the benefit approach to taxation is accepted. The scope for this approach would appear to be very limited in developing economies. A somewhat different point of view is presented by S. Andic and A. Peacock, "Fiscal Surveys and Economic Development," *Kyklos*, 19, no. 4 (1966), 620–41. They maintain that an optimal program must be defined in terms of both taxation and expenditures considered jointly.

A DEVELOPMENT MODEL

To analyze the effects of indirect taxation on the attainment of the goals of the developing economies, a development model must be employed. This requirement inevitably presents a dilemma. Should we choose a simple model that is mathematically solvable if the coefficients are available and that has relatively limited data requirements? Or should we adopt a more complex model that includes more of the significant determinants of development but also has many variables that cannot be quantified and much greater data requirements so that a mathematical solution is not feasible? The great dangers with the first type of model are that it will be misused and that it will provide quantitative answers that will not reflect actual behavior because significant determinants are omitted. But so little knowledge of the significant coefficients (e.g., elasticity of demand for imported goods in a particular developing economy) is now available that precise quantitative analysis is not possible. There is therefore little merit in simplifying a model to the point at which it might theoretically become solvable. Thus the model presented here—which is, of course, only one of many possible—is too complex for quantitative solution. But by calling attention to a number of determinants of development it may help to avoid serious errors in framing tax policy.

In summary form: the rate of economic growth, defined as the annual increase in per capita real income (Y/N), is a function of:

1. The rate of capital formation: the annual increase in total capital stock (K); $\Delta K = I$ (investment).

2. The incremental capital output ratio (ICOR): the relationship between an increase in capital stock and the consequent increase in output $(\Delta K/\Delta Y)$.

3. The rate of technological change (t): the rate of increase in new available technology, which affects the quantity of output that can be obtained from a given quantity of factor units.

4. The rate of increase in quantity and quality of natural resources, labor, and entrepreneurial activity (r). Improvement in the quality of labor depends in part on improved consumption patterns and improved health.

5. Modifications in the institutional environment (v).

Thus the basic relationship may be expressed as

$$\Delta Y = f (\Delta K, \Delta K/\Delta Y, t, r, v).$$

The actual coefficients will vary with the circumstances of the country and are difficult to ascertain with accuracy.

Each of these determinants requires a brief analysis.

1. The Rate of Capital Formation

The annual net addition (I) to a country's stock of capital goods, K, is controlled by (a) the potential or "required" rate of capital formation permitted by the rate of savings and the rate of net inflow of foreign capital, which sets the maximum, and by (b) investment opportunities that determine the actual level of investment. This may coincide with or be less than the potential rate.

Specifically:

a. Potential or full-employment capital formation, I_p, is a function of (1) the rate of savings (S/Y) and (2) the net flow of foreign capital. Real capital formation cannot exceed the sum of the excess of income over consumption (net savings) plus the sum of foreign capital available for investment.

b. Actual capital formation, I_a, which cannot exceed I_p, consists of two parts, private investment (I_{av}) and governmental investment (I_{ag}). Private investment depends upon (1) the potential rate of return from capital investment, which determines the willingness of business firms to undertake real investment; (2) the availability of entrepreneurship; (3) the willingness of entrepreneurs to take the risk of investment; (4) certainty of expectation of future earnings; and (5) the extent of mobilization of money capital to permit potential entrepreneurs to obtain the necessary funds.

The expected rate of return depends upon potential sales of the product and thus upon total income and expenditure patterns, the extent of foreign competition, expected trends in national income and population, and expectations of political stability, among other elements. Governmental investment is determined through the governmental decision-making process.

2. ICOR: The Incremental Capital-Output Ratio

The significance of a higher stock of capital goods for growth in per capita real income is measured by ICOR ($\Delta K/\Delta Y$). ICOR, in turn, depends upon:

a. The nature of the new capital goods relative to demand for goods to be produced with them. As an extreme example, construction of a sugar mill that lies idle from the time it is completed because of lack of sugar cane adds nothing to output. A factory producing goods for which demand is sufficient to allow capacity operation has a low $\Delta K/\Delta Y$ ratio, that is, the amount of capital necessary for a unit of additional output is low. The contribution is even greater if the investment facilitates the development of additional industrial or agricultural activity, as do certain types of processing.

b. The allocation of total investment between infrastructure and capital that results in additional output of physical goods. The direct additional output from investment in infrastructure may be slight, although this investment may be essential before other forms of investment can take place. Once the basic infrastructure is completed, additional capital formation is likely to result in a much greater rise in output and thus ICOR will be lower.

c. The scale of operations of the capital employed. With economies of scale, the larger the market and thus the scale of operations, the greater the additional output per unit of additional capital.

d. The ability to import capital equipment. Since most developing countries cannot produce capital equipment, investment must take a relatively primitive form, with low output per unit of input of capital, unless capital goods can be acquired from the outside. The ability to import capital goods is a function of (1) total exports, (2) inflow of foreign capital, (3) imports of consumption goods and services, and (4) net depletion of foreign exchange reserves.

e. The organization of inputs. Failure to maximize organizational efficiency will reduce output per unit of additional capital.

3. Technological Change (t)

Distinct from the effects of a greater stock of capital goods are those of changes in technology; capital formation involves in part the embodiment of these changes, although some of the changes may occur without capital formation. In a developing country, technology is largely "borrowed" from abroad, and therefore developments within the country have little significance for the existence of improved technology. Education, however, may play a major role in the introduction of the new technology.

4. Increases in Quantity and Quality of Other Resources (r)

These include:

a. Natural resources. Discovery and development of new natural resources allow increased output per capita.

b. Labor supply. An increase in the supply of workers from a current given population allows greater output per person (though perhaps less per labor-hour). This additional supply may result from a greater intensity of labor, a willingness to work longer periods, a shift of underemployed persons in the agricultural sector to the commercial-industrial sector, and an increased willingness of women to enter the labor market. Improved health standards also increase the supply of labor-hours. An increase in population, on the other hand, while leading to greater output by raising the labor supply, also increases the number of persons among whom the total output is distributed. The net effect on Y/N is therefore unpredictable.

c. Quality of labor. Higher levels of skill and education appear to constitute a major source of rise in per capita real output. Thus investment in educational facilities may have substantial effects on development, as will immigration of skilled workers. Improved food supplies and health facilities play an important role in improving the quality of labor.

d. Management skill. This is of particular importance for economic development.

e. Use of resources in government. For example, use of resources for tax collection and other administrative purposes may decrease.

5. General Environment (v)

Economic development is influenced by changes in the overall environment: in the attitudes of persons toward abandoning traditional procedures, in the organization of markets, in the legal framework, in family relationships, in elimination of tribal hostilities.

POTENTIAL EFFECTS OF TAXATION ON DETERMINANTS OF GROWTH

Taxation affects economic development in two major ways: by altering the determinants of economic development and by permitting the financing of current governmental activities and governmental or government-financed private investment without the undesirable effects of other methods of financing.

Our primary concern in this study is with indirect taxes. Since the principal alternative is direct taxation, the most suitable approach is to compare the relative effects of these two general forms, specifically indirect taxes and income taxes. Indirect taxes, under the assumptions, enter into the development model in the form of higher prices for consumption goods relative to the prices paid factors (factor incomes). Accordingly, the reduction in real income necessitated by absorption of resources by government is distributed in relation to consumer expenditures on the taxed goods. In contrast, income taxes enter the model by reducing disposable income, the amount of tax being related (in proportional or progressive fashion) to the income earned. The appropriate comparison is between indirect taxes and income taxes of equal yield in real terms.

1. Capital Formation

a. Potential Capital Formation. (1) The private sector S/Y ratio. All taxes are likely to affect the overall private sector rate of savings or S/Y ratio, and the level of potential private investment. To the extent that taxes can be established in such a manner as to raise the S/Y ratio, the potential rate of private sector capital formation will be increased. There is always danger of the reverse: that taxes will primarily absorb income that would otherwise be saved, that is, that tax payments will be regarded as a substitute for saving rather than for consumption and thus provide an incentive to consume more and save less.

Indirect taxes, under the assumptions, are directly related to consumer spending rather than to receipt of income. Accordingly, it is frequently argued that such taxes will reduce consumption more and savings less than income taxes and will therefore allow a higher private sector S/Y ratio than an income tax yielding equivalent revenue. An income tax, since it applies to the return from saving, reduces the net return from saving, whereas an indirect tax affects the real return from saving only when the earnings are spent on consumption. This argument is less valid than it may appear to be. It is now generally recognized that a reduction in the net return from saving does not necessarily reduce the amount of saving. Both income and substitution effects operate, and persons may save more to reattain previous incomes. Thus a consumption-related tax has no inherent advantage. But for several reasons indirect taxes are likely to have a greater effect:

(*a*) Indirect taxes have a greater relative impact on families spending high percentages of their incomes. Many of these persons must reduce consumption because they have no margin of saving or because their saving is of a contractual nature and they cannot reduce it easily. Direct taxes have a greater relative impact on families with larger margins of savings.

(*b*) To the extent that income taxes are progressive, their relative effect in curtailing saving is likely to be greater. The more progressive the tax, the more significant becomes the substitution effect, since the sacrifice necessary to maintain the old level of income becomes progressively greater. Indirect taxes are not directly progressive relative to income, even if the overall pattern is progressive.

(*c*) Indirect taxes may be made progressive relative to consumption of the category of purchases most substitutable for saving—namely, luxury consumer durables. Indirect taxes, even if not highly progressive relative to overall income, may be progressive relative to the types of expenditures that increase rapidly as income rises.

(*d*) The money illusion may be important with indirect taxes. Persons may continue to spend the same amount on consumption despite the price increase and absorb the entire tax through a reduction in net consumption expenditure. There is no similar phenomenon with income taxes.

(*e*) The motives for savings may be unrelated to future consumption. Persons may regard a current escape from indirect taxes by not consuming as a permanent avoidance of the tax rather than mere postponement. With these motives, the volume of savings is unaffected by the return on savings, the substitution effect does not operate, and the income effect will dominate. Mere accumulation per se, the desire to develop and expand a business, and the desire for an emergency reserve are significant goals not related to returns.

(*f*) So long as business firms are able to shift forward the indirect taxes that rest on them directly or indirectly, the taxes will not reduce business savings, an important segment in total savings. Income tax structures that include corporate incomes, as virtually all do, have a greater impact on business savings.

The net difference, therefore, between indirect and income taxes will be influenced by a number of considerations: the effect of a net reduction in the returns from savings on the total volume of savings, the progressivity of the two forms of tax, the importance of the money illusion, the significance of various motives for savings, and the importance of savings by business firms. While no a priori conclusions are possible, there is at least a presumption that indirect taxes will usually permit a somewhat higher S/Y ratio than income taxes yielding the same revenue.

(2) The flow of foreign capital. To the extent that taxes reduce the net return from foreign capital and absorb earnings of foreign-owned businesses or any funds that would otherwise be expatriated, they reduce the outflow of capital and increase the net inflow (positive or negative). Taxes also affect the flow of foreign capital by lessening inflation and government borrowing and by increasing the confidence of foreign investors.

Indirect taxes have no direct effect on the earnings of foreign-owned enterprises, whereas income taxes reduce the returns and make investments by foreigners less attractive. At the same time, however, income taxes provide a means to absorb a portion of the earnings from these investments and check the outflow of money capital. The net effect depends on the relative strength of these two forces.

b. Actual Capital Formation. Taxes may affect investment incentives and therefore the ability of an economy to attain the potential rate of capital formation:

(1) Rate of return on real investment. Any tax that reduces the net return makes investment less attractive and, other elements given, is likely to reduce its volume.

Income taxes, if not shifted forward to consumers, directly reduce the rate of return. Indirect taxes, per se, reduce earnings by lowering total consumption. The latter effect is in general offset by the government's expenditure of the funds. If with a balanced budget the offset is not complete and unemployment develops, a reduction in the level of the taxes should restore investment, full employment, and the rate of return, although some of the advantage of indirect taxes in allowing a higher S/Y ratio is sacrificed when this occurs. Expenditure of the funds does not automatically eliminate the reduction in the rate of return due to income taxes, and a reduction in the level of taxes may not accomplish the offset or may do so only if the deficit is very large. Indirect taxes are therefore likely to have some net advantage, the extent depending upon (1) the sensitivity of real investment to the rate of return, (2) the ability of the government to adjust the level of indirect taxes sufficiently to offset any net deflationary effect arising from their greater impact on consumption, and (3) the relative propensities to consume of the persons affected by the two forms of tax.

There are two other possible sources of difference. High excise taxes on commodities offering particularly high rates of return may depress total investment so drastically that changes in the level of taxes cannot offset the effect. On the other hand, protective import duties raise the rate of return on investment in industries producing the protected products, while income taxes have no similar reactions.

(2) Availability of entrepreneurship. This is little affected by either form of tax except as modified by other factors discussed in this section.

(3) Willingness to take risk. When returns from all investments are reduced by taxes, the substitution effect encourages persons to take less risk (since they receive less compensation for risk-taking); the income effect encourages them to take more risk to maintain their incomes. A proportional income tax may increase total risk-taking rather than reducing it. The more progressive the income tax, the greater is the likelihood of an adverse effect. Indirect taxes have no similar impact on return, but may reduce risk-taking by reducing confidence in the prospects of the market.

(4) Certainty of expectation of future earnings. Taxes directly reduce expected future earnings and may affect expectations of future profits by their influence on political stability. A tax that creates widespread popular opposition may endanger the existing government and bring about its defeat or an armed revolt, with possible chaos and a government less (or in some cases more) favorable to private investment. Neither major form of tax holds an obvious advantage in this respect.

(5) Availability of money capital to business firms. Mobilization of capital is often imperfect in developing economies, with inadequate mechanisms for transfer of funds to persons who wish to use it. Therefore taxes on business incomes, which primarily absorb funds that would otherwise be used for expansion, particularly restrict capital formation. Indirect taxes have less adverse effect of this type.

2. The Incremental Capital-Output Ratio

By affecting ICOR, taxes will alter the rate of increase in output resulting from a given rate of capital formation.

a. The Nature of Capital Investment. Taxes may alter this in a number of ways. Taxes may favor, accidentally or deliberately, certain forms of investment over others, particularly through differences in tax rates, in impacts on markets, or in allowable deductions for depreciation and depletion.

Income taxes offer greater opportunities for directing real investment into the most productive channels through tax credits and adjustment of depreciation allowances. Indirect taxes may accomplish this goal to some extent if placed on capital goods at varied rates, but this approach may restrict overall investment. Excises on particular consumption goods will deter investment in these fields.

b. Scale. All taxes, by reducing private sector consumption, reduce the possibilities of attaining economies of scale when government purchases are made for other purposes. Indirect taxes offer greater risk of reducing attainment of economies of scale because they are likely to concentrate on manufactured goods, particularly consumer durables, for which scale is important.

c. Importation of Capital Goods. Taxes may reduce the importation of capital goods by making them more expensive, or taxes may increase such imports by raising the supply of foreign exchange available to buy them.

Indirect taxes, particularly customs duties, offer a major potential advantage in reducing the consumption of imported luxury goods, thus lessening the drain on foreign exchange and facilitating the importation of goods required for optimal capital formation. Income taxes dampen luxury consumption somewhat but not to the same degree, because the tax liability is not directly related to expenditure.

d. Organization of Inputs. One of the greatest dangers of taxes for ICOR is their possible influence upon factor combinations and methods of organizing production. If taxes are not neutral among various alternative combinations, the use of favored ones will be artificially increased, to the detriment of maximization of output from given resources. Alternatively, taxes may at times facilitate optimum factor combinations by stimulating firms to greater efficiency or by making price and social costs more nearly equal.

Indirect taxes, particularly sales and excise taxes with direct impact upon business firms, offer greater hazards in this area than income taxes. As discussed in subsequent chapters, it is very difficult to design sales taxes that will be entirely neutral among various structures of production and distribution. Income taxes may have some effect on the incentive to maximize efficiency, but they are more easily designed to treat the alternatives uniformly.

3. Technological Change

Since developing economies import most new technology, taxes are not likely to affect technological change by altering research activity, as they may do in more developed economies. Taxes may restrict technological change by favoring some methods of production over others, and by restricting capital formation they may check the embodying of new technology.

4. Factor Supplies

Taxes may increase or reduce the total quantities of factor supplies available for use in production.

a. Natural Resources. The nature of the tax structure may significantly affect the willingness of persons to undertake the discovery and exploitation of natural resources, in light of the heavy risk often involved. Income taxes reducing the returns may discourage development. On the other hand, certain forms of taxes on land, primarily those independent of current earnings, will encourage more intensive use of land and may bring better utilization by forcing the breakup of large estates. In other instances, however, such a breakup will reduce output. Effective utilization of forest land will also be affected.

Indirect taxes offer less discouragement to the development of new natural resources than income taxes, but at the same time they offer less potential for encouraging it by varying depreciation and other allowances. Neither indirect nor income taxes have the advantages enjoyed by taxes on land.

b. Labor Supply. Taxes may alter the total supply of labor-hours available and the relative supply of various types of labor. Their influence on the total supply is generally believed to be slight. The income effect encourages people to work more as their incomes are reduced by taxes; the substitution effect encourages them to work less and enjoy more leisure. The net effect cannot be determined analytically. If people seek only a fixed living standard—as some groups in developing economies may do—higher taxes will lead them to work more. If they are highly ambitious to raise their income levels, there is greater danger of adverse effects.

Indirect taxes have similar effects, but the less direct connection between the earning of the income and the payment of the tax lessens the influence. When saving is an important objective and is undertaken primarily for motives other than future consumption, indirect taxes are likely to have less adverse impact than direct taxes. But in an economy where additional income is desired solely for additional consumption, this advantage is lost. The primary difference is likely to arise out of the difference in the progressivity of the two taxes and the ability of direct taxes to force subsistence workers to seek employment or sell produce, since they must pay taxes in money. Indirect taxes have no such effect.

Taxes that alter the relative gains from various occupations may affect the relative flow of workers into them. Taxes highly progressive relative to income may reduce the flow into occupations requiring extensive training if monetary motives are dominant but may have little effect if other motives control the decisions. The treatment of the income of wives may affect their willingness to enter the labor market. Taxation of monetary income while subsistence income is untaxed increases the attractiveness of the latter and may drive some persons out of the commercial sector, but taxes on persons solely in the subsistence sector may force them into the commercial sector. Taxes on "incentive goods"—those urgently desired by persons with low incomes—may lessen their willingness to leave the subsistence sector; taxes on basic necessities may drive low income workers below subsistence and impair their ability to work.

c. *Quality of Labor and Entrepreneurial Skill.* While the quality of the labor force is greatly influenced by governmental expenditures, the potential effects of taxes may be minor. The tax structure, however, may affect the willingness or even the ability of persons to obtain additional education and training for themselves and their children and of employers to train new personnel. Tax structures and levels may affect the willingness of expatriates to come to the country or may drive highly trained personnel from the country. Indirect taxes that reduce the consumption of goods essential for health and energy will reduce the overall quality of the labor force.

d. *Resources Used for Tax Administration.* Resources—particularly labor, skilled management talent, and capital equipment—utilized for collection of taxes and compliance with taxes are not available for use in production. Thus the fewer resources so used, the greater the potential output of the economy.

In developing economies, many indirect taxes can be collected with adequate efficiency at less cost than direct taxes and thus with less drain of resources from other uses. The primary reason is that the number of taxpayers—importers, manufacturers, or merchants—is smaller. Import duties can be forced through the "bottleneck" of customs houses. While withholding (PAYE) greatly simplifies the collection of income taxes, the tax must still be collected from a larger number of taxpayers, which makes evasion easier and increases the need for control if enforcement is to be effective.

5. General Environment

Taxes may be effective in upsetting traditional patterns. If they must be paid in money, they may lead subsistence farmers to sell produce. A head tax on cattle may force pastoral tribes to market their cattle. A progressive tax on the number of wives may check polygamy. Income taxes appear to have a greater potential effect than indirect taxes because they can be adapted to personal circumstances.

POTENTIAL EFFECTS OF TAXATION UPON THE RATE OF GROWTH:
LEVEL OF GOVERNMENTAL EXPENDITURES

To the extent that particular taxes allow the raising of more money than others, they increase the potential contribution of governmental activities toward economic development. The size of the tax base and a host of political, economic, and administrative considerations determine the potential yield of various taxes,[5] and the effectiveness of administration influences the actual yield. The most significant merit of indirect taxation is its ability to raise much more revenue than would be politically, economically, and administratively feasible with direct taxes.

This conclusion is valid to some extent in developed economies; it is much more significant in developing ones. The political strength of the wealthier groups is often sufficiently strong to restrict increases in direct taxes. High direct taxes may restrict savings, real investment, and development. The administrative complications, especially for incomes other than wages and salaries and for those from larger firms, are so great that large collections are difficult. In countries in the early years of economic development, most of the people are living at bare subsistence levels, with limited money income. The level of literacy is often low. While poll or graduated personal taxes may raise some revenue, no direct tax can, as a practical matter, yield large sums. Indirect taxes on imports and domestic sales provide a much more effective way of reaching this large semisubsistence population. Only by exacting some contribution from this group can economic development proceed at the fastest possible rate.

The revenue elasticity of the yield relative to changes in national income varies with different forms of taxes. The yield of some does not increase as fast as national income, and thus constant rate changes are necessary to maintain relative revenue. Inertia and political considerations restrict these changes. Taxes—particularly those on income—that have a revenue elasticity of more than 1 ensure that the government will automatically receive a growing share of total national income as development continues. To the extent that consumption lags behind income as income rises, indirect taxes offer less revenue elasticity than direct taxes. But the lag is likely to be much less in countries in the early years of development than in more developed ones.[6]

5. See J. R. Lotz and E. R. Morss, "Measuring 'Tax Effort' in Developing Countries," *International Monetary Fund Staff Papers* 14 (November 1967), 478–99.

6. Dharam Ghai found revenue elasticity for excises to exceed that for income taxes in Uganda for the period 1951–63. His projection to 1970, however, showed elasticity of less than 1. *Taxation for Development* (Nairobi: East African Publishing House, 1966).

G. S. Sahota found a surprisingly high 1.6 revenue elasticity figure for union government excises in India in the 1951–52 to 1957–58 period, much higher than the figures for the income tax. *Indian Tax Structure and Economic Development* (New York: Asia Publishing House, 1961), pp. 16–17.

TAXATION AND THE DISTRIBUTION OF INCOME AND WEALTH

In any economy, the tax structure, which determines the pattern of reduction in real income arising from governmental use of resources, has a major impact upon after-tax patterns of income and wealth distribution. The distributional pattern depends not only on the immediate changes in disposable incomes and in prices of consumer goods relative to factor incomes, but also on secondary changes in relative factor incomes, which are often difficult to ascertain. Even the more direct effects are not easily traced, in view of the uncertainty of the actual effects that taxes have on commodity and factor prices. Despite these problems, the distributional patterns of various taxes appear to differ substantially. Highly progressive income taxes will alter distributional patterns more than universal flat-rate consumption taxes. High customs duties and excise taxes on luxury goods will cause different patterns than more general levies. The pattern of land taxes will be different in many countries from that of other levies.

By widely accepted standards—especially in many developing countries—income and wealth are regarded as the most acceptable measures of taxpaying capacity. But luxury consumption is also widely accepted as an alternative, in part as a proxy measure of income and wealth, in part as a significant measure in itself. In addition, all consumption over bare subsistence may be regarded as an indicator of some ability to pay. Thus indirect taxes are acceptable, if properly designed, as one suitable instrument for reaching persons on the basis of ability. But alone they are inadequate measures, particularly in those countries in which some persons have large incomes that are used for purposes not reached by indirect taxes, such as land, gold or precious stones, foreign travel, personal servants, or investments abroad. Such persons can be reached only by taxes on income or wealth. Similarly, consumption-related taxation is inadequate in reaching families with vast holdings of land and concentrations of wealth.

While indirect taxes are inadequate, by usual standards, as sole measures of tax capacity, the case for primary use of them as a second-best substitute is strengthened if income and land taxes cannot be enforced effectively, as is often true in a developing economy. Primary difficulties arise with the self-employed, including business and professional men and farmers. Records are inadequate; literacy is low; in some countries the businessmen are primarily persons of foreign origin whose loyalty to the government and interest in the development of the economy may not be strong. Outright bribery, common in some countries, may be more prevalent with direct taxes. Thus, indirect taxes, if administered reasonably well, may in fact be more equitable than direct taxes that are poorly enforced. Accordingly, it may be acceptable to rely on them more heavily than would otherwise be regarded as optimal.

TAXATION AND RESOURCE ALLOCATION

Virtually any tax will have some effect upon resource allocation; even a uniform income tax will reduce consumption—and thus production—of some goods more than others because of differences in income elasticity. The relative tax burden by income level will affect the nature of the cutbacks in production. These effects are anticipated and accepted. But taxes may also have more positive effects. Levies such as excises that alter relative prices of various consumption goods will obviously affect consumption patterns and resource allocation. These changes may be desired—developing economies often seek to lessen luxury consumption—or they may be unintended. Taxes that alter the costs of producing some products compared with others will likewise affect relative prices and resource allocation.

Indirect taxes offer greater potentialities than direct taxes for influencing allocation of resources to priority uses but, if improperly designed, may divert production into nonoptimal patterns. Excises or higher sales tax rates can be used to reduce the production of goods not regarded as essentail for development and thus to channel resources into the production of higher priority goods under the assumption that demand is not perfectly inelastic. If the demands are highly inelastic, the output of untaxed goods will fall as well as that of the taxed goods. By the same token, excises on goods not regarded as undesirable from a development standpoint will reduce output of these goods relative to others and thus create an "excess burden." General sales taxes with no exemptions and uniform rates have little or no diverting effects, resembling income taxes in their influence on resource allocation.

The greatest danger to optimal resource allocation from indirect taxes is created by customs duties. Even though imposed for revenue purposes, they are almost certain to provide some unplanned and unwanted protection and stimulate the development of inefficient domestic production.

TAXATION AND STABILITY

Per unit of revenue, some taxes have more anti-inflationary effect than others. The ideal tax from this standpoint is one that curtails consumption by a sum large relative to the amount of the tax but that neither reduces work incentives nor leads to pressures to increase wages or other costs. Such taxes are difficult to design. In general terms, the overall anti-inflationary effectiveness depends upon the extent to which spending is reduced, the effects upon incentives, and the effects upon costs.

Indirect taxes dampen inflationary pressure by raising prices relative to factor incomes; income taxes do so by reducing disposable income and thus the ability to consume. There is no inherent advantage of one approach over the other except for the frequently lower revenue elasticity of the indirect taxes, which weakens their automatic stabilizing effect. Indirect taxes, which are related to consumption rather than income, may induce people to consume less and save more, as noted above. On the other hand, by raising prices of consumption goods they may generate demands for wage increases, which in turn increase cost-push inflationary pressures. As with growth, the greatest contribution of indirect taxes is the greater total revenue they make possible, thus lessening the danger that expenditures will outrun revenue and produce inflationary pressure.

The overall revenue elasticity of taxes relative to changes in national income is important for stability as well as for governmental revenues. A high degree of elasticity ensures that revenue will rise more rapidly than prices in an inflationary period and thus dampen inflation. On the other hand, revenue will fall more rapidly than income in periods of unemployment, reducing the downward pressure on national income without the need for legislative action to reduce tax rates.

SUMMARY OF ADVANTAGES AND DISADVANTAGES OF INDIRECT TAXES

In the attainment of the objectives of developing economies, indirect taxes offer several major advantages:

1. They make possible greater governmental revenue for financing of infrastructure and capital investment and permit a higher rate of economic development than would otherwise be possible without resort to excessive creation of money.

2. They may restrict luxury consumption more effectively (per dollar of revenue) than other taxes, allowing a higher rate of savings and capital formation. This effect is particularly facilitated by the use of high rates on luxury purchases.

3. They can be used to restrict importation of luxury goods more effectively than other taxes, thus conserving foreign exchange for purposes more significant for economic development.

4. They require less administrative effort for effective collection and reduce the drain on resources for this purpose. Because the collection is more effective they may be less inequitable relative to direct taxes than they are in more developed economies.

5. As luxury consumption is a relatively good measure of taxpaying ability in most developing countries, they provide a more equitable distributional effect than they do under other conditions.

6. By their selective nature on particular forms of consumption, they facilitate the control of resource allocation.

7. They may be less harmful to incentives than direct taxes.

Other advantages are likely to be somewhat incidental.

The greatest weakness of the indirect taxes is their inability to reach high concentrations of income and wealth as effectively as direct taxes.

Accordingly, they can appropriately play a greater role in countries characterized by relatively equal distribution of wealth and income (such as many tropical African countries) than in those with marked disparities. Indirect taxes may also distort the organization of productive factors with a consequent loss of efficiency in production, and they can create consumer "excess burdens" and discriminate against families on the basis of preferences. They offer less potential than income taxes for influencing the direction of capital investment and the use of savings and for luring people out of the subsistence sector. Finally, as explained in subsequent chapters, implementation of indirect tax structures to attain desired objectives encounters many problems. There is always the danger that customs duties, the easiest levies to collect in early years of development, will produce unwanted protection and loss of efficiency.

Objectives in Framing Indirect Tax Structures

An optimal indirect tax structure may be defined as the one that best facilitates the attainment of the objectives of the particular society. The optimal structure and rates of taxes, therefore, depend upon the goals accepted in the society, the relative weights attached to the different goals, and the coefficients in a development model that adequately explains growth in the particular society. Optimality of indirect taxes can be considered only in terms of the overall tax structure, and therefore simultaneous optimal adjustment of other elements of the structure is assumed. Optimality can be defined only in terms of a particular economy at a given time, in view of differences in objectives and in coefficients in the development model.

Accordingly, generalizations about an optimal system are of limited significance. Nevertheless, given the usual objectives—rapid economic growth, acceptable patterns of income distribution, optimal resource allocation, and reasonable stability—and given what appears to be the general nature of the functions in the development model, several statements of conditions necessary to attain the optimum are possible.

1. Optimal Growth

a. Attainment of total tax revenue consistent with the maximum rate of economic growth. Expenditures and taxes should be extended to the point at which the estimated marginal contribution to growth from use of resources in the governmental sector is equal to the marginal loss in growth from transfer out of the private sector. This level can be ascertained only very roughly.

b. Maximization of the rate of capital formation in the private sector, given the ratio established between private and governmental spending.

Indirect taxes are likely to increase the S/Y ratio and thus the potential rate of capital formation. Care must be taken to ensure that the depressing effects of lowered consumption upon capital formation do not prevent attainment of the potential rate of capital formation. Clearly, indirect taxes should be designed to avoid adverse effects on real capital formation. For example, they should not be applied to capital goods and artificially increase the cost of real investment. In one major respect indirect taxes can increase the profitability of investment—that is, by protecting industry against foreign competition. But this gain must be balanced against possible adverse effects on resource allocation.

c. Minimization of the incremental capital-output ratio. Since importation of capital goods is usually essential for optimal investment, maximum restriction of importation of luxury consumer goods is advantageous. The indirect tax structure must not interfere with optimal organization of factor inputs by making some methods of production or organization of economic activity more expensive relative to others. The effects of indirect taxes on the scale of production must be considered, as well as the effects in stimulating import substitution that would reduce efficiency in use of resources.

d. Minimization of adverse effects on the introduction of new techniques of production. This objective requires that indirect taxes not increase the relative cost of new capital goods necessary for the embodiment of technological change.

e. Maximization of the supplies of factors. Taxes should be designed to avoid or minimize adverse effects on factor supplies and if possible to increase the supplies. Thus taxes must not destroy labor incentives, as they might if commercial sector goods were made too expensive relative to labor incomes. They must not push workers below subsistence levels or interfere in other ways with improvements in the quality of labor. The drain of resources for compliance with and administration of the taxes must be minimized.

2. Optimal Equity

The pattern of distribution of the tax burden must coincide with the patterns regarded as optimal. By usual standards, this requires a distribution progressive relative to income and thus concentration of tax upon spending in the higher income levels, with minimum levy on the consumer spending of subsistence groups, which make up much of the population in developing countries. Whether these groups should be burdened at all is a matter of the society's attitudes. Apart from overall patterns, avoidance of discrimination among individuals on the basis of unacceptable criteria is necessary as well as enforcement adequate to prevent extensive evasion.

3. Optimal Resource Allocation

To the extent that indirect taxes can bring resource allocation more closely in line with desired patterns, they will facilitate the overall attainment of goals. Thus differentiation of rates between imported and domestic goods and among various domestic products must coincide with desired patterns of reallocation. Higher taxes on luxury goods, for example, will aid in transfer of resources to production of goods more important for development.

4. Stabilization

Overall stabilization is assisted if the revenue elasticity is maximized, a result accomplished in part by including in the base of the tax expenditures that rise rapidly as income rises. Indirect taxes must also be designed in such a way as to minimize stimulation of wage increases.

THE NEED FOR TRADE-OFFS

Structural features that further certain requirements may also do so for others; high rates on luxury goods may increase the equity of the structure, facilitate optimal resource reallocation, and restrict demand for imported goods. Duties on imports may lessen consumption of luxuries and at the same time aid domestic investment. But frequently the various requirements conflict, and trade-offs are required to obtain an optimal balance among them. There are many possible instances of need for trade-offs:

1. Potential versus actual capital formation. Taxes that increase the S/Y ratio increase the potential rate of capital formation but, by reducing consumption, may make actual attainment of it more difficult.

2. Protection versus efficiency. Taxes that discriminate against imported goods encourage domestic investment and industrial output but reduce efficiency in the use of resources since some goods are being produced within the country at greater cost.

3. Administration versus equity, restriction of luxury consumption, and organization of production. Requirements for the most efficient compliance and enforcement may conflict sharply with other needs. Making a sales tax rate uniform over a wide range of goods, for example, simplifies collection but lessens the equity of the tax and its ability to restrict the consumption and importation of consumer durables. Higher rates on luxuries and exemption of basic necessities make the operation of the tax much more difficult. Exclusion of producers goods from tax may be difficult to accomplish administratively.

4. Revenue versus equity. Maximum revenue may require a very broad-based tax; the pattern of the burden may be regarded as contrary to accepted principles of equity.

5. Equity and incentive effects. High taxes on certain luxury items—incentive goods—may be desirable on the bases of equity and restriction of consumption, but may make people less willing to seek higher incomes.

6. Political versus economic considerations. Programs that drastically reduce consumption and importation and increase governmental revenue may offer great potential for aiding growth, but they may give rise to such strong political protests that implementation becomes impossible. Even a fear of effects on political stability may lessen real investment by reducing the certainty of future profits. Governments have sometimes been overthrown because they increased consumption taxes too drastically. The ability of a government to carry through a program of optimization of indirect tax structures, therefore, depends upon the reaction to the program and the government's ability to withstand protests. These, in turn, are influenced by the general popularity of the government, attitudes toward the use of the revenues, the extent to which the public is convinced of the benefits of the policies, and the acceptability of governmental institutions.

OVERALL PROBLEMS OF DEVELOPING OPTIMAL INDIRECT TAX SYSTEMS

The attainment of an "optimal" indirect tax structure is impossible, except by sheerest accident. The best that can be attained is a rough approximation, one that avoids obvious departures from the optimum.

The first difficulty is the inability to attain precise specification and quantitative weighting of various objectives. How much weight shall be given to rapid growth compared with equity, for example? Such decisions can be made only by a government itself, reflecting, at least in a democracy, its interpretations of the consensus of thought in the society. The decisions are usually made only implicitly and crudely, with no attempt at quantitative weighting.

Second, since the coefficients of the development model are not known in any economy, the magnitude of the effects of various policies in the attainment of the goals cannot be measured. More specifically, information is lacking in varying degree on the following:

1. The significance of an increase in the S/Y ratio for the rate of growth. It is now rather evident that feasible increases in S/Y in developed economies have relatively little effect on economic growth, but this conclusion is not necessarily valid in developing countries.

2. Relative effects of different taxes on real investment.

3. Effects of changing tax policies on expectations of future earnings from investment.

4. Price and income elasticities of demands for various goods. These are significant for the effects of tax policies designed to restrict consumption and importation of luxury goods.

5. ICOR and the effects on it of changes in input combinations, scale of operations, and other determinants.

6. Optimal factor combinations and the degree of interference with their attainment by various taxes. If, for example, a particular type of indirect tax increases vertical integration in production, what is the actual effect on total output?

7. Effects of various taxes on the labor supply.

8. Administrative requirements and the potential effectiveness of enforcement.

9. The distribution of the burden and thus the acceptability of the pattern of income redistribution resulting from various taxes. The taxes may not be fully reflected in consumer prices, and factor prices may change; and accurate data on consumer expenditures by income group are often not available even in developed economies.

10. The significance of various taxes for resource allocation, partly because the optimality of the allocations before the tax is not known.

11. The effect of higher indirect taxes in stimulating wage increases.

Thus any precise establishment of an optimal system is impossible. But consideration of the various objectives, the requirements for their attainment, and the various elements determining growth should help to minimize the adverse features of a tax structure and approach the goals more closely than a purely haphazard system. Present-day knowledge permits nothing more. The ideal—an adequate econometric model with all coefficients available and with simulation of alternative taxes until the overall optimal structure is ascertained—is very far from realization.

SUMMARY OF REQUIREMENTS

Subject to all the limitations stressed above and to the requirement that taxes be adjusted to the circumstances and objectives of the particular society, the following general rules for indirect tax structures would appear to have validity:

1. Revenues from indirect taxes should be maximized subject to the constraints noted, with accompanying maximization of other tax revenues.

2. The taxes must apply to a wide range of mass consumption goods if revenues are to be maximized.

3. Taxes should be uniform on consumer expenditures on various goods except where there is specific justification for differentiation.

4. Much higher rates should be applied to goods consumed primarily in the higher income groups for equity, restriction of luxury consumption, and protection of foreign exchange.

5. Taxes on "incentive" goods—those the lowest income groups are striving to obtain (for example, bicycles in many countries)—must not be so high as to discourage attempts to increase incomes.

6. Indirect taxes should be designed to restrict importation of luxury consumer goods to make foreign exchange available for developmental purposes. The foreign exchange position and the merits and limitations of protection should determine the extent to which duties should be used to encourage import substitution.

7. Rate differentiation must be tempered by its adverse effects on effective operation of the taxes.

8. Taxes should not apply to capital goods except when designed to discourage unwanted types of real investment or to discourage excessive capital intensity.

9. Taxes should be neutral among various methods of production, organization of production, and distribution except when certain methods are deliberately to be discouraged.

10. Taxes should have the lowest possible costs of compliance and enforcement, subject to attainment of the other objectives.

11. The taxes must be politically acceptable to avoid endangering the stability of the government. Educating the public to the need for the taxes is a significant element in the success of a tax program.

SUPPLEMENTARY REFERENCES

Bird, R. M. *Bibliography on Taxation in Developing Countries.* Cambridge: Harvard Law School International Tax Program, 1968.

_____. *Taxation and Development. Lessons from Colombian Experience.* Cambridge: Harvard University Press, 1969.

_____, and Oldman, O. *Readings on Taxation in Developing Countries.* Rev. ed. Baltimore: Johns Hopkins Press, 1967.

Brochier, H. "Les Problèmes de L'Impot Indirect dans les Pays en Voie de Développement." *Revue de Science Financière,* 57 (July–September 1965), 369–85.

Hicks, Ursula. *Development Finance.* London: Oxford University Press, 1965.

Hinrichs, H. H. *A General Theory of Tax Structure Change during Economic Development.* Cambridge: Harvard Law School International Tax Program, 1966.

Musgrave, R. A. *Fiscal Systems.* Chaps. 5, 6. New Haven: Yale University Press, 1969.

Organization of American States. *Fiscal Policy for Economic Growth in Latin America.* Joint Tax Program, Organization of the American States/Inter-American Development Bank/United Nations Economic Commission for Latin America. Baltimore: Johns Hopkins Press, 1965.

_____. *Problems of Tax Administration in Latin America.* Joint Tax Program, Organization of the American States/Inter-American Development Bank/United Nations Economic Commission for Latin America. Baltimore: Johns Hopkins Press, 1965.

Peacock, A. T. "Fiscal Policy for Economic Development in Theory and Practise." In A. T. Peacock, ed., *Public Finance as an Instrument for Economic Development.* Paris: Organization for Economic Cooperation and Development, 1965.

Peacock, A. T., and Hauser, G., eds. *Government Finance and Economic Development.* Paris: Organization for Economic Cooperation and Development, 1965.

Prest, A. *Public Finance in Underdeveloped Countries.* London: Weidenfeld & Nicolson, 1962.

2.

The Role and Structure of Customs Duties as a Source of Revenue

One of the oldest forms of taxation is the customs duty, imposed upon the importation of goods.[1] As stressed by Hinrichs, simple direct taxes, such as the poll tax, are the pioneer forms of taxation, but customs typically came to play a major role in tax structures as development progressed from the most primitive years.[2] Customs duties now constitute a major revenue source for developing economies, yielding on the average about half of indirect tax revenues and a third of total tax revenues, as shown in table 2–1. As explained later in the chapter, customs decline in importance as development continues.

Customs duties enter the development model as supplements to the prices of imported finished products and imported inputs. With given exchange rates and world export prices and in the absence of domestic production, prices to consumers rise by the amount of the customs duties, and the duties reduce real income in proportion to consumer spending on the dutiable goods, as domestic indirect taxes do. There are obviously potential exceptions. If exchange rates were flexible, the reduction in the volume of imports would increase the foreign exchange value of the country's money, thus reducing the "burden" of the tax on consumption and shifting a portion to the producers of export commodities. Since flexible exchange rates are virtually unknown in developing economies, this possibility is not a significant one. If the duty stimulates domestic production, domestic prices rise without revenue yield. The "burden" on consumers is no longer a share of the costs of governmental activities but an excess burden produced by

1. From a collection standpoint, duties resemble fees or charges; they constitute payment for a specific privilege and are collected before the privilege is granted. But they are classified as taxes, not fees, because the amounts bear no relation to the cost of related governmental services.
2. Hinrichs, *General Theory of Tax Structure Change.*

TABLE 2–1.   RELIANCE ON CUSTOMS DUTIES IN DEVELOPING ECONOMIES (BY GNP CLASS)

Estimated Per Capita GNP, U.S. $	No. of Countries	Customs Duties as % of:[1]	
		Total Indirect Tax Revenue (Average)	Total Tax Revenue (Average)
Under 101	20	52 (59)	35 (41)
101–200	11	50[2] (59)	32[2] (39)
201–500	19	51[3] (57)	33[3] (35)
500–850	9	38	18
Over 850	15	12	4

Source: See table A–1, appendix. Data are for latest year available in 1965–69 period.
Note: Information by country is given in table A–1 in the appendix.
[1] Figures in parentheses give total collections at customs, including sales tax revenue collected at importation.
[2] Nine countries; customs duty collections not segregated from other collections at customs for 2.
[3] Eighteen countries; customs duty collections not segregated from other collections at customs for 1.

loss of efficiency in resource utilization. But the basic assumption of distribution of governmental costs in relation to consumer spending on taxed goods appears to be a reasonable one.

MERITS OF THE USE OF CUSTOMS DUTIES FOR REVENUE PURPOSES

Customs duties offer several advantages to a developing economy of particular importance in the earliest years of development.

1. Customs duties provide a technique for attaining the objectives of indirect taxation (noted in the previous chapter) that is administratively more feasible initially than domestic taxes. As a consequence, the need for trained administrative personnel is less and the potentiality of effective enforcement is much greater. Customs administration, as subsequently noted, requires some highly trained personnel, but relative to revenue the number is small compared with that required for most domestic taxes. The reason for the difference is that imports may be forced through the "bottleneck" of a few custom houses, since the tax must be paid before the goods may enter the country. As a consequence, a relatively small trained staff plus the unskilled personnel required to make sure that goods actually pass through custom houses can operate the tax.

Because of the ability to enforce payment more effectively, in the early years of development the total potential revenue from duties is much larger than that from domestic indirect taxes. Use of customs, or at least collection of indirect taxes at customs, allows a larger yield even after a country has attained a substantial degree of development.

2. Customs duties are particularly effective devices for accomplishing a major objective for economic development: restriction of imports of consumption goods, particularly those of a "luxury" nature, and of capital goods not regarded as significant for economic development. To the extent that high duties on such goods reduce their importation, they produce no revenue, but they may significantly aid development more easily than alternatives such as prohibition of importation. At the same time the duties may increase the overall S/Y ratio; if luxury goods are not imported and are not produced in the country, persons may save more of their incomes. Influence upon the types of capital goods imported may result in a lower incremental capital-output ratio (ICOR) than would otherwise be attained. Furthermore, by reducing the demand for foreign exchange the duties will lessen the tendency for foreign exchange crises to develop, with the consequent need for drastic controls over imports or unwanted devaluation.

3. Since the duties do not apply within the domestic sector of the economy, they are less likely to interfere with incentives for domestic production and with the organization of inputs in production than are domestic indirect taxes. By varying the rates of duty on different types of capital goods, the government can use the customs system to influence relative investment in various lines of industry in conformity with the development plan.

4. At the same time, by discouraging importation of the taxed goods, the duties encourage import substitution—the establishment of domestic industries to produce the high duty products—if the duty equals or exceeds the cost differential between domestic and foreign production, given the exchange rates. Such protective effects may conform with overall development plans. As subsequently noted, however, they may also be undesirable.

5. Finally, in a developing economy customs revenues meet accepted standards of equity to a reasonable degree, far more so than in highly developed countries. So long as most goods consumed by the higher income groups but not by the lower are imported, a duty on all except basic necessities (most of which may be domestically produced anyway) is likely to be the most effective way of placing a heavier burden on the higher income groups. In developing countries there are commonly sharp differences in the consumption patterns of higher and lower income groups, in contrast with highly developed countries. In view of the difficulties most developing economies have in administering progressive income taxes, a system of customs duties may be far more equitable in practice, however desirable the introduction of an income tax may be. The same may hold in comparison with a poorly administered domestic indirect tax.

Customs duties are not without objectionable features, particularly as development continues, as will be noted later in the chapter.

To summarize, in terms of the development model presented in Chapter 1, customs duties offer the following advantages:

Effects on Determinants of Growth

S/Y ratio. Since many luxury goods consumed in a developing economy are imported, taxing them will discourage luxury consumption and increase the S/Y ratio.

Investment. By providing protection, even though not deliberately sought, duties encourage domestic investment (although perhaps at the expense of efficiency in resource use). They also avoid the adverse effects on domestic investment that both direct and internal indirect taxes may have.

Importation of capital goods. Duties on consumption goods free foreign exchange for capital goods essential for development. This represents perhaps the greatest contribution of duties.

Resources for tax collection. Duties, because they are relatively easy to enforce compared with domestic indirect taxes, require fewer resources for administration.

Effects on Total Governmental Revenue

Particularly in the earliest years of development, duties allow a government to collect much more revenue than could possibly be obtained from other sources and therefore to obtain more resources for development.

Equity

Duties are relatively equitable by usual standards in the earlier years of development when most luxury goods are imported.

OPTIMAL TARIFF STRUCTURE: INTERNATIONAL CONSTRAINTS

In framing its tariff structure, a country is subject to certain international restraints that must be considered as well as its domestic requirements. For centuries countries imposed tariffs without the restraint of international agreements, although they might be wary of possible retaliation. Since World War II, however, several steps have been taken to increase uniformity and cooperation in the tariff field. The first was the creation in 1948 of GATT—the General Agreement on Tariffs and Trade—to liberalize restrictions on the flow of trade. The agreement provides:

1. A generalized MFN (most favored nation) rule whereby concessions given to one signatory country will be shared with all others. Exceptions are concessions (a) under existing preference systems, such as those of the British Commonwealth, and (b) within customs unions and free trade areas.

2. Stress on tariff reductions made through negotiations among particular countries, with agreement that duties reduced through negotiations are not to be raised again except to prevent dumping or the destruction of a domestic industry. This escape clause is sometimes used to sabotage the general intent.

3. Prohibition of quantitative controls of imports except when required (a) to restore the balance of payments, (b) because of domestic restrictions on agricultural output, and (c) when essential for economic development planning of less developed countries.

4. Prohibition of indirect discrimination against imports or artificial assistance to exports. Thus internal taxes must apply equally to imported and domestic goods, and refunding of taxes on exports is limited to indirect taxes, which are presumably reflected in the prices of the goods.

5. Provision of machinery for the settlement of disputes.

In subsequent years, following the first United Nations Conference on Trade and Development (UNCTAD), GATT has stressed the responsibility of the more developed countries to aid in the growth of the less developed ones.

Most Western countries, developed and developing, are contracting partners of GATT. Developing countries may hold observer status, and several have preferred this to full membership. A member gains the advantages of cooperation with other countries but of course subjects itself to restraints in the tariff field, although these are not particularly significant for duties designed primarily for revenue. The primary restriction is on applying different tariff rates to imports from various countries, except as covered by the special provisions.

GATT has no real power to enforce its rules, and many countries— including the United States and Canada—have not always followed them strictly. If a country complains of a violation, the GATT headquarters in Geneva attempts to get the countries to reconcile their differences. If an offender will not agree to follow the terms of the agreement, members may withdraw their concessions to it. But in practice, in part because of generous escape clauses and the loosely-knit nature of the organization, violations are frequent and are often ignored. Nevertheless GATT has made significant contributions to freer trade.

To make GATT policies more specific, the Customs Cooperation Council was formed in 1950, with close ties to the Organization for Economic Cooperation and Development (OECD), and headquarters in Brussels. The council has accomplished two major tasks: the development of a uniform customs classification, called the Brussels Tariff Nomenclature (BTN), and the adoption for custom valuation of the open market selling price with CIF (that is, delivered) basis. Most contracting parties of GATT have become members of the council and have accepted the two conventions,[3] and other countries that are not members have adjusted their tariffs to the BTN basis.

OPTIMAL TARIFF STRUCTURE: DOMESTIC REQUIREMENTS

Given the international restraints, the structure of the tariffs must be such as to obtain the maximum contribution toward the attainment of the goals of the society.[4]

Vertical Consistency

Goods may be imported in finished form or in various stages of production from basic materials on. If relative rates are not established with care, that is, if the effective protection rates of tariffs are not recognized instead of nominal rates the structure may retard development.[5] If a relatively heavy duty is placed on the product at an early stage of production and a lower rate at subsequent stages, an incentive will be given to import the finished product instead of the materials, which will be tax free in the production process in the foreign country. Even if the country does not deliberately seek to encourage fabrication within the country, it scarcely wishes to discourage it. To avoid this, materials usually bear little or no duty while the finished products bear a much higher rate. But if import substitution develops as a result, with materials imported, the duty revenue may be entirely lost. There may be some gain (or loss) to the economy from the protective effect, but the revenue is gone, and while the total foreign exchange spent on the goods will be less (by the amount of domestic value added) it may still be substantial. This effect is particularly

3. The chief exceptions are Canada and the United States, which have very complex tariffs and have traditionally used constructive valuations extensively and an FOB basis. The United States became a member of the council in 1968, but has not modified its tariff structure.

4. One of the few analyses of this question is to be found in H. Bachmann, *The External Relations of Less Developed Countries* (New York: Praeger, 1968).

5. The effective protection rate expresses the relationship of the tariff to domestic value added rather than to gross value, taking into consideration both the input coefficients and the tariffs on the inputs. In other words, the effective rate is the percentage increase in value added per unit made possible by the tariff structure compared with the free trade situation. A nominal rate of 50 percent on wool cloth represents a 25 percent effective protection rate if the imported wool constitutes 50 percent of the value of the cloth, a 50 percent effective rate if the wool is also subject to a 25 percent duty. The question of effective rates has been discussed at length in the literature in recent years; see, for example, B. Belassa, "Tariff Protection in Industrial Countries," *Journal of Political Economy*, 73 (December 1965), 573–94; W. M. Corden, "The Structure of a Tariff System and the Effective Protective Rate," *Journal of Political Economy*, 74 (June 1966), 221–37; R. J. Ruffin, "Tariffs, Intermediate Goods, and Domestic Protection," *American Economic Review*, 59 (June 1969), 261–69; and H. G. Grubel and H. G. Johnson, "Nominal Tariffs, Indirect Taxes and Effective Rates of Protection," *Economic Journal*, 77 (December 1967), 761–76.

objectionable if, as frequently occurs, the domestic production involves little more than packaging, assembling, or blending, with little domestic value added—the "cake mix" import situation. The cost in the form of lost revenue and lessened suitability of the revenue system may be very great. The solution in such instances is either continued taxation of imported materials or an excise tax on the finished product.

Horizontal Patterns

Use of several rates of duty may facilitate attainment of the goals of the tariff system. First, high rates can be established for protective purposes. Second, higher rates can be placed on goods consumed primarily in the higher income groups to provide a more progressive distribution of the tax burden. In practice the selection of goods for higher rates is frequently not based on a study of consumption patterns, although in earlier years of development virtually all imported consumer goods are bought by higher income groups. Third, higher rates can be imposed on those goods whose use hampers economic development or at least makes little contribution to it, such as liquor. Selection of goods for the higher rates is somewhat arbitrary, but the usual high rates on liquor and tobacco reflect a consensus on the negative contribution of these goods. Fourth, goods regarded as making particular contributions to development, such as sources of needed vitamins or medicines, can be freed of duty or given low rates. Bicycles can be treated similarly if they increase worker mobility; contraceptives, if they reduce the birth rate. High rates can be applied to products such as motor fuel to finance governmental activities related to the use of the product.

Rate variation may also be desired to lessen inequality of ratios of duty to final consumer expenditures on various goods. Suppose that a government wishes to have the same duty burden on consumer expenditures for radio sets and cosmetics. The former are imported directly by retailers, who sell them to the final consumers with a margin (and thus value added) of 30 percent of the retail price. Perfume, however, is imported by wholesalers, who advertise it extensively and repackage it in expensive containers. The total margin, we assume, is 60 percent. If the commodities were subject to the same duty rate, the effective rate on cosmetics would be only half that on perfume. Thus a higher rate is required on those goods with high domestic value added.

Rate differentiation, no matter how carefully designed, has certain disadvantages. Application of the tariff is more complicated; a single rate would simplify many aspects of operation. Differentiation of customs duties, like that of excise and sales taxes, results in arbitrary lines between closely related products, with discrimination on the basis of consumer preferences and possible undesired distortion of resource allocation. Critics of differentiation also argue that the variation produces a less desirable pattern of import substitution—inevitable to some extent, even when not sought—than a uniform rate. A uniform rate would automatically stimulate production of those commodities for which the country had the least relative disadvantage and would reduce consumption of the least desired imported goods. Tariff differentiation substitutes the government's decisions about development for the automatic ones of the market economy. Apart from protective aspects, a uniform rate would reduce imports of those goods least desired by consumers.

To the governments of developing economies these arguments are untenable, under the philosophy that the governments must substitute their decisions for those of the market to speed development. The imports with the most elastic demands may be those highly important for growth; those with the least elastic demands may be ones of little consequence. The demand for milk needed for child health may be far more elastic than that for liquor. Furthermore, development must be based on an overall integrated plan; the priority for import substitution must go to those goods most essential for the plan. Differentiation is usually regarded as necessary for equity, to place relatively heavier burdens on the higher income groups and to free from tax most of the purchases of the lowest income groups.

While rate differentiation is essential in light of the goals, it is desirable to limit the number of separate rate classes to a few, perhaps three or four, apart from special cases such as liquor. Fine distinctions cannot be justified in terms of the goals, and administratively the use of a small number of rates is imperative. Many tariffs have grown up with numerous rates and fine distinctions that multiply complications with no gain.

Necessities

If revenue maximization were the sole goal in the establishment of a tariff, duties would be placed on articles widely purchased by the lowest income groups. Textile products often constitute the largest category of imports in terms of monetary value and are widely consumed. In food-importing countries, certain basic foodstuffs such as rice, powdered milk, or coffee may be important. The demand for these products may be highly inelastic, and import substitution may not be encouraged by low rates—or at all. Taxation may thus be highly productive of revenue. But such a tax may be contrary to accepted standards of equity because it places a disproportionate burden on the lowest income groups, which may be considered to have no tax capacity. Taxation of these basic items may result in wage increases, shifting forward the burden of the duty and increasing costs in export industries. On the other hand, a government may desire some contribution from these groups and regard customs duties as more effective than income, poll, or graduated personal taxes in reaching them.

Capital Equipment

In view of the importance attached to increased investment in developing economies, capital equipment is usually freed from duty or subjected to a low rate except when protection of domestic producers of the equipment is desired. Similar policies are also usually followed for agricultural, electric power, and commercial transport equipment (except for motor trucks, which are frequently subjected to some duty, partly on the benefit basis). The only significant objection raised to this policy of exemption of capital equipment is that application of a duty would encourage less capital intensive methods of production, particularly important if duties on basic necessities raise labor costs. This argument is not easily resolved; it is considered at length in chapter 7.

A major complication arises with dual-use goods—ones that may be used for either consumption or production, with the ultimate use unknown at the time of importation. There is no ideal solution. Establishment of liability for duty on the basis of ultimate use seriously complicates the enforcement of duties because the use may not be known at the time of importation and because statements of importers about use are difficult to check. Another approach is to allow manufacturers to import such items for production duty free and to apply duty to other importations of the goods, refunding the duty if the goods are subsequently sold for industrial use.

SPECIFIC VS. AD VALOREM RATES

Most early tariffs used specific rates; the Swiss tariff remains completely specific down to this day. A specific duty may apply on the basis of units of product (cigarettes) or measured units (for example, square feet).[6] Specific rates have the primary advantage of ease in application; no valuation is necessary, and no evasion of duty by understating values is possible. This basis has additional merit when the aim is to obtain a uniform amount of duty per unit of the product regardless of price, as is true with motor fuel, based upon the benefit principle, or alcoholic beverages, on which the duty is linked with the alcoholic content on a sumptuary basis. Most tariffs continue to use specific rates for liquor and tobacco products, petroleum and petroleum products, motor vehicle tires, and in some instances fabricated metal in various forms. As noted below, specific rates are also used in conjunction with ad valorem rates on certain classes.

Specific rates are subject to many limitations, however, which make their general use progressively more difficult as a country develops. One is

6. Or arbitrary units of value established by law and not adapted to actual sales value, as the *aforo* of the Argentine tariff for many years.

that some classes of commodities are made up of a large number of items of different character, use, and value. Hardware is an excellent example; there are thousands of different items. Specific rates would require a tremendous number of separate entries and would constantly become obsolete as products changed.

Second, specific rates discriminate against cheaper varieties of a product because the duty is a larger percentage of their selling price than are those of expensive types. This not only discourages use of the cheaper brands but also makes the customs system regressive, since the lower income groups will buy more of the cheaper brands and types. If the levy has a benefit or a sumptuary basis, the consequence may be regarded as acceptable, but otherwise it is contrary to usually accepted standards of equity. To meet this problem, tariff items are sometimes broken down into subitems based on price and quality (a common practice with cigarettes).[7]. But this procedure complicates application of the tariff and requires determinations of value, thus losing much of the advantage of the specific duty.

Third, with a specific tariff structure, uniformity of duty to consumer expenditures—or intended variations from uniformity—is virtually impossible to attain. This is true even when a tariff is created, but it is particularly so after a lapse of time as relative prices shift.

Fourth, the absolute rates of specific duties become obsolete as prices change. The problem is particularly severe in a period of rapid inflation. The ratio of duty to selling price falls in proportion to increases in the prices of the goods; tariffs are rarely revised rapidly enough to offset this effect.

Fifth, maintenance of vertical consistency in the tariff is difficult. Materials may easily be overtaxed relative to finished products and domestic producers injured.

Finally, specific duties produce one operational problem not arising with ad valorem rates—the need for physical measurement. This is easy with some products but is time-consuming with others (bolts of cloth, for example).

Because of these limitations, ad valorem rates have become dominant in most tariffs despite the valuation problem. Specific rates are retained mainly for high duty commodities for which sumptuary or benefit considerations are important and which are relatively uniform in price and quality and limited in categories. Some countries, however, have retained many specific duties, more for reasons of inertia and tradition than logic. In other instances, specific duties have been retained in combination with ad va-

7. There are eighteen classes of cigarettes in the East African tariff.

lorem duties: a certain amount per physical unit plus an ad valorem percentage.

Many countries, including most developing ones, have retained *minimum* specific rates for many commodities. The primary rate is ad valorem, but the duty cannot be less than a designated specific figure. This dual system is employed primarily for textiles, clothing, shoes, and cheaper kitchenware, to protect revenue on very cheap items imported from India, Hong Kong, Taiwan, and other Asian countries. Domestic value in these countries is difficult to ascertain and dumping and collusion of importers and exporters are frequently suspected. The use of a relatively low specific minimum avoids some difficulties of the specific approach, but it does complicate the application of duties and results in a relatively high burden on economy items of certain types of garments or shoes.

In summary, the ad valorem approach is greatly to be preferred as a general rule. Specific rates, if used at all, should be confined to a few well-defined categories with little variation in quality or price and with high duty rates, which increase the tendency to undervalue. Specific rates are most justifiable when benefit (motor fuel) or sumptuary (liquor) considerations are important.

CLASSIFICATION

If a tariff applied at a uniform ad valorem rate to all commodities, no classification would be necessary. But in practice such a policy would be contrary to usually accepted goals of tariffs.

1. For the goal of protection, a government desires to tax finished products more heavily than materials, parts, and other producers goods and to protect certain industries without imposing high rates on goods that the country cannot produce or can produce only at serious disadvantage.

2. Governments will tax "luxuries" more heavily than necessities, in the interests of equity of burden distribution and to conserve foreign exchange.

Classification can be established in very broad categories or in relatively narrow ones. This latter policy may be a result of domestic production of only certain subclasses of the items (certain sizes of tires), the desire to make concessions to certain countries and not to others (in exchange for concessions by the former), and in some instances to attain distributional goals. A progressive scale can be established for motor vehicles on the basis of purchase price or engine capacity.

Forms of Classification

No single system of classification can satisfy all the goals. Several bases are used:

1. Specification of a commodity by name—for example, matches, malt extract, and molasses.

2. Specification of a broader class of items by designation of the nature of the articles—wheeled toys, or railway track fixtures and fittings. The difference between this and the first basis is only a matter of degree.

3. Establishment of items by content—tube and pipe fittings of aluminum, yarn of sheep's wool, or fabrics of cotton. General categories established in this fashion usually have final "other" classes to pick up non-specified items made from the materials.

4. Specification by general use or specific use in a certain instance— "vegetable materials *of a kind* used primarily in brushes," "essential oils *for use in* the manufacture of perfumery." In the second instance the duty is determined by the *actual* use, in the former by *general* use.

5. Other bases include: (*a*) weight or capacity, for instance, engine capacity of motor vehicles; (*b*) value per unit; (*c*) state of preparation (assembled or not); (*d*) whether packaged or in bulk; (*e*) specific purchaser (such as a hospital); and (*f*) whether the good is of a kind made in the country.

Tariffs typically have catchall or "not otherwise specified" categories to reach items not listed (for example, all articles of wood not otherwise specified) or not falling within any category. With some tariffs this class is highly significant.

Complications Produced by Classification

Classification of commodities complicates the operation of a tariff.[8] This result is in part inevitable and in part is aggravated by the extent and nature of the classifications employed.

1. The Meaning of Terms. Terms are not always unambiguous or generally accepted. This is true even of apparently clear-cut terms such as bread. But particular problems are encountered with broader categories, such as farm machinery or vehicles, and with categories with qualifying adjectives such as "ornamental." Decisions can be made on particular items, but these may not be uniformly applied, and new products and forms of products are constantly being developed.

2. Determination of Appropriate Classification. Duty status often rests upon the interpretation of the nature of the good. Is a sundial, not mentioned in a tariff, a timepiece or an ornamental object for garden use? Are fancy snap fasteners for garments clothing accessories or jewelry? Are aluminum household trays aluminum hollow ware or "other" aluminum

8. Good examples are found in the Canadian-American Committee study by F. Masson and H. E. English, *Invisible Trade Barriers* (Washington: National Planning Association, 1963).

products? In the broader categories, questions are numerous. Is a particular piece of equipment "other machinery" or "other products of iron or steel"? The use, content, and nature of categories may overlap, and questions of primary determination arise. Descriptions of classes often end with the phrase "and the like," one always open to interpretative questions.

3. *Interpretation of the Contents Basis*—what something is made of. How rigidly is the category to be defined? Does the presence of a tiny amount of silk thread in a garment mean that it is not made of cotton and thus must bear a higher rate? When a commodity is made up of several ingredients and the tariff statement uses the term "made primarily of," is this to be interpreted in terms of weight, volume, or what? In some instances the contents may be very difficult to determine, for example, the species of spruce from which particular lumber was milled. In other instances the exporter may be unwilling to reveal secret formulas.

4. *Mixed Commodities*. A simple instance is a dual-purpose article— a combination pen and pencil. Many questions arise over parts and accessories, either attached to a product or shipped separately. Is a radio antenna a portion of the car or a separate item subject to a separate duty? Shipments of parts for assembly or for repair and replacement may contain articles (bolts and nuts) that can be used for other purposes; do these constitute parts or not? Special containers with other uses (a household pail in which detergents are sold) may or may not be subject to duty separately.

5. *Classification by Use*. The statement "of a kind generally used for" is highly subjective, and interpretations may differ. Classification on the basis of use may create no problems if the good is imported by a processor using it for one purpose. But if it is imported by dealers who sell it to others, the use is not known at the time of importation. Many goods can have uses for which exemption is not desired as well as uses for which it is.

6. *The Qualification "of a Kind Made within the Country."* One aspect is the breadth of the category; does the domestic category have to be exactly the same or only similar, serving the same purpose? How much production must there be in the country to constitute "made within the country"? (Ten percent of total consumption is sometimes used as a rough guide.)

Some Consequences of the Classification Problems

The classification problem creates several undesirable results:

1. Because of questions, customs clearance and settlement of liability are delayed.

2. The exporter and importer are often uncertain about liability, particularly when a firm is considering exporting to the country for the first

time or when new products are developed. Because of the uncertainty, the firm may not undertake the venture or may lose heavily if it does.

3. It is difficult to treat all importers uniformly, especially when new products are involved. Various customs officials will interpret the classification differently, and much time may elapse before this is discovered by higher authority.

4. Innovation may be restricted. Firms may be reluctant to change products or methods because of uncertainty and possibly higher duty. The exact nature of a product or processing methods may also be altered solely to reduce the duty, with consequent loss of economic efficiency. The textile sections of the tariffs of some countries produce sharp differences in duties between materials that are essentially identical but have been produced on different types of equipment.

5. The classifications may operate differently than intended and produce undesired results. Interpretations may be different from what the government intended when the legislation was enacted. The classifications may become obsolete; trade in the "standard" type of a product receiving a low rate may give way to others subject to much higher rates. Classifications may not produce expected results. The engine capacity basis for taxing motor vehicles, for instance, encourages adjustment of engines to give the same horsepower with lower cubic capacity. This may result in imports of more expensive cars with lower engine capacity and increase, rather than decrease, the drain on foreign exchange.

Solutions

Some of the problems noted are inherent in any classification system. But they have been aggravated by governmental policy, and adjustment of tariffs and procedures can ease them.

1. Much of the difficulty stems from the contents and intended use bases for classification. In some instances these bases are imperative, but minimizing them will reduce the problems and adverse effects. The contents basis can produce particularly serious effects on resource allocation when two articles capable of serving the same function have widely different duties because their contents are different.

2. The use of numerous fine subdivisions of categories is the source of endless difficulty. Many of these divisions arise from a desire to protect some items of a class and not others; rarely do they arise from revenue considerations. Attainment of this protection must be tempered by consideration of the consequences for operation of the tariff system.

3. Many tariffs have large numbers of rates with only minor differences. The problems are lessened by minimizing the number. The fewer the rates, the fewer the interpretative questions.

4. Adequate procedures for ensuring uniformity among custom houses, for giving prompt interpretative answers, and for settling disputes quickly are imperative. Nonuniformity and delays can be disastrous to firms.

5. Use of common sense, with reference to legislative intent, facilitates satisfactory interpretations.

Brussels Nomenclature

Since exporters typically sell to a number of countries, uniformity in tariff classification facilitates the conduct of foreign trade. In the late fifties, the Customs Cooperation Council, in preparing the Brussels Tariff Nomenclature (BTN), sought to develop a generally acceptable classification system that would avoid the unworkable delineations of many tariffs, as well as other complications. The tariff contains 1,095 headings (about 1,600 individual items) grouped into 99 major categories. It is much less complex than the United States and Canadian tariffs (neither country has accepted the BTN), but it looks much more complicated than those of many less developed countries, such as those of East Africa before the change to BTN in 1968. Despite the greater complexity, however, the BTN causes fewer interpretative problems than the simple tariffs, which have fewer specific categories so that many commodities fall into "other" classifications.[9] A further advantage of the BTN is that its structure facilitates compilation of data of imports by use, as required for input-output and national accounts data, although the actual duty does not ordinarily depend upon the specific usage. The BTN also facilitates international comparisons of trade statistics.

The transition to BTN requires careful planning, first to convert the tariff itself to the new form without making undesired changes in rates and then to educate customs personnel and importers to it. Great Britain in 1958 and East Africa in 1967 and 1968 provided a six-month "instructional" transition period during which importers were asked to indicate both old and new classes to gain experience with the new system before the actual change was made. Requiring the exporter to indicate the BTN class number on the invoice facilitates the task of importers. The advantages of the change are great—particularly that of uniformity—while the transitional problems are minor.

VALUATION

Were all duties imposed on a specific basis and were there no concern with dumping—that is, the sale of goods into the country at prices much

9. This has been the experience in East Africa, for example, according to officials of East African Customs and Excise.

lower than they are sold elsewhere—no customs valuation would be necessary. But the broad customs systems of today necessitate ad valorem rates, and even if they did not, fear of dumping would lead to some valuation effort.

In developing and developed economies alike, the question of customs valuation is of prime importance in view of the very high rates (100 percent or more on certain products, with 40 to 75 percent common). When sales taxes are collected at importation as well as on domestic sales, as in Ghana, Uganda, and Mali, for example, the pressure to reduce liability is increased still more.

Undervaluation takes two forms. The first is deliberate understatement of value below the actual sales figure or below the open market value in order to evade the full duty. The second is sale by the exporter below what may be regarded as a reasonable selling price in order to dispose of a portion of his output in the foreign market in competition with domestic firms. This second form is more appropriately regarded as avoidance rather than evasion. If tariffs were established for revenue only, this variety of undervaluation might well be ignored, just as the same practice is for sales taxes, but from a protective standpoint it is very important.

Invoice Price

There are several possible approaches to valuation, as noted below. The simplest value figure to employ is the actual invoice price, since it is readily available and clearly defined. Clearance is simplified and speeded. With this approach, transport costs to the border or port may be excluded (FOB) or included (CIF). The former was the traditional approach, for reasons not obvious. Its effect is to eliminate the cost of transport from the originating country, including sea freight and land freight within the country of origin. FOB lessens the advantage of suppliers close at hand by offsetting to some extent the differences in transport costs, thus facilitating the entry of more distant suppliers into the market and increasing competition.

The trend has been toward CIF or, for many countries, CIF-port, in part because this basis was endorsed by the Brussels Convention. The CIF base is larger, and thus lower duty rates will accomplish desired objectives. More significantly, by using a base closer to the figure of consumer expenditures on the goods, CIF provides a more uniform ratio of duty to these expenditures. Transport costs reflect real resource use; to the extent that the duty covers a broader range of real costs, the less discriminatory it is relative to various production and distribution techniques and relative to consumer expenditures on various goods. CIF offers one operational advantage; goods are commonly invoiced on a delivered basis, and thus the invoice value does not require adjustment for duty.

While most countries today use the invoice value as the principal measure for calculating duties, they supplement it in varying degrees by other measures. A few, particularly Canada and the United States, make extensive use of other bases. Partly these other approaches are designed to prevent evasion through understatement of selling price, either through collusion of buyer and seller or through joint control, and partly to prevent the use for duty purposes of actual prices lower than those regarded as fair or reasonable.

Equivalent Selling Price

A second general approach is the *domestic value*—the use of the domestic price of the commodity in the exporting country. The figure sought is that at which the commodity normally sells under the same conditions in the domestic market. Thus if the commodity is sold more cheaply abroad, the customs duty will apply to the home market figure. This is the basis of the Canadian rule; if this figure exceeds the invoice price it must be used. The South African tariff and ones derived from it are similar. Zambia, for example, abandoned this rule only in 1967.

The concept of the somewhat similar *export value,* which serves as the basis for United States tariffs since their simplification, is the price at which goods are offered for export in the foreign country under ordinary conditions.

Use of either of these bases greatly complicates the operation of the customs system. If the rules are taken literally, appraisers need to determine the export or domestic price of each commodity being imported. Ascertainment of domestic selling prices is particularly difficult. There are often wide ranges of distribution channels and selling prices; none may have the same characteristics as the export market. Export sales are often made in larger quantities, and thus some costs are lower; selling activities may be very much less, the advertising of the product being undertaken after import. The principal domestic market for the goods may not be clearly defined. Goods for export may not be identical with those produced for the home market (for example, cars produced in Great Britain for sale elsewhere have the steering wheel on the left side instead of the right). There have been many disputes over whether certain domestic taxes (sales, excise, purchase, and other indirect taxes) should be included in the value or not. Even money conversion problems are troublesome with dual or widely varying exchange rates.

Constructive Values

When actual values are unacceptable and neither domestic nor export values are ascertainable or acceptable, purely constructive value figures are employed. Usually the approach is to estimate the cost of production in the producing country and a "normal" profit margin. Discounts from total costs may be allowed. The difficulties of determining cost figures and of deciding what costs to include are far greater than those of ascertaining the domestic or export selling price. The time and effort required are tremendous.

A final alternative sometimes used, especially by the United States, is the domestic selling price of the commodity or a similar one in the importing country. This figure may be easier to determine than other constructive figures but may be far removed from (and perhaps much higher than) the more appropriate figure. This approach has primarily been used to increase protection.

The use of any figure other than the invoice value has several disadvantages. Determination is often difficult, expensive, and time-consuming, since information must be obtained from the exporting country, often by a visit of an appraiser. This is costly for any country; it is impossible for most developing economies importing from a number of supplying countries. Apart from the problems of obtaining data, there are difficult matters of principle, such as determining appropriate discounts from the domestic price, and uniformity of treatment is hard to achieve. Furthermore, the procedure creates great uncertainty for the importers and exporters. A firm is never sure of what the dutiable value will be, and the delay before final determination is often substantial (years, in some instances, when court action is involved). Meanwhile the goods will have been sold, and if the duty is much higher than expected the firm may experience severe losses. By the nature of the problem the final action must usually be rather arbitrary and thus hard to predict. Valuation problems are among the most serious obstacles to the free flow of international trade.

This analysis suggests that the actual invoice value should be used as the basis of the valuation system, with departures only when there is strong evidence of deliberate understatement through error, collusion, or common ownership of buyer and seller. This rule is desirable in developed countries; it is imperative, in view of personnel shortages, in developing countries. Some review is obviously necessary or evasion will occur, but these cases can usually be spotted by trained appraisers (valuation officers) and adjusted without resort to detailed examination of prices, margins, and costs in the exporting countries. Such procedures are required only as a last resort in instances of major attempts to defraud. As noted, the CIF basis simplifies customs operation and has become increasingly advantageous as more countries have adopted it. Prevention of dumping is essentially a protective question and thus will not be considered in detail in this study. Enforcement of antidumping rules should not be placed upon customs officials but be related to complaints by domestic firms, which would be investigated in cooperation with the customs agency by a special unit in the ministry or department of trade and commerce.

SUPPLEMENTS TO CUSTOMS DUTIES

A number of countries, particularly in Latin America and former French Africa, apply various supplements to customs duties. A consular invoice fee is common. If a small charge unrelated to the value of the goods is made for approval of the invoice by the consulate, the practice has a limited justification. But generally the requirement for consular invoices is unfortunate. The consular fees of a number of countries are a substantial percentage of the value of the imports, often without exemptions.[10] The fee is collected at the time of importation rather than by the consular offices in the exporting country. It is essentially an ad valorem supplement to the duty and is, in fact, an additional duty providing substantial revenue.

This policy is objectionable in many respects, but primarily because it complicates the duty structure with no gain whatever. Moreover, the merits of the use of specific rates are lost if the goods are also subject to ad valorem duties. Articles that would as a rule never be subjected to duties, such as basic necessities and industrial machinery, are covered by the fees. The level of the overall duty appears to be less than it actually is. And the fees are so obviously higher than any costs of the consular services that importers resent them.

Another type of supplement is a requirement for stamps of substantial value on each consular invoice, bill of lading, bill of entry, or other document. The amounts are frequently independent of the value of the invoice and thus burden small shipments unfairly. But the main objection is the lack of rationale; these stamp requirements are a reflection of the policy in many countries of taxing every possible object and activity instead of concentrating on a few major taxes. As a consequence the number of taxes and fees becomes great while none operates effectively. Virtually all stamp taxes constitute unnecessary sources of nuisance.

The imposition of substantial automatic fines or penalties for unintended errors is another practice that infuriates importers and accomplishes little. For example, some countries have very complex tariffs that are difficult to understand and interpret; if an importer classifies a good differently than the customs officer believes appropriate, he is subjected to a substantial penalty although he did not intend to defraud. Obviously such policies are indefensible and, by creating ill will, lessen the cooperation of importers and brokers with the customs administration.

CUSTOMS PROCEDURES

The administration of customs resembles that of fees or charges more than that of taxes, since payments are made to obtain a specific government action, the release of goods from customs.

---

10. The Venezuelan fee, for example, is 3.5 percent of the value on larger shipments.

Entry Form and Procedure

The entry form or bill of entry is the basic document in customs operation. It is prepared by the importer or his agent from information on the invoice and the arrival notice and is submitted to the customs officer at the port of clearance, together with the invoice and the arrival notice. The form is specified by the customs department, but importers are usually expected to have their own forms printed. The invoice is mailed by the exporter to the importer, while the notice of arrival is sent by the carrier to the importer.

The importer includes a calculation of the duty on the bill of entry. The customs clerk checks the bill of entry and the accompanying documents, accepts payment,[11] and turns the bill over to a customs officer or appraiser who reviews it for accuracy. If it is found to be accurate it is sent to the site of the goods, which are then released by the customs officer or transport firm. Copies of the bill of entry and other forms go to the central audit unit of the customs agency for a final review to provide a check on customs officers and to increase the likelihood of uniformity among various ports of entry.

Physical Control

Initial control is exercised at the border point. Goods may be cleared at this point, or they may be shipped in bond to the destination consigned to a bonded warehouse, and cleared at the custom house at the destination. Normally the importer cannot obtain release of the goods until the bill of entry has been filed and the duty paid. Exceptions are made, however, when goods are imported in carload lots by large firms, which may receive the goods directly and subsequently pay duty to customs.[12]

The extent of actual physical examination of the imported goods by customs officers varies widely among different countries. Smaller shipments are often examined by the customs officer at the time of release. The primary rule for larger shipments is to retain at the time of initial clearance one package in ten for detailed examination. In other instances every tenth shipment is examined. Some types of shipments, of course, require no examination or only a cursory one, such as carloads of coal. When examination is made, several elements are checked, including the nature of the commodity to be sure that it is labeled and reported correctly and the physical dimensions when rates are specific or specific plus ad valorem. A

---

11. In Canada and some other countries, clearance takes place before payment. Canada requires bond and allows 72 hours after clearance for payment.

12. Regulations may require that the seal on the car not be broken without customs approval; this is often given by telephone. Exceptions to the regulation are made for bulk shipments of coal, oil, ore, and the like.

major problem with textiles is underreporting of the actual measurements. If a reasonable number of shipments is not physically examined, exporters will learn of this and tend to misstate the contents to reduce the duty.

The speed of clearance varies with the circumstances. Many countries seek to clear within 24 hours except when some packages are retained for detailed examination, when several days may be required. Other countries regard two or three days as the maximum under ordinary circumstances. Final liquidation of liability is often not completed until the audit or checking branch in customs headquarters reviews the entry, and this is likely to take several weeks or even months. If the importer protests the duty assessment and appeals to a higher authority and then to the courts many months or even years may elapse before the final settlement.

Other Documentation

In addition to the invoice (on the form prescribed by customs for the particular type of shipment) and the bill of entry, several other documents are relevant for clearance. The shipping line's *manifest* lists all goods consigned to a particular port, and the goods unloaded and their invoices are checked against the manifest to ensure that nothing is unloaded without proper identification. The *certificate of origin,* a statement of the country in which the goods originated, is required when duty depends upon origin or when imports from certain countries are banned.

The United States and some other countries require, except on smaller shipments, a consular invoice prepared in the exporting country giving details about the goods and certified by the U.S. consul in that country. The theory is that the consul is in a better position to judge value and other characteristics than the customs officers. Actually consular checking becomes routine, and the system appears to contribute little while creating cost, nuisance, and delay for the shipper.

The Role of Brokers

In any country an importer is free to clear his own goods through customs, and in some countries this is a relatively common practice, especially on the part of larger firms. But in most countries customs brokers play a major role, serving as agents for the importers in the clearing of goods for a fee. The brokers, who are typically licensed, are experts in customs work and seek to keep familiar with changing procedures and requirements as well as to remain on good terms with customs officials. Accordingly, the ease and speed of clearing as well as the duty assessed may depend in part on the attitude of the local customs officials toward the particular customs broker.

CUSTOMS PERSONNEL

Customs departments require a wide range of personnel, from border guards, who are essentially policemen, to persons highly trained in valuation and other techniques of control. Apart from the clerical, warehouse, and guard personnel, the principal classes include:

1. Customs officers (sometimes called inspectors), who examine goods for physical identification and make the initial checks of the bills of entry. Others check baggage of persons entering the country. A high school education is usually required.

2. Examining officers (or senior customs officers, under some classifications), who check the bills of entry and invoices much more closely than the customs officers at the time of payment of duty. They also serve as officers in charge of ports and larger border posts.

3. Valuation officers or appraisers, who review the value figures shown on the invoices and bills of entry in case of doubt and carry on detailed investigations of values when necessary. The size and importance of the valuation section vary with the nature of the tariff and the availability of personnel. In many developing countries there is a severe shortage of persons trained for this type of work.

4. Auditors or review personnel, senior headquarters staff with substantial experience who review the work of the examining officers and seek to ensure uniformity.

5. Investigators, who visit business firms to audit their invoices and check inventories to uncover possible violations or smuggling. This work is usually on a sample basis.

6. Collectors, the senior personnel in charge of the major custom houses.

The senior personnel may rise through the ranks or may be recruited from university graduates or commercial employers. Customs personnel typically are hired after graduation from secondary-schools, receive in-service training, and remain in the service as a career in view of the highly specialized nature of the work.

Adequate compensation for customs personnel is essential. Inadequate salaries cause a loss of trained personnel and greatly increase the likelihood that they will accept bribes or, in some disorganized countries, actually seize goods for personal use. Paying the examining officers a portion of the fines assessed, the practice in some Latin American countries, is particularly objectionable since it discriminates among individuals in the service and leads to excessive penalties and extra assessments.[13]

13. If a maximum per month is set, customs officers have an incentive to apply penalties until they have reached the maximum and then cease for the rest of the month. This was reported to occur widely in Venezuela. See C. S. Shoup, *The Fiscal System of Venezuela* (Baltimore: Johns Hopkins Press, 1959), chap. 9.

It is often difficult to prevent bribery of customs officials. There are frequent chances for differences of opinion and close contact between the importer (or his broker) and the customs personnel. The importer cannot obtain his goods until the assessed duty is paid; the officer is therefore in a position to seek a bribe, and the importer may regard the bribe as cheaper than higher duties and penalties and endless delay.

THE GENERAL PROBLEM OF ENFORCEMENT

Escape from payment of required duties arises in several ways, some of which have already been discussed:

1. Misclassification

Importers have an incentive to classify goods in duty-free or lower-rate categories. Ambiguity of classifications facilitates misclassification, since the importer can say that he was classifying on the basis of his identification of the goods. An adequate physical check on imports is necessary to minimize misclassification, but the expense usually prescribes a sample basis.

2. Underreporting of Magnitudes

With specific rate tariffs, the importer has an incentive to understate the dimensions or the number of units. Again, a physical check is necessary. But this may be time-consuming, especially when the duty is established on a basis such as length of cloth on a roll.

3. Understating the Value

This is discussed in detail in the section on valuation. This is one of the most difficult problems of customs operation with ad valorem tariffs, particularly if a basis other than the invoice price is used, but may occur even with this basis if there is collusion or common interest between exporter and importer.

4. Misstatement of Country of Origin

This is likewise difficult to detect. The problem represents a strong argument against such differentiation.

5. Smuggling

From the days of the first customs duties, smuggling in a great variety of forms has been the primary form of escape. Goods may be smuggled in bulk across unguarded borders, by sea, land, or air, or they may pass through control points concealed from the customs officers. The extent of smuggling depends on several elements:

a. The Country's Borders. A country with very lengthy coastlines is particularly vulnerable, since a complete patrol is impossible. The Philippines, with thousands of small islands, has one of the most difficult problems in the world. A lengthy land border, such as that between the United States and Canada, also presents problems, particularly when there are many isolated crossings that cannot be guarded economically or when a metropolitan area spreads over the borders with numerous points of entry possible. The ideal situation is one in which there are only a few routes of entry into a country, but few countries are so fortunate.

b. The Volume of Border Traffic. When the number of persons crossing the border is very large, control becomes more expensive and more difficult, especially in times of peak travel. The Detroit-Windsor and Niagara Falls borders and that at Tijuana, Mexico, are good examples.

c. Nearby Sources of Supply. Smuggling is most effective if cheap sources of supply are close at hand, particularly on islands off the coast, so that small boats can slip in at night. Fernando Po has long been a source of supply for smuggling to Nigeria, and Zanzibar was once the main source for the East African countries. Hong Kong and the Indonesian islands supply the Philippines over longer distances.

d. The Level of Duties and Internal Taxes. There is a direct relationship between the level of duties and the extent of smuggling. If duties are low, the gains from smuggling are limited and there is little danger. A low tariff country such as Zambia has virtually no smuggling problem while the Philippines, with high tariffs, has particular difficulty. Domestic taxes on sales of commodities aggravate the problem. In some instances the potential for smuggling places a limit beyond which a tariff cannot go without causing loss in revenue (or loss in protective effect). Other price differentials have similar effects; if farm policies in one country push food prices far above those in a neighboring country, smuggling will be encouraged even if tariffs are low. Direct controls on imports will also produce smuggling.

e. The Nature of the Commodities. It is obviously easier to smuggle some goods than others. A country's problems will be severe if there are great advantages in smuggling valuable articles that can be easily concealed or that can be transported by means hard to detect, such as in small boats or in small planes flying across the border at night. Diamonds have traditionally been a major item of smuggling because they can be so easily concealed.

f. The Attitudes of Neighboring Governments. Effective control of smuggling depends in part on the cooperation of governments in the countries from which smuggling occurs; thus their attitudes and general level of law enforcement affect the volume of smuggling. If a neighbor is glad to see a disrupting influence in the country (as for example in southern Africa), it will do nothing to help. If a neighbor's law enforcement level is generally low, its government may be powerless to aid even if it wishes to do so.

Control of Smuggling

Control of smuggling takes several forms:

1. *Border Inspection and Patrol.* The greater the inspection at customs posts and the patrol of coastlines and borders, the less easy is smuggling. But there are obvious limitations to expansion of this activity. One is cost; as border patrols are increased the marginal returns fall, and a point is quickly reached at which additional outlay will produce little net revenue. Since it is impossible in practice to patrol an entire border intensively at all times, smugglers can easily outwit the border patrols. Similarly, inspection of persons, baggage, and small parcels entering the country becomes uneconomic if extended very far and is a source of strong complaints and interference with tourist travel. No one likes to have his person searched carefully, and detailed inspection of all baggage is very time-consuming.[14]

2. *Internal Checks.* Commodities smuggled on a large scale must be sold through retail outlets. Accordingly, surprise inspections of vendors may turn up merchandise on which duty has not been paid. But with many small vendors selling on stands or on the sidewalks and streets, inspection will unearth few smuggled goods.

3. *Marking Requirements.* Internal control is aided if imported goods must be marked to show that duty has been paid. This is feasible with a few types of items but impossible with others, and the time and cost involved usually prevent its use on any scale. In fact, most countries have been moving away from stamp or other marking requirements on cigarettes and liquor, the items for which they were typically required.

4. *Investigation in Foreign Countries.* Large-scale smuggling and smuggling of valuable items can often be controlled most effectively by investigations of the countries of origin. This is most effective with the cooperation of the foreign country, which may be able to spot sources of illicit supply to other countries, but it may take the form of a strictly underground investigation. Countries usually do not publicize this type of activity; it appears to be most common with diamonds and narcotics. This work is usually beyond the capacity of a small country, but cooperative activity with neighbors may be feasible.

5. *Complaints of Competing Firms.*

14. Both the United States and Canada now spot check only and find this policy more effective than examining all baggage.

LIMITATIONS OF CUSTOMS DUTIES AS SOURCES OF REVENUE

While customs duties offer significant advantages to developing economies, they are also subject to limitations.

Economic Effects

Duties may give rise to several adverse economic effects. The most significant is unwanted protection. A customs duty, by its nature, taxes one source of commodities (imports) but not the substitute (domestic products) and thus favors the latter. This effect in some instances may be regarded as consistent with development plans, even if the primary motive for the tariff is revenue. But in other situations, the consequence may be highly undesirable from the standpoint of domestic use of resources. The great danger is that stress on revenue in the tariff design will lead to substantial distortion of domestic production from the patterns that are desired for economic development.

Second, optimal adjustment of tariff rates to establish vertical relationships consistent with desired objectives may be hard. Intermediate goods may be used for several purposes and the use not identifiable at the time of importation. The desired impact on those used for some purposes may be quite different from that desired for others. A particular product may be imported in a number of different stages of completion. While a sales tax can be confined to finished products, a duty cannot if some commodities are not to escape completely. Unsatisfactory vertical relationships encourage firms to push functions forward past the point of importation, a consequence that may aid development in the country but may reduce efficiency, optimal resource allocation, and revenue.

A third source of adverse economic effects is the varying ratio of import price to final consumption expenditure on the commodities, which results from variations in the ratios of domestic values added to selling prices. No workable tariff structure can prevent this variation. As a consequence, a distortion of consumption patterns may result with possible excess burden.

Finally, if customs duties are changed frequently, merchants will be subject to losses or gains on their inventories. The consequence is a distortion in business methods, particularly a tendency to speed up imports when higher duties are expected and to curtail them when a reduction is anticipated. Floor stock taxes on inventories and refunds are possible on only a few major items such as motor vehicles.

Equity

While customs duties may be far more acceptable on equity grounds in developing countries than in highly developed ones, there are nevertheless certain difficulties in terms of usual standards of equity. The uneven ratio of tax to final consumer expenditures (except as deliberately sought) arising out of differences in domestic values added may be regarded as inequitable as well as a source of potential distortion of resource allocation. Moreover, on some products the duty may result in lower prices net of tax, the foreign exporter absorbing some of the duty to be able to stay in the market. In a sense this is advantageous to the country, but it produces an unequal tax burden relative to consumer spending. The duty structure may not succeed in placing a heavier burden on the higher income groups if they concentrate their expenditures on domestic goods and services, foreign travel, and other purposes not reached by the customs duties. Finally, if exchange rates are flexible and the duties reduce imports, the rate of exchange may rise, thus making exports of the country more expensive to foreign buyers and transferring the burden of the duties to the producers of export commodities. This consequence is unlikely in most developing countries.

Administration

As noted in detail in the preceding pages, despite the inherent administrative advantages of duties in developing countries compared with other levies, there are limitations, particularly when smuggling is feasible. Most of the other problems center around valuation and the necessity to use constructive values to some extent, even if a policy of accepting the invoice value is followed whenever possible. Domestic consumption taxes can be applied to actual prices in a much larger number of situations.

Exports and Revenues

A final consideration is the dependence of governmental revenues upon export markets. Since foreign exchange limits the ability to import, a decline in exports will result in governmental measures to restrict imports and thus the base for duties. The imports most likely to be restricted or banned are precisely those most productive of import revenues, since the government will give priority to basic foodstuffs and producers goods important for expansion. Thus the decline in duty may be substantially greater than the percentage decline in exports and available foreign exchange.

THE DETERIORATION OF CUSTOMS AS A SOURCE OF REVENUE

Despite the limitations noted in the preceding section, customs constitute an acceptable revenue source, by usual standards, in the earliest years of economic development. But analysis suggests and empirical studies support the thesis that they become progressively less acceptable in terms

of development goals as the process of development continues and ultimately deteriorate in productivity of revenue.

The primary difficulty, once development has progressed to the level
at which domestic industrial production becomes at all significant, is the
unwanted import substitution that the tariffs inevitably produce. Production
springs up behind the duty walls even if the rates are no more than 25 or
30 percent, but particularly if they reach 75 and 100 percent. This danger
is small early in development but increases rapidly as it continues.

Partly as a result of this import substitution, but primarily as a result
of ongoing development itself, the revenue productivity of customs at given
rates falls as development progresses. Development inevitably involves an
increase in the ratio of domestic value added by manufacture to total
gross domestic product (GDP), given typical development objectives. Only
in an economy that elects to remain an agricultural producer, exporting
farm products and importing manufactured goods, would this rule not be
valid, and in the modern world such a policy is virtually unknown. The
consequence is a decline in the ratio of imports of manufactured goods to
GDP or GNP and possibly even a decline in the ratio of total imports to
GDP. As expansion continues, the percentage of imports consisting of
materials and parts rises and that of finished products falls (although the
latter may rise in absolute terms). This has been demonstrated by the
work of Simon Kuznets[15] and Harley Hinrichs[16] and, in the most intensive
studies of its type, by Jonathan Levin for Colombia[17] and Stephen R.
Lewis, Jr., for Pakistan.[18] In Colombia, manufactured consumer goods of
all types fell from 43 percent of total imports in the 1920s to 9 percent in
the 1960s. In Pakistan, by 1964, industrial development had reduced the
potential yield from duties by about one-third compared with 1951-52.

For a considerable period this revenue loss is offset by higher imports
of other goods and by higher duty rates, as shown in table 2-1. Only the
countries above the $500 level show a drop in the relative importance of
duties. But some countries will reach the point at a much earlier level of
development, and ultimately virtually all countries reach this point.[19] The
tendency suggested by table 2-1 is borne out by the use of simple correla-

15. "Quantitative Aspects of the Economic Growth of Nations," *Economic Development and Cultural Change,* 15 (January 1967), 44.
16. *General Theory of Tax Structure Change.*
17. "The Effects of Economic Development on the Base of a Sales Tax: A Case
Study of Colombia," *International Monetary Fund Staff Papers,* 15 (March 1968),
30-101.
18. "Revenue Implications of Changing Industrial Structure," *National Tax Journal,* 20 (December 1967), 395-411.
19. In India, for example, customs duty revenue as a percentage of total national
tax revenue fell from 27 percent in 1950-51 to 18 percent in 1968-69. W. R. Mahler,
"Sales and Excise Taxation in India" (Ph.D. diss., Syracuse University, 1969), p. 14.

tion analysis by R. A. Musgrave in his *Fiscal Systems*.[20] He found no correlation between GNP and relative reliance on customs duties for countries below $600 GNP but significant correlation (inverse) for his entire sample of countries. When his technique (equation 41)[21] is applied to data collected for this study, similar results are obtained. There is no correlation for the group below $500 GNP but substantial correlation for the entire group:[22]

For all countries included:

$$CD/T = e^{1.4954} \; Y_c^{-.458} \qquad R^2: .46$$
$$(-7.49)$$

For countries with GNP under $500:

$$CD/T = e^{-.71917} \; Y_c^{-.00050} \qquad R^2: .00$$
$$(-.00501)$$

T = tax revenue; CD = customs duty revenue; Y_c = per capita GNP.

The ratio of total imports to GDP typically rises during earlier years of development and, according to the studies of Kuznets and others, may continue to do so indefinitely. In other countries, such as the United States, they ultimately begin to fall. The changing structure of imports is basically responsible for the deterioration of the customs source. In some areas, such as Central America, development of a common market has caused further declines in customs revenue.

The changing import structure also results in a loss in the equity of this revenue source. Domestic production of some goods will develop, perhaps with high import content, perhaps with little or none (jewelry may be an example in a country having the necessary materials). Thus customs revenue will be obtained on the consumption of some goods and not on others, and people concentrating their expenditures on imported goods will be discriminated against. The rule that virtually all imports are luxury goods and all luxuries are imported, accepted in the very early years of development, loses validity as development continues.

20. New Haven: Yale University Press, 1969.
21. *Ibid.,* p. 145.
22. Examination of the data by country in table A-1 in the appendix shows considerable individual variation from the standard pattern, but most of the extreme cases can be explained by rather obvious factors. India, Pakistan, and Brazil have a low degree of "openness" (ratio of foreign trade to GDP), mainly because of their size, and they have well-developed internal excise and sales tax systems. The French Equatorial African countries have come to rely heavily on sales taxes collected mainly at importation; if these items are added to duties, per se, the figures are typical. With the highly developed countries, there is a close inverse correlation between size of the country and reliance on duties.

Approaches to a Solution

The more extreme and undesirable forms of "cake mix" import sub-stitution such as assembly, involving very little value added, can be checked to some extent and a country's revenue protected by placing duties on the materials and parts. If the government desires to encourage assembly and similar operations it can retain some differential between the duty on the parts and that on the finished products, thus providing some revenue and yet some protection. In other words, careful attention must be given to effective protection rates. If the nation does not desire protection, the duties can be made equivalent. Such adjustments are often difficult to implement satisfactorily, particularly when the parts may be used for a number of purposes, and the adjustment complicates the tariff structure if widely employed. Furthermore, such adjustments do nothing to check undesired import substitution involving a smaller import content.

A more drastic approach, emphasizing the distorting effects of import substitution on resource-allocation, proposes to eliminate customs duties as a source of revenue as soon as a country reaches the level of development at which import substitution appears. Tariffs would be retained for protective and foreign exchange purposes alone, yielding some revenue only incidentally.[23] The revenue duties would be replaced by internal indirect taxes of the types discussed in subsequent chapters. This approach does not preclude *collection* of a substantial portion of the indirect taxes at the time of importation. If, for example, excises are imposed, they can be collected on imported products at customs and on manufacturers' sales for domestic products. Sales taxes can likewise be collected in part at importation, an important practice in the various former French African countries and in Uganda. Collection at importation may be final, or it may constitute a credit against subsequent tax liability, as explained in subsequent chapters. By this means the merits of collection of much of the revenue at importation are preserved and all unwanted import substitution is eliminated, tariffs being designed solely for the other goals, primarily protection and foreign exchange.

This step is a drastic one that most countries are unwilling to take. The usual procedure is to introduce domestic taxes to supplement customs duties as domestic production increases. These are usually applied to both domestic and imported goods, and thus, if no tariff adjustments are made, the degree of protection existing at the time the levies are established is preserved. Rarely are customs systems revised as the domestic taxes are

23. Note, for example, the paper by H. G. Johnson, "Fiscal Policy and the Balance of Payments," in A. T. Peacock and G. Hauser, eds., *Government Finance and Economic Development* (Paris: Organization for Economic Cooperation and Development, 1965), pp. 157-72.

established. This approach protects the customs revenue against the effects of import substitution and avoids the substantial adjustments required with the alternative method. But in terms of development goals it is an inferior technique because, while it solves the revenue problem, it does not necessarily eliminate unwanted import substitution.

SUPPLEMENTARY REFERENCES

The literature on customs duties as a source of revenue and on operational aspects of customs duties is very limited; the references noted below are in part directly relevant to more developed countries.

Bachmann, H. *The External Relations of Less Developed Countries.* New York: Praeger, 1968.

Blake, Gordon. *Customs Administration in Canada.* Toronto: University of Toronto Press, 1957.

Crombie, Sir James. *Her Majesty's Customs and Excise.* London: George Allen and Unwin, 1962.

Edwards, C. T. "The Future Role of Import and Excise Duty Taxation in the States of Malaya and Singapore." *Malayan Economic Review.* 11 (April 1966), 29-41.

Elliott, G. A. *Tariff Procedures and Trade Barriers.* Toronto: University of Toronto Press, 1955.

Hinrichs, H. H. *A General Theory of Tax Structure Change During Economic Development.* Cambridge: Harvard Law School, International Tax Program, 1966.

Lewis, S. R., Jr. "Revenue Implications of Changing Industrial Structure." *National Tax Journal.* 20 (December 1967), 395-411.

Masson, F., and English, H. E. *Invisible Trade Barriers.* Washington: National Planning Association, 1963.

Organization of American States. *Fiscal Survey of Colombia.* Baltimore: Johns Hopkins Press, 1965.

Organization of American States. *Fiscal Survey of Panama.* Baltimore: Johns Hopkins Press, 1964.

Shoup, C. S. *The Fiscal System of Venezuela.* Baltimore: Johns Hopkins Press, 1959. Chapter 9.

3.

Excise Taxation

As industrial development begins in a country, experience suggests that it centers in the production of commodities that previously yielded considerable customs revenue, for the obvious reason that these commodities offer a relatively large and stable domestic market. Manufacture of beer and cigarettes is usually first, followed by certain types of distilled spirits and, in some countries, wine. A petroleum refinery often follows closely. These products are ones of widespread consumption, and the economies of large-scale production are not such as to require a market of the size necessary for many basic industries. As domestic production of these commodities develops, a country stands to lose substantial revenue unless equivalent taxes are levied on domestic production, and typically this is done. As import substitution continues, the question of further expansion of excises beyond these basic commodities becomes urgent.

A word on terminology is necessary. As domestic levies on particular commodities developed historically, they were usually imposed on production (rather than sale), with specific rates; accordingly, the term *excise* came to mean a tax imposed in this fashion rather than any tax levied on domestic production or sale. Subsequently, however, the concept has broadened to cover taxes on the sale as well as the production of particular commodities, with either ad valorem or specific rates.

Traditionally, excises are applied only to domestically produced goods. When they are imposed, their rates are established at levels related to the customs duties, usually somewhat lower than the latter. When excises are imposed, customs duties on the goods are often raised to maintain a desired level of protection. Some modern excises are applied to both imported and domestic goods.

This discussion assumes that excises are shifted forward to the final consumers of the products. If merchants use constant markup percentages in establishing prices, the price increase to the consumer will exeed the amount of the tax. If markups are fixed monetary amounts rather than percentages, or if the excise tax is kept separate from the price base to which the percentages are applied, the price rise will equal the tax. In either instance the prices of the taxed goods will rise relative to untaxed goods, and real incomes will decline in relation to expenditures on taxed goods. This assumption is oversimplified, since the prices of some factors specialized to the production of the taxed goods will fall, but it is a reasonable first approximation.

Table 3–1 indicates the relative revenue importance of excise taxes in a group of developing economies, with figures for developed countries included for comparison.

Excises can be grouped into several classes: sumptuary (the traditional levies on liquor and tobacco), benefit based (motor fuel), services, miscellaneous special, and extended systems.

SUMPTUARY TAXES: LIQUOR AND TOBACCO

The earliest excises, and the most important in terms of revenue, are those on beer, wine, liquor, and tobacco products. In a sense these are, at least from a political standpoint and in part from an economic one as well, ideal objects for taxation. Use is typically widespread, even in the early years of development, and the demand is relatively inelastic. Consumption of the commodities is considered to contribute little to economic development and is therefore regarded as undesirable and in some countries morally objectionable. Frequently—but not always—the number of producers is small and easily subject to control, and thus administration is not difficult. The most urgent direct motive for the introduction of sumptuary excises, however, is the need to compensate for the loss of major sources

TABLE 3–1. RELIANCE ON EXCISE TAXES (GNP CLASS)

Estimated Per Capita GNP, U.S. $	No. of Countries	Excise Taxes		Excise Taxes and Misc. Indirect Taxes	
		As % of Indirect Tax Revenue	As % of Total Tax Revenue	As % of Indirect Tax Revenue	As % of Total Tax Revenue
100 or less	16	24	15	28	19
101–200	9	30	17	33	21
201–500	16	29	20	36	23
501–850	8	36	15	42	20
Over 850	15	46	15	..[1]	..[1]

Source: See table A–1, appendix. Data are given for latest year available in 1965–69 period.
[1] Miscellaneous included in other categories.

of customs duty, since these commodities are highly productive of customs revenue.[1]

Nature of the Taxes

Almost without exception, other than in a few countries in which inflation has been severe, excises are imposed with specific rates and thus upon physical units. There are several reasons. One, historically the primary explanation, is ease of application. No valuation is required; only the physical quantity need be ascertained. Avoidance of the valuation problem is particularly important because of the high rates. But related has been the principle, partly arising from the sumptuary nature of the levy, that the amount of tax should be uniform per unit of the product or constituent element of it—that the "tax penalty" a person should pay for using the goods should be related to physical quantity. Another consideration of more recent concern is the desire to avoid distorting effects on distribution channels that arise with ad valorem taxes at the manufacturing level, as explained in detail in chapter 4. The distortion is potentially very severe because of the high rates of duty.[2] Finally, the specific rate has the political advantage of obscuring the actual ratio of tax to selling price, which is often 100 percent or more of price net of tax.

The specific rates are the source of some complaint, particularly over their discrimination against the cheaper brands of the commodities such as cigarettes, which has distorted resource allocation by lessening relative use. At the same time, since the cheaper brands are used primarily by the lower income groups, the taxes are more regressive than otherwise. The purchaser pays no more tax on the most expensive whisky than on the cheapest; thus the relative after-tax price differential is lower. But there has been widespread belief that for distilled spirits a cheap product is not in the public interest because it increases drunkenness among the lower income groups. Partly for this reason, taxation on the basis of physical units is so widely accepted that the complaints are usually disregarded. The exception is cigars, whose extensive variety has led to adjustments in terms of the selling price of the product, with tax on a per-pound basis. This solution is only a partial one because of quality differences. While cigarettes are usually taxed at a single rate, some countries, particularly when the variation in the quality is significant, have set up several rate classes, the rate varying according to the selling price.

1. For example, in Singapore (1968), tobacco yielded 44 percent of customs revenue, liquor 20 percent, petroleum 15 percent, all other 21 percent.
2. This consideration alone led the Canadian Royal Commission on Taxation to conclude that the Canadian excise levies should not be converted to an ad valorem base. *Report of the Royal Commission on Taxation* (Ottawa: Queen's Printer, 1966), 5, 87–88.

The units to which the tax applies are often constructive rather than actual. With distilled spirits the tax is usually applied to a 100-proof gallon (50 percent alcohol by volume). The aim is to make the tax uniform on the basis of the actual object of the tax, the alcohol involved. Beer in many countries is taxed on the actual volume, but in others on the worts—the unfermented mixture of malt and other ingredients—which in turn determines the alcoholic content of the finished product. With wine the adjustments are much less precise. Typically two rates are provided: one for table wine less than 25 proof (12.5 percent of actual content), and the other for dessert wines (port, sherry, etc.) more than 25 proof (these wines are typically about 20 percent alcohol). Champagne and other sparkling wines draw a much higher figure, often comparable to that on distilled spirits. Tobacco products are more frequently taxed on actual weight or individual units.

The unusual treatment accorded alcoholic beverages, which originated in the United Kingdom, was in part a product of long-obsolete control measures. The methods used are not necessarily objectionable in terms of the rationale of the taxes; the main criticism is that the actual burden of the tax is not at all evident to legislators or others. The statement that a levy is 10 shillings per 36 gallons of worts conveys little meaning. Even the proof basis is confusing.

These excises sometimes apply to the sale of the product but more frequently to its production or its withdrawal from bond for sale. Liquor, for example, is usually taxable when withdrawn from a bonded warehouse where it was stored for aging. In Great Britain and some other countries, beer is taxed at the worts stage, that is before fermentation and sale, but the time lag is much less than in the production of liquor. The timing of collection is not too significant, but collection at an early stage has disadvantages. The producers have more capital tied up in taxes in inventory, and later losses and damage to goods may require adjustments that are either arbitrary (a certain percentage) or complex. Taxation at the time of sale is preferable.

Control measures in the liquor, beer, and tobacco tax fields are usually drastic compared with those for other taxes. Rigid licensing requirements are established; firms cannot produce the commodities without specific authorization, and licenses may be denied if evasion is feared. Inspection is continuous or frequent. In some larger plants, a full-time excise inspector is on duty to measure and check operations. The firm is usually required to submit detailed plans of the plant, paint pipes different colors to indicate contents, and follow other rules relating to the handling of materials. The controls seek to make sure that nothing is produced without payment of excise, that nothing (such as sugar) is added after the application of tax that will increase the alcoholic content, and that the product is not diluted. Thus the control of liquor excises, unlike other taxes, which depend almost entirely on the examination of records, rests primarily upon actual observation. This complex system is a result of great difficulties with enforcement in the early years of excises, when firms deliberately sought to evade. Whether the need for such controls remains—despite the high excise rates—is doubtful. The firms are typically large. Even in less developed countries, control through examination of records and occasional checks on physical output should be adequate, but this method may prove to be more expensive than physical control given shortages of audit personnel.

Some countries—including the United States in the past—require that stamps be placed on packages and containers for control purposes. The stamps are purchased from the government and applied to containers as evidence that the tax has been paid. If inspectors find unstamped units, the lack of stamps constitutes prima facie evidence of evasion. This type of control is most useful as a check against smuggling (if imported goods have a comparable requirement) and against the sale of illicit products through regular outlets. But the trend has been away from stamps. They are a source of substantial nuisance and cost to the producers. They are unnecessary for most production since control can be maintained by other means, and they are not particularly useful against illicit production, which normally will not be marketed through usual channels anyway.

The other aspect of control, particularly of alcoholic beverages, is prevention of illicit production—bootlegging. This is a source of evasion in all countries, but far more in some than in others. Beer (of a kind) and wine are the types most easily made on a noncommercial basis. In some countries household production is so widespread that control is impossible, and production in smaller quantities is either exempted by law, as in Zambia,[3] or routinely escapes with little serious effort to tax. The palm wine of West African countries and the opaque beer of Central Africa are good examples. Distilling typically is on a somewhat larger scale and makes more use of commercial outlets. Control is thus somewhat easier. In the United States, the lower income areas of large cities and the hill country of the upper South have traditionally been the primary sites of illegal production. Control is possible only by use of agents, with considerable undercover work. Unusual purchases of sugar often provide a lead. Regardless of control techniques, the possibility of illegal production places a limit on how high the taxes can go. Illicit liquor has the further disadvantage that its quality is often poor and it is sometimes dangerous.

The Rationale of Sumptuary Excises

The primary argument for excises on alcoholic beverages and tobacco products is their revenue productivity. They yield substantial sums relative

3. Production in quantities of 50 gallons or less is exempt.

to overall revenues with little harm to economic development. The only economic danger is that, in light of the inelasticity of demand, the tax may be paid out of funds that would otherwise be used for milk for children or for food important for adequate nutrition. The seriousness of this objection cannot easily be assessed, since consumer behavior is difficult to determine. Interview surveys are useless; no one is going to admit that his drinking deprived his children of food. All that can be said is that this danger is a limiting factor in raising these levies.

The other objection concerns equity. While these goods may be regarded as luxuries, they are widely consumed in the lower income groups. As a consequence the absolute burden on the poor is likely to be significant, and the burden may well be regressive. This is particularly true of cigarettes and beer. Consumption of higher-priced distilled spirits is likely to be small in the lowest income groups. A related question is whether placing a substantial portion of the burden on those who consume large amounts of the taxed goods is consistent with usual standards of equity. Despite these questions, however, the taxes are widely accepted on equity grounds as suitable elements in the tax structures of developing as well as more developed economies.

From an administrative standpoint, the taxes are easy to collect so long as the number of producers is small. If producers are numerous, smaller firms must be exempted or expensive measures taken to prevent substantial evasion. In any event, the possibility of small-scale production places a limit on potential rates since revenue will decline if rates exceed a certain level.

In summary: resting as they do on somewhat nebulous concepts of "avoiding adverse effects" and "burdening persons on goods they could well do without," sumptuary levies have limited justification. But their revenue productivity is so high, the evidence of adverse effects so slight, and their accord with widely accepted standards of "justness" in taxation so great that they play a major role in most tax structures. The limit is set primarily by revenue considerations, that is, by the losses that may result if rates are so high as to stimulate illicit production and smuggling.

TAXATION OF MOTOR FUEL

Motor fuel is typically a major source of customs revenue before a refinery is established in a country and is an early object of excise taxation once refining is undertaken. Unfortunately many countries, including the United Kingdom, have never defined a precise philosophy of motor fuel taxation, and policy inconsistencies and controversy result. The primary justification of taxing motor fuel relates to benefit and resource allocation. A government's provision of roads is in part a commercial activity, like the provision of electric power. Charging the users for the product is justified on equity grounds and required for optimal resource allocation. As experience in many countries has effectively demonstrated, levies on motor fuel are more suitable for accomplishing this goal than collection of tolls. Requiring users to pay lessens the need to rely on other taxes that are likely to have adverse economic effects, particularly on incentives. Levies directly related to benefit, like other prices, are less likely to distort economic behavior than are compulsory payments unrelated to governmental services.

Use of benefit-related levies also facilitates governmental decision-making on roads and is likely to result in more optimal allocation of resources to roads than are more conventional means of financing. Failure to charge users makes transport costs artificially cheap and distorts location decisions.[4] Finally, in developing countries that have railways, benefit-related charges aid in attaining optimal use of the two forms of transport. To provide free roads while railway charges cover all costs will shift traffic uneconomically to the former. The same considerations are relevant in planning new rail and road construction. These justifications apply to all road use, private and commercial; in fact, so far as resource allocation is concerned, the argument for user levies is even stronger for commercial vehicles than for private ones, since the motives for using private cars in preference to commercial carriers are such that substitutability is not high.

In addition to the benefit-based levy on all fuel used on highways, fuel used for private cars can justifiably be subject to an additional tax on abil-

---

4. A. R. Prest, *Transport Economics in Developing Countries* (New York: Praeger, 1969). A different view is expressed by A. A. Walters; see, for example, "The Cost of Using Roads," *Finance and Development*, 6 (March 1969), 16–22. Walters argues that users should pay only short-run marginal costs for which they are responsible (e.g., maintenance and congestion costs), not the costs of road construction, on the basis that once roads are built a charge sufficiently high to cover long-run marginal costs and thus construction costs would prevent optimal use of the roads. If they are not used to capacity, a charge in excess of the marginal cost arising out of additional maintenance would result in poor utilization of resources.

This argument would result in very low user charges, if any at all, since so long as roads are not used to capacity the only short-run marginal cost is for very minor additional maintenance. Such a policy is objectionable in several ways. It deprives the government of a guide to investment in new roads; if existing charges cover only added maintenance, the roads will be overused relative to their long-run costs, and new roads will be built and others replaced on the basis of erroneous measures of demand. Other taxes used in place of user charges are likely to have even greater adverse effects on the economy (because of the widespread acceptance of the latter on the benefit basis) and are objectionable from an equity standpoint because the road users—so far as private cars are concerned—are in the higher income groups. Even more seriously, given the limited potentials for tax revenue in developing countries, reliance on taxes other than user charges to finance roads will almost certainly result in less total revenue, in the pulling of resources away from other urgently required governmental functions, and in a lower level of road construction. Finally, to use the short-run-marginal-cost rule for roads but not for railroads will result in an uneconomic allocation of traffic between the two modes of transport. The Walters argument is essentially a static one that disregards the significance of present traffic for investment in new roads and the ultimate need to replace existing roads.

ity grounds. Purchases of motor fuel are a good measure of luxury consumption and thus of ability to pay. In developing economies, the typical subsistence farmer or low-paid unskilled worker does not own a car (whereas he is likely to consume both cigarettes and beer). Persons in higher income levels are likely to do more driving than those in middle income levels and to use cars that consume more gasoline.

The optimal structure of a motor fuel tax is complicated by the multiplicity of fuels and the use of the same products for both highway and nonhighway purposes. With gasoline (petrol or motor spirit) the problem of nonhighway use is not serious, since industrial use is limited. Gasoline used for boats and private planes can justifiably be taxed because of governmental services provided for them. Usually the only significant exception is farm use. If this is substantial, provision for a refund upon application by farmers may be regarded as desirable, although such a system may involve some evasion. Avoidance of exemptions and minimizing refunds are imperative. If every worthy cause (ambulances, fire engines) is allowed an exemption the base of the tax and the effectiveness of administration are destroyed, as occurred initially in the United Kingdom.

Control of heavier fuels, particularly diesel fuel, is much more troublesome because of their importance for nonroad use—railways, electric power generation, and industry—and their similarity to heating fuels. But failure to exempt nonhighway consumption will have undesirable effects on industrial use, prevent optimal selection of fuels, and produce such opposition to the tax as to endanger its revenue possibilities.[5] There are two principal approaches: the refund method, as described for gasoline, and the taxing of only that diesel fuel sold for highway use. The choice depends on the relative importance of highway and nonhighway use and the nature of the motor transport industry and of the nonhighway users. If the latter are few in number (railways, power plants), specific exemption for them, with registry as licensed purchasers and with close audit, is feasible. If there are many nonroad users, including smaller firms, the refund method is preferable, particularly to permit collection of the tax from the refinery. If there are only a few large road users, all sales can be exempted except those made to these firms, with a careful audit of buyer and seller. This method is dangerous in most countries, however, because highway transport firms are often small and collection from dealers permits evasion. Control may be facilitated if the oil sold to nonhighway users tax free is marked chemically in a certain way to permit checking. Great Britain has found this technique useful. While circumstances dictate the exact method, some

5. In a number of countries, such as the Philippines, the tax on diesel fuel is nominal. As a consequence, strong artificial incentive is given to use diesel vehicles, and commercial motor transport is excessively cheap relative to its real costs, with consequent overdevelopment.

technique must be employed; no satisfactory system of motor fuel taxation is economically or politically feasible otherwise.

A major question is that of relative benefit-based rates on diesel fuel and gasoline. Superficially it would appear that uniformity per gallon is required; but the diesel engine provides greater ton-mileage per gallon of fuel. Accordingly, to place the same burden per ton-mile, the tax on diesel fuel must be higher than that on gasoline by 33 percent or more.[6] Diesel vehicle users complain that a higher rate is discriminatory, but this is an instance in which uniformity of rates is discriminatory. Since, with minor exceptions, diesel fuel is used for commercial purposes only, no ability-based supplement is desirable. Therefore if a country seeks no more in the way of ability-based taxes on motor fuel than an amount equal to a third of the benefit-based tax, the two levies can be made uniform. But the difference in rationale must be recognized.

There is a small group of diesel-powered cars, primarily certain types of Mercedes. If gasoline is taxed more heavily than diesel fuel for ability reasons, the diesel car is favored. The only practicable solution is a special heavy license fee on diesel (or other nongasoline) private cars.

Control of motor fuel taxes is relatively simple compared with many other excises, apart from the nonhighway use problem noted above. Typically, petroleum products are produced by one or a few refineries, and the tax is applied to their sales on the basis of periodic (monthly or other) returns. Little direct inspection of the plant is required except in case of doubt. There is no need to collect from dealers except under some approaches to taxation of diesel fuel. Illicit production is impossible.

The rates are universally specific, as is logical in terms of the benefit basis. Since there is little quality or price variation, simplicity also dictates the use of specific rates for the ability-based portion as well. The homogeneity of product and the small number of firms make this one of the easiest of all taxes to operate; the only complication is created by the use of fuel for nonhighway purposes.

Motor Vehicle License Charges

Closely related to motor fuel taxes are annual levies upon motor vehicles, usually designated as license charges or fees. There are two justifications:

Benefit. The license tax is a standby charge, a supplement to the motor fuel tax for the privilege of using the roads. In addition, for larger vehicles, graduated license charges compensate for the failure of fuel con-

6. The figure is based on studies reported in U.S., Congress, House, *Supplementary Report of the Cost Allocation Study,* 89th Cong., 1st sess. H.D. 124 (Washington, D.C., 1965). This study showed a differential ranging from 17 percent for small trucks to 45 percent for the largest ones.

sumption, and thus of the motor fuel tax, to rise as rapidly as weight. Without some compensation, the burden on the larger vehicles will be less per ton-mile than that on the smaller. Theoretically, the additional charges on the larger vehicles should be established in relation to the additional highway costs for which they are responsible. But these are seldom ascertainable in a developing economy, and thus a reasonable rule-of-thumb guide is a rate structure such that the burden per ton-mile will be similar regardless of a vehicle's size. In countries with light automobile traffic and dirt or lightly paved roads, large vehicles are likely to cause disproportionate damage to roads and the burden per ton-mile should at least be as heavy as that on cars.

License fees suffer from one limitation: the charge is not related to the mileage traveled. To adjust for mileage, as some governments do with a special ton-mileage tax, makes the highway tax structure much more complex to operate and thus is not advisable in the earlier years of economic development. Actually, large transport trucks are usually kept busy most of the time; specialized equipment is the type less likely to be using the roads much of the time, and relative taxes on these vehicles can be adjusted accordingly.

There is little justification for varying the license charge on automobiles on a weight basis, since the weight differences are not great enough to affect road costs. Car length—which affects parking space requirements—is a more significant measure. But relative fuel consumption is of concern, particularly in countries not producing petroleum, suffering serious foreign exchange shortages, and seeking to discourage the use of cars that have high fuel consumption. One method is to adjust the license charge on the basis of engine capacity. This approach has merit, but it does encounter one difficulty: engine capacity and fuel consumption are not perfectly correlated because of differences in design. Some low capacity engines have high fuel consumption because of high speed revolution. American cars in particular have high engine capacity for their speed of rotation and thus are unreasonably penalized by a tax related to engine capacity. Accordingly, if horsepower is used, the rate differences should be moderate and the graduation should stop at a level that blankets most larger cars in a single group.

Ability. Possession of a private motor vehicle may be regarded as a measure of wealth and ability to pay and thus suitable for a tax in addition to that on motor fuel. But if such a measure is employed, neither a flat rate nor rates graduated according to weight or horsepower are satisfactory as there is no correlation between either of these measures and value, particularly in a country where there are many old cars. For cars of any one year there is of course a correlation, but there is also a substantial deviation: some of the most expensive European cars have low weight and engine capacity compared with those of American cars of equivalent or less value. Such correlation as exists for one year is lost as time passes, and high rates on heavy cars will force the junking of heavy old cars. The goal of discouraging importation of expensive cars is best served by a high tax on the initial purchase rather than high annual taxes.

Yet some variation in the annual levy is warranted. Since annual valuation is not feasible except in developed countries with highly organized markets for used cars, a simple solution is a system of licensing with some graduation according to engine capacity and with the charge diminishing with the age of the car down to a flat minimum. This is only a rough approximation to the desired goals, but it is preferable to heavy charges related to weight or horsepower but not to the age of the car.

EXCISE TAXES ON SERVICES

Excises are commonly imposed on particular types of services, primarily those regarded as luxuries. Entertainment and hotel taxes are among the most popular, along with taxes on airport departures and transport services. Levies on betting are closely related. Moderate hotel and motel services are suitable levies from an equity standpoint, since they are paid primarily by the upper income levels and by tourists, and they are not difficult to enforce, since hotels are usually licensed. Rates can be varied by class of hotel—"luxury," "first class," "other," as is common in Latin America. Some problems arise in distinguishing transient hotel facilities from lodging occupied for longer periods and from boarding houses with more or less permanent residents. A country concerned with developing its tourist trade must use some discretion in the choice of rates or tourists may be discouraged from coming, with possibly serious adverse effects on foreign exchange and employment. Entertainment taxes, again at reasonable rates, have perhaps even greater merit in view of the "luxury" character of the base and the greater concentration of expenditures in the higher income levels.

Taxes related to transport are of much more doubtful merit. Airport departure taxes are particularly annoying to tourists, coming as they do when the person is leaving and may have no local currency. Higher landing fees charged the airlines will accomplish the same objective. Taxes on domestic passenger transport have the unfortunate effect of favoring the higher income groups able to use their own motor vehicles, and by diverting business they lessen the ability of transport firms to provide good service and increase the deficits of state-owned railways. The poorest people are frequently the ones who are forced to use public transport. A tax on freight service is highly objectionable, as is any levy applying within production processes. The worst economic effect is the diversion of traffic from public carriers to vehicles owned by the shippers, with a consequent avoidance of tax. Quite apart from this objectionable feature is the lack of any rationale whatever for a levy on freight transport, a levy which has the overall effect of artificially increasing the cost of transport and lessening regional specialization. Such a tax is completely different in character and effect from a charge on motor vehicles for the road costs for which they are responsible and the inclusion in railway freight rates of costs of construction and maintenance of the rail lines. These charges reflect real economic costs for which the transport services are responsible; general taxes on transport service do not.

Taxes on betting have merit by usual standards but may direct gambling to small-scale illegal and unregulated forms.

MISCELLANEOUS SPECIAL EXCISES

A few countries have imposed relatively high excises, comparable to those of a sumptuary nature, upon other commodities regarded as particularly suitable measures of tax capacity. Sugar is an outstanding example; Somalia obtains 15 percent and Mauretania 6 percent of total tax revenue from levies on sugar (1968 budget figures). Great Britain traditionally placed a heavy excise upon tea and the Scandinavian countries upon candy. These taxes are open to the obvious criticism of discrimination against persons with high preferences for the taxed goods and the potential excess burden arising from distortion of consumption patterns.

A form of tax related to excises that spread from Europe to many developing countries is a stamp tax on various kinds of documents, including legal documents such as deeds and mortgages, receipts, and bank checks. The rates are normally relatively low, often a fixed amount unrelated to the face value of the document. Others are graduated according to the value. Similarly, Latin American countries frequently require that certain legal documents be prepared on special paper that must be purchased from the government at prices far in excess of cost.

The stamp taxes and stamped paper requirements for legal documents have at least a limited merit, since they involve documents for which certain governmental action is necessary; they are, accordingly, related to fees. Stamp taxes on receipts and bank checks, on the other hand, not only have no justification but are objectionable in several ways. Their nuisance is substantial, and they are not related to ability to pay in any usual sense. But most significantly, they discourage the use of the documents involved; business firms are less inclined to give receipts (unless the customer insists) if a stamp must be applied. Receipts consist more and more of cash register slips; to apply stamps to all these is a serious nuisance. Taxation of bank checks similarly encourages people to pay in cash instead of by check. Both of these effects reduce the potential evidence for the enforcement of sales and income taxes, which are far more significant as sources of revenue. In other words, a minor tax in effect sabotages the enforcement of major taxes.

EXPANSION OF AN EXCISE SYSTEM

As import substitution continuès, customs revenues will be lost on a growing range of products extending far beyond liquor, tobacco, and motor fuel. One solution to this problem is the establishment of additional excises in fields in which import substitution has occurred and which are regarded as particularly suitable for taxation on equity, economic, and administrative grounds.

Additional Coverage

The additional coverage takes two principal forms, which may be used separately or jointly:

Luxury consumption goods. The items selected for tax may be those regarded as a good measure of taxpaying ability because of their luxury characteristics. These may be nondurables; soft drinks are often singled out for taxation early as their use becomes widespread. Bakery products are other examples. Consumer durables such as radios, phonograph records, motor vehicles, and electrical appliances are often regarded as suitable objects for taxation. Domestic production frequently involves no more than the assembly of imported parts, with limited value added and contribution to the domestic economy.

Items of widespread use. Countries may tax items of widespread use to maintain revenue without high rates. Clothing and textiles are frequently the largest, or one of the largest, categories in customs revenue. Since most developing countries can produce these products, especially clothing, with reasonable efficiency, import substitution occurs early in the development process. Sugar is another product of widespread use frequently subject to tax because of its revenue productivity, plus some thought that it is not in the "absolutely essential" class. Taxation of sugar may be regarded as a substitute for the taxation of products made with it.

Taxation of luxury items fits the usual standards of equity and the desire to stimulate savings through a reduction of luxury consumption. Use of the second type of excise, especially when applying to all forms of cloth, cheap or expensive, at the same rate, can be questioned in terms of equity. It is the type of tax that can be justified only if a country seeks as a matter of policy to force everyone at all income levels to curtail consumption in order to aid development.

Characteristics of Expanded Excise Systems

An expanded system of excises differs substantially from the more traditional types. First, the rates are relatively low, partly because demand elasticity is likely to be greater and thus revenue maximization may be reached at a lower tax rate (relative to the prices of the goods). Furthermore, there is no intent to penalize the use of the goods as there is with liquor and tobacco. Since rates are lower, controls over the firms are less severe. Physical inspection of the type used with liquor and beer is rarely employed, enforcement depending on audit.

Rates are frequently specific as long as the number of categories covered is relatively small and the goods are homogeneous. For example, in the East African excise system, the rate on sugar is 22.40 Kenyan shillings per hundredweight; on packaged biscuits, 25 Kenyan cents per pound; on soap, 25 shillings per 100 pounds; on fabrics, 25 cents per square yard; and on paints, 4 shillings per gallon.[7] As the excises are extended further, some ad valorem rates must be employed, since many categories contain so many nonhomogeneous items that a specific basic is unacceptable. In the more developed countries, most excises (except liquor, tobacco, and motor fuel) have ad valorem rates.

The union government of India has extended excise taxation further than any other country; excise revenue rose from 0.7 percent of total national income in 1950–51 to 4.3 percent in 1966–67, and from 17 percent to 51 percent of Union government revenues. As of 1968–69 there were some 75 different excises, including the traditional levies and ones on various luxury goods and on a number of items of widespread usage.[8] Ten of the excises—those on diesel oil, tobacco products, sugar, motor fuel, yarn and fabrics, iron and steel, kerosene, tires and tubes, cement, and matches—yielded 76 percent of the total excise revenue. Several excises provided less than 0.01 percent of total excise revenue; the 9 with the lowest yield provided a combined revenue of less than 0.5 percent of total excise tax revenue. Most of the excises have specific rates.

Merits of the Broadened Excise Approach

The extension of excises beyond the traditional sphere offers the direct and obvious advantage of replacing duty lost on the commodities as import substitution occurs. As noted, this is of particular importance when domestic production involves nothing more than assembly, blending, or packaging. At the same time, excises discourage excessive import substitution. In these instances they are, in a sense, alternatives to continued taxation of the parts and materials, and are more satisfactory when goods may

7. The Kenya shilling contains 100 cents; 1 shilling equals 14 U.S. cents.
8. See W. R. Mahler, "Sales and Excise Taxation in India" (Ph.D. diss., Syracuse University, 1969), chaps. 3–8. The following sample gives some idea of the coverage: motor fuel, sugar, steel ingots, coffee, tea, cement, footwear, soap, paper, paint, glass, glassware, yarn, phonograph records, film, cosmetics, motor vehicles, cloth, plywood, and fuel oil.

be produced with various alternative materials and parts, with the method based in part on relative duty rates. Furthermore, commodities may be imported for other uses as well, as previously noted.

Compared with the major alternative, a sales tax, excises offer easier administration so long as the number of excises is relatively small and specific rates can be employed. Collection of specific rates at the manufacturing level is possible without discriminating between imported and domestic goods or among various distribution channels. Excises can be limited to those fields in which effective, inexpensive collection is possible, avoiding the products of many small artisan establishments sold directly to the users or through small shops.

Excises can be (but may not be) confined to products regarded as suitable in terms of equity, and rates can likewise be adjusted on different commodities in terms of the objectives. By contrast, exemptions and rate differentiation seriously complicate the operation of sales taxes.

Limitations to the Excise Approach

The basic weakness of the excise approach is the growing complexity and loss of inherent advantages as the system expands. So long as the coverage is limited the excise system is simple to operate, but the revenue possibilities are likewise limited. As the coverage expands, the advantages are lost and the disadvantages magnified.

More specifically, the limited coverage of the excise approach not only restricts revenue possibilities compared with a general sales tax but inevitably discriminates against those with relatively high preferences for the taxed goods and leads to a possible distortion of resource allocation from more preferred goods. With some goods taxed and others untaxed, persons preferring the latter will be favored and relative consumption and production of them will increase, with a possible loss of economic welfare. These objections are relevant for any economy regardless of its level of development.

As the system expands the specific-rate basis becomes increasingly unsatisfactory. As noted in the analysis of customs duties, a specific rate is satisfactory only with homogeneous, uniform-price commodities. As excises are extended they apply to more and more goods that do not fully meet these requirements, with consequent restraint on economy varieties, greater regressiveness in distribution of the burden, and inequality of burden relative to consumer expenditures. Some categories, such as many food products and hardware, are so varied that either a wide range of separate excises must be established or ad valorem rates introduced. Detailed classifications impede administration and quickly become obsolete as new products develop and others change.

Collection at the production level, which is necessary for most excises if administration is to be simple, has some disadvantages even under specific rates. Margins between manufacturer's price and final retail sale price vary, and thus the ratio of tax to consumption expenditure will not be uniform nor conform, except by accident, with any desired patterns of non-uniformity. Furthermore, the markup methods of wholesale and retail pricing common in most countries lead to pyramiding, that is, increases in prices to consumers greater than the tax as markup percentages are added to purchase prices that include the tax. With the scope of excises expanded to the scale at which ad valorem rates become necessary, the evils of collection at the manufacturing level become much more serious. With the tax applied to value uniform treatment of imported and domestic goods and of firms using different distribution channels is virtually impossible, as is explained in detail in the next chapter. The discrimination will almost certainly distort production and distribution methods away from the optimum.

Finally, the excise system's lack of generality permits undesired import substitution on commodities not yet subject to excises. If excises are not introduced until domestic production is under way, the domestic producers will protest the excises strongly and may be driven out of business. Optimal resource use requires that unwanted import substitution be avoided.

As an excise structure expands the point is reached, sooner or later, at which the disadvantages of further extension, particularly the complexity, exceed those of a more general type of levy that, because of broader coverage, offers greater revenue potential and protection against undesired import substitution. Determining this point is difficult, and different countries have followed substantially different policies. Among the major determinants are the following:

1. The nature of domestic production, especially the range of commodities affected by import substitution. The smaller the number, the more feasible is the use of excise taxes.

2. The nature of the production and distribution structure, particularly the importance of small-scale artisans and retail shops. The more extensive the small-scale production, the greater the advantage of utilizing a few excises instead of a sales tax.

3. The extent to which commodities suitable for excises are consumed in patterns that provide an acceptable distribution of tax.

4. The capacity of the administrative structure to deal with the larger number of firms encountered under a sales tax.

5. The urgency of the need for revenue, given other tax sources and requirements for economic development. The broader base of the sales tax offers greater potential for revenue at politically acceptable tax rates.

6. The dangers of unwanted import substitution. This criterion, perhaps the most significant, is the one commonly neglected in planning tax policy.

Relative Importance of Various Excises

Table 3–2 shows the relative importance of various excise taxes for those countries for which information is available. The data of this table are of limited significance. A failure to show revenue from a particular source may indicate that domestic production has not yet developed or that a customs duty is collected on importation of materials instead of an excise on domestic production. Or the article may be subjected to a high rate in

TABLE 3–2. RELIANCE ON MAJOR EXCISE TAXES (COUNTRIES FOR WHICH DATA ARE AVAILABLE)

Country	Percentage of Total Excise Tax Revenue			
	Tobacco Products	Alcoholic Beverages	Motor Fuel	Other
Under $850 GNP				
Congo (B)	0	18	82	0
Malagasy Rep.	0	30	30	40
Mauretania	6	4	37	53
Ghana	41	23	0	36
Mali	16	6	51	27
Senegal	15	7	62	16
Sierra Leone	71	25	0	4
Somalia	44	1	0	55
Zambia	31	56	12	1
Iran	0	11	64	25
Ceylon	38	34	0	28
Malaysia	9	18	68	5
Singapore	0	26	44	30
Panama	10	49	29	12
Trinidad & Tobago	0	55	43	2
Venezuela	32	45	10	13
Guyana	0	0	98	2
Over $850 GNP				
Austria	38	11	51	0
Belgium	24	15	53	8
Denmark	29	23	17	31
France	20	19	51	10
Germany	29	10	47	14
Italy	27	2	43	28
Japan	11	33	24	32
Luxembourg	36	5	44	15
Netherlands	35	20	40	5
Norway	13	23	15	49
Sweden	17	28	30	25
Switzerland	15	2	53	30
United Kingdom	34	21	26	19

Source: See table A–1, appendix.

the sales tax structure rather than to an excise. With the data as given, the relative importance of the major levies varies widely. Motor fuel levies yield more than half the excise revenue in 6 of the 17 countries; liquor taxes do so in 2 and are the largest source in 2 others; the tobacco tax is dominant in 2. In the developed countries, motor fuel and tobacco taxes are the chief sources, with liquor substantially less; only in Japan is it the major item.

RELIANCE ON EXCISE TAXES AS GNP INCREASES

The importance of excise tax collections has been shown in table 3–1 for various GNP classes. The yield rises, in early years of development, as a percentage of total tax revenue and then falls; as a percentage of indirect tax revenue the figure rises initially, stabilizes, and then rises sharply. The initial rise is attributable to the development of excises as import substitution occurs, and to the peculiarity that sales taxes are currently more important in the lowest income countries than in the next higher group. In the latter, excises are more important than sales taxes. The ultimate drop in the percentage of total revenue reflects the declining importance of indirect taxes; as a percentage of indirect taxes, excises rise in the highest group (despite the more general use of sales taxes) because customs revenue drops so sharply.

Use of the Musgrave regression technique shows no significant relationship between relative reliance on excise taxes and per capita GNP:

For all countries included:

$$ED/T = e^{-2.27096} \; Y_c^{.04956} \quad\quad R^2: .01$$
$$(.6899)$$

For countries with GNP under $500:

$$ED/T = e^{-3.402} \; Y_c^{.28636} \quad\quad R^2: .07$$
$$(1.63)$$

T = tax revenue; ED = excise tax revenue

Table A–1 in the appendix provides data by individual country, showing a very wide variation. This variation reflects several influences. The former French West and Equatorial African countries have developed sales tax systems, for example, while many of the African countries of the British Commonwealth have introduced excise systems in lieu of a sales tax. Domestic production of commodities typically subject to excises has developed in some countries earlier than in others. Some continue to use customs duties to tax the products despite domestic production, as for example, through the taxation of imported petroleum rather than through an excise on the motor fuel.

Supplementary References

The literature on excise taxation, other than the critical analysis of the "excess burden" argument, is very limited.

Boothalimgam, S. *Final Report on Rationalization and Simplification of the Tax Structure.* New Delhi: Government of India Press, 1968.

Crombie, Sir James. *Her Majesty's Customs and Excise.* London: George Allen & Unwin, 1962.

Cutt, James. *Taxation and Economic Development in India.* New York: Praeger, 1969.

Report of the Royal Commission on Taxation (Canada), vol. 5. Ottawa: Queen's Printer, 1966.

4.

Sales Taxes at the Manufacturing Level and the Wholesale Level

The inherent inadequacies of excise systems in protecting revenue as domestic production develops, in preventing unwanted import substitution, and in providing a simple system of internal indirect taxes suggest the need for a more general levy on sales, and many developing countries have introduced this form of tax, as shown in table 4–1.

The simplest step from an excise tax structure is to a general levy at the manufacturing level plus application of this levy to imports to ensure the desired relationship between taxes on domestic and imported goods. At first most of the tax will be collected at customs, but the application to domestic manufacturers as well will avoid the difficulties of sole reliance on customs. An alternative way is to establish the tax at the wholesale level, applying it to sales by manufacturers, wholesalers, or importers to retailers and to importation by retailers or final consumers (or to importation at all stages, with a subsequent credit against tax on domestic sales).

THE MANUFACTURING AND IMPORT LEVEL

The manufacturers sales tax was first established by Canada in 1923, Argentina in 1935, the Philippines in 1936, and Pakistan in 1951. It has been introduced in more recent years by Colombia (1965), Ghana (1965), Uganda (1968), Tanzania (1969), and South Africa (1969). It is used as a levy on firms selling in more than one state of the Union Douanière et Economique de l'Afrique Central (UDEAC). There are manufacturing elements in the sales taxes of the Indian states.[1] The tax is also used in Greece and South Viet Nam and has been used at times by France, Chile, Finland, and other countries. It is being used, at least temporarily, by Nicaragua.

1. The taxes in Rajasthan and Madhya Pradesh are often classified as manufacturers taxes. They are more appropriately designated wholesale sales taxes, as tax is not applied to sales by a manufacturer to a wholesaler.

TABLE 4–1. RELIANCE ON SALES TAXATION BY GNP CLASS

Estimated GNP Per Capita, U.S. $	No. Countries Included	No. Countries Using Sales Tax	% Total Tax Revenue from Sales Tax		% Indirect Tax Revenue from Sales Tax	
			All	Users	All	Users
100 and under	20	13	14	21	20	33
101–200	11	8	11	15	17	21
201–500	18	9[1]	8	16	13	25
501–850	8	4[1]	9	19	16	37
Over 850	15	14	13	14	41	45

Source: See table A–1, appendix.
[1] One additional country uses the tax but breakdown of yield by type of tax is not available.

Structure and Administration

✗ This type of sales tax has its direct impact on the economy in the form of tax supplements to prices of imports or of goods sold by taxable manufacturers. Thus the prices of these goods rise relative to factor incomes and to services and commodities not subject to tax. The assumption in this discussion is that these supplements are transferred forward to the retail prices of the taxed products, either by identical amounts or with percentage markups applied.

This tax applies to the sale by the manufacturer of taxable goods plus the importation of goods (usually, by persons other than registered manufacturers), although Colombia applies tax to sales by the importer rather than to the importation. Since the levies are designed to be single stage in nature, various techniques are employed to prevent multiple application of tax to the same commodity. Under the "suspension" rule as used in Canada, Uganda, and Pakistan, for example, the tax applies only to the sale of final products, since manufacturers can buy materials and parts free of tax. Under the second, or value-added technique, which employs features of the value-added tax discussed in chapter 6, sales by manufacturers of all goods, finished or not, are subject to tax, but manufacturers are allowed to deduct from their figures of taxable sales the cost of taxed materials and parts purchased during the year. This method is used in Argentina, Greece, and the Philippines (but the deduction is allowed in the Philippines only if the tax has been paid at the same rate on the materials). Alternatively, as in Colombia since 1966 and South Viet Nam, firms are authorized to deduct from tax liability the tax paid on materials and parts purchased during the period.

There is little to choose from between the suspension and value-added approaches so long as they are set up properly. The suspension method is in some ways simpler, but it may be more difficult to control in countries in which enforcement is not highly effective. The value-added technique permits collection of a considerable portion of tax at importation and therefore lessens evasion, and like the value-added tax proper it offers the advantage of facilitating cross checking among firms. Since only manufacturers are liable for the tax, no tax applies at subsequent stages in distribution channels. Sales for export are usually—but not always—exempt.

Rates. Tax rates are typically high compared with those of many other sales taxes, as they must be if they are to raise significant revenue. Canada uses a single rate, 12 percent in 1970, and Viet Nam applies a 6 percent rate. Other countries use rate differentiation in an effort to place a heavier tax on goods regarded as luxuries. The least differentiation is in Ghana, with a 7.5 percent rate on goods subject to excises, 10 percent on imports, and 11.5 percent on other domestically produced goods. The primary rate in both Uganda and Argentina is 10 percent, with reduced rates of 5 percent in the former and 3 percent in the latter and higher figures of 15 and 20 percent in each (plus, in Uganda, some specific rates).[2] Tanzania likewise uses a basic rate of 10 percent, luxury rates of 15 and 20 percent, and some specific rates. The principal rate in Nicaragua is 10 percent, with a range from 5 percent to 70 percent. The basic figure in Colombia is 3 percent, with 8 and 15 percent figures; the Philippines, with a 7 percent basic figure, has rates of 30 and 50 percent on luxury goods. The basic figure in Greece is 7 percent, with reduced rates of 5, 3.6, and 1.8 percent on widely used goods. Pakistan uses a 15 percent basic rate, with 20 percent on luxuries plus a 25 percent defense surcharge. Rates are sometimes higher on imported than on domestic goods, as, for example, in Colombia.

Exemptions. Unprocessed food does not fall within the orbit of a manufacturers sales tax, since no manufacturing is involved. Taxing it when sold by farmers or retailers would significantly alter the structure of the tax. Beyond unprocessed food, exemptions vary. On the one extreme, Canada exempts almost all foods except a few items such as candy regarded as luxuries. Greece exempts basic foodstuffs. But in the developing economies—Uganda, Tanzania, Ghana, Colombia, and the Philippines are examples—the practice is to exempt only basic unprocessed foods (and milk) and to subject all other food to tax. In Ghana a line is drawn on the basis of whether or not foods are packed in airtight containers, an approach that conforms with usual equity standards. In developing economies, basic subsistence consists primarily of unprocessed food; by exempting this food the burden on the lowest income groups and the discrimination against those

2. The Uganda and Tanzania acts are unique in that a separate rate is specified for each item of the East African tariff (which uses the Brussels Tariff Nomenclature). The tax in Nicaragua is also imposed on specified tariff items.

who must buy their food compared with those who produce it themselves are greatly reduced or eliminated, as is regressivity of the tax.

Apart from foods, exemptions of consumer goods are usually relatively limited, confined largely to drugs and books.

A manufacturers tax, per se, is not applicable to services under the usual definition of manufacturer. The term could be defined to include the rendering of services, of course, but to do so would bring within the tax structure a type of establishment substantially different from the usual manufacturing concern in terms of size, records systems, and other characteristics. A separate tax on services is likely to prove more satisfactory than incorporating services within the production tax. If uniformity of tax relative to consumer expenditure is desired, the rate must be lower on services since it applies to the final price to consumers.

The tax treatment of producers goods varies. All of the manufacturers sales taxes exclude, by various techniques, the materials and parts becoming physical ingredients of goods produced. Uganda and Tanzania exempt many materials unconditionally; more commonly they are exempted conditionally according to use. Failure to exclude materials would result in some characteristics of the turnover tax. Canada (currently, and for most of the life of its tax), Ghana, and Uganda exclude industrial and farm machinery from the scope of the tax, but Colombia, Greece, the Philippines, and Argentina do not. The issues involved are the same with all forms of sales tax and will be discussed in chapter 7.

Administration. All manufacturers, as defined, are required to register for purposes of the tax. The practice on the registration of wholesalers varies; Canada originally registered many of them and then reverted to a practice of doing so only if more than half of their sales were conditionally exempt (primarily sales to manufacturers). Other countries register only a few. The aim of registering some wholesalers is to avoid tax refunds when goods sold on a taxable basis by manufacturers are resold for conditionally exempt purposes (such as for use as materials or for export). In fields in which wholesalers are relatively large compared to manufacturers there is also an administrative advantage.[3] More typically, however, wholesalers are more difficult to control than manufacturers. Registration of all wholesalers would convert the levy into a wholesale sales tax.

The number of taxpayers (other than importers) depends on (1) the relative development of manufacturing in the economy, (2) the practice with respect to the registering of wholesalers, and (3) the policies followed

3. Richard M. Bird in *Sales Taxation in Colombia* (Cambridge: Harvard University, Center for International Affairs, 1966), pp. 28–29, argues that in Colombia the wholesale level would have been preferable, because of the small number of wholesalers relative to manufacturers. Other observers have questioned his conclusions.

in exemption of small firms, as discussed below. Reported numbers of tax-paying firms (not including importers) are shown in table 4–2.

Collection. Tax is collected on imports in conjunction with duties and from domestic producers on the basis of returns. Filing periods are monthly in Uganda, Ghana, the Philippines, Canada, and Nicaragua; bimonthly in Colombia; and annual, with monthly payment, in Argentina. The return is due on the 15th in Uganda and Nicaragua, the 20th in the Philippines and Argentina, the 25th in Ghana, the 30th in Colombia, and the last day of the month in Canada, the date in all cases being in the month following that for which the return is due. The monthly payments in Argentina are made on the basis of the return for the preceding year as adjusted for inflation, with reconciliation with actual sales made at the end of the year.

Major Problems: Taxpaying Firms

Definition of Manufacturing. The concept of manufacturing is not easily defined in simple fashion to attain the desired results. Canada does not define it at all but merely lists certain borderline activities as being covered. Uganda defines manufacture (article 58) as "to subject any physical matter to any process . . . which materially changes such matter in substance, character or appearance. . . ." Regardless of legal definition, the core meaning of the concept is the change in the physical form of goods other than by agricultural activity. The principal question arises over extractive activity such as mining and lumbering, and processing that involves merely assembly, blending, packaging, or reconditioning. Mining and lumbering are normally not covered by the law. Activities such as assembly and packaging are usually defined to be manufacturing if the article changes form or is placed in a container (as differentiated from a bag or basket). No matter where the line is drawn, questions of interpretation are inevitable. There is, economically, no clearly definable line between manufacturing and various service activities.

TABLE 4–2. REGISTRANTS FOR MANUFACTURERS SALES TAX

Country	Population (million)	Estimated Per Capita GNP, U.S. $	Registered Taxpayers
Uganda	8	100	130
Ghana	8	230	500
Colombia	19	280	8,250[1]
Nicaragua	1.8	330	400
Argentina	23	780	60,000[2]
Canada	20	2,240	46,000

[1] Includes importers.
[2] As reported. The figure would appear to be extremely high.

Small Firms. In many developing economies, small artisan producers are very common. The relative surplus of labor and shortage of capital make hand production of shoes, furniture, clothing, and many other products economical, whereas in developed economies efficiency requires mass production industries. The small producers typically operate in their homes, helped by members of the household and apprentice labor. Frequently the artisans are illiterate and keep no records. Even the more educated ones who do have records can easily conceal the correct data since they are not subject to outside audit as are larger enterprises and only one or a few persons are involved in any falsification. Thus effective control of these firms for tax purposes is impossible. The problem is more complex than with retailers under a retail sales tax. Small retailers can at least be subjected to tax on their purchases so long as they are made from registered suppliers. But artisans frequently obtain their raw materials from nonregistered producers or sellers. Even if their materials are taxed, the value the firms add to the product is usually much greater than that added by retailers.

There is no ideal solution. If no exemption is provided, the smallest firms will escape anyway, and the line between payer and nonpayer will be haphazard and irregular. A formal exemption of firms with sales below a certain figure provides a more systematic solution. But the line is arbitrary, and checks to ensure that concerns just above the line are registered is difficult. Some firms may move back and forth across the line. There is always the danger that a firm will divide into several firms to stay below the line—a simple practice with the extended family system common in many developing economies. This is reported to be a significant source of tax evasion in India.

Actual practices vary. Canada simply excludes certain types of businesses (such as blacksmiths and opticians) and manufacturers with sales under specified figures—$3,000 a year in some fields, $1,000 in others. In the highly developed Canadian economy, little competitive disturbance results. The Philippine law exempts very small firms (those with sales under about $540 a year) as do the Indian states.[4] Colombia and Ghana exclude small firms informally rather than by law; in the latter, the so-called wayside firms—small establishments—are simply not registered.

Nicaragua has no exemption, but in fact small firms are not reached. Uganda employs the most systematic program. There is no exemption by volume of business; sales in industries in which small firms are numerous (shoes, furniture, clothing, and bakery products, for example) are ex-

---

4. The exemption figures for manufacturers on the basis of annual sales volume are 5,000 rupees (about $500) in Madhya Pradesh and Rajasthan, 10,000 rupees (about $1,000) in West Bengal and Punjab, and 20,000 rupees ($2,000) in Gujarat.

empt but their raw materials are taxed at twice the normal rate.[5] This rule is based on the assumption that the processing doubles the value of the products. Larger firms in the industry may register if they wish and pay tax on their sales. Tanzania uses the same technique. This approach does not solve the problem entirely, as some materials will be bought from unregistered firms and the value added will differ among firms, but it does lessen the competitive disturbances produced by outright exemption. It does not solve the problem of the small firm in other industries.

Fortunately, the artisan problem becomes progressively less serious as an economy develops. In Colombia, for example, the output of artisans fell from 27 percent of total manufacturing output in 1925 to 20 percent in 1940 and 13 percent in the early 1960s.[6]

The Valuation Problem

The most serious problem in the satisfactory operation of a sales tax at the manufacturing level is that of valuation, that is, the specification of the taxable price. Under usual standards, the aim with any sales tax is to provide uniform treatment of alternative methods of organization of production and distribution in order to avoid inequity and distortion of choice of methods. Such distortion results in loss of efficiency in the use of resources, which developing economies can ill afford. Discrimination against some methods of organization compared with others creates a differential burden that is hard to shift. Difficulty arises with the manufacturers tax because its impact comes early in the production-distribution flow. Some manufacturers may prefer to integrate forward, undertaking wholesale and retail activities. But if they do, the taxable price may be higher than that for nonintegrated firms. The result will be discrimination against the integrated firms, which may be forced to contract their scope of operation.

All firms are given an incentive to push as much activity and cost as possible beyond the point of impact of the tax so as to reduce liability. Those firms not in a position to do so are subject to discrimination. As the transfer occurs, revenue from the tax falls, and the rate must be increased to maintain the same revenue. If this happens, the pressure to transfer activity forward increases. Some firms may gain control over distributors and sell to them at artificially low prices to reduce the tax still more. There may also be widespread differences among industries in integration patterns; the overall tax relative to consumer spending will be greater in the industries in which economic forces require forward integration.

Solutions. Most countries using this form of tax have made little attempt to solve the problem except to seek to raise the taxable price to open

5. On textiles, 15 percent instead of 10.
6. J. Levin, "Effects of Economic Development," p. 87.

market levels when sales are made at artificially low prices between jointly controlled companies.

The most concerted effort has been made by Canada.[7] Companies in various industries are allowed to apply the tax to the transfer of goods to "unlicensed wholesale branches"—frequently existing on paper only— rather than to actual sales. Two rules are employed for establishing the taxable price on such transfers:

1. When frequent sales are made to independent wholesalers, manufacturers may use the prices actually charged on such sales as the basis for prices on the transfers, which occur when sales are made to retailers or consumers.

2. In other industries (typically about 25), a system of discounts is prescribed whereby manufacturers selling to retailers or consumers may reduce the price for tax purposes by a specified percentage, which is determined on the basis of study of typical margins in the field.[8]

This system achieves only rough equality, since the deductions are based on standard prices and percentages, not actual ones. No adjustments are allowed in industries in which sales through wholesalers are not significant, and thus the overall burden on products of these industries is greater than that in fields in which discounts are authorized.

Whereas Canada seeks to adjust the taxable price backward to the typical manufacturer-to-wholesaler level, Uganda brings the taxable price forward to the typical wholesaler-to-retailer level. The tax is applied to the wholesale price, which is defined as "the price . . . the goods would fetch on a sale made by a wholesaler to a retail trader" (article 13). In accordance with this rule, a 10 percent supplement is added to the actual sales price by manufacturers to wholesalers but not to the price on sales to retailers or final consumers. Ten percent is also added to the import price except, presumably, for imports by retailers or final consumers.

The Argentina law allows adjustment in limited instances, but the requirements are so rigid that the provision is not significant.

In the United States, similar problems arose with the manufacturers excise taxes. No adjustment was provided by law except on direct sales to final consumers. On sales to retailers, the Internal Revenue Service permitted manufacturers to transfer the goods to a sales subsidiary, which in turn sold to retailers, and to apply the tax to the price charged the sales subsidiary so long as this was the same figure charged independent whole-

7. See *Report of the Royal Commission on Taxation,* vol. 5, chap. 28; J. F. Due, *The General Manufacturers Sales Tax in Canada* (Toronto: Canadian Tax Foundation, 1951), chap. 6. There has been very little change since 1951.

8. In practice the discount is applied to the tax rate rather than to the taxable price. The result is the same.

salers or represented a discount below the price-to-retailer figure regarded by IRS as reasonable.

No approach can meet the problem entirely. There are many possible distribution methods and channels, and any type of adjustment based on averages is certain to favor some firms and discriminate against others. Any firm shifting more than typical amounts of activity beyond the impact of the tax is favored.

One particularly troublesome case is that in which large retailers integrate backwards, performing wholesale functions and buying cheaply in large quantities from manufacturers. While this is a manufacturer-to-retailer sale, clearly no downward adjustment in price is warranted; yet in practice this situation cannot be distinguished from that of forward integration by manufacturers. The problem is aggravated with private brand merchandise of large retailers, who often supply research and designs and undertake all advertising activity. Accordingly the retailers buy at prices lower than the usual manufacturer-to-wholesaler price. This has been a major issue in Canada, where large-scale retailing and private brands are particularly important. One partial solution—as followed in Colombia—is to define the retailer in such instances to be the manufacturer. But this procedure can easily result in overtaxing private brands.

The other difficulty with the policy of allowing adjustments is the consequent complexity. This has been a major source of complaint in Canada, where the system is far more complicated than necessary. But at best the task of the manufacturer in calculating his tax liability is complex, there are certain to be many questions of interpretation, auditing is difficult, and new opportunities for evasion are created. Yet failure to make adjustments at all will lead to loss of efficiency in production.

Imported vs. Domestic Goods. Part of the problem centers on the relationship of imported and domestic goods. The usual—but not universal—policy is to apply the tax to imports at the time of importation. Of the countries using this tax, only Colombia does not do so, instead collecting the tax on the sale by the importer. But the point of impact on imports is not necessarily equivalent to point of impact of tax on domestic goods. Activities of domestic manufacturers, such as advertising and wholesale distribution, may be performed for imported goods by wholesalers and retailers, and imports will be favored relative to domestic goods. The Philippines seeks to meet this problem by applying a 100 percent markup for tax purposes to the CIF duty-paid value of imports of luxury goods, 50 percent on semiluxury goods, and 25 percent on other goods. These figures are, of course, highly arbitrary and unequal.

On other imported goods, distribution activities will be undertaken by the foreign exporter, and the goods will be imported directly by retailers at relatively high prices compared with those of domestic goods. Thus imported commodities will sometimes be favored, in other instances domestic goods. In Canada, one group of firms has complained for many years that the sales tax favors imported goods; another group argues the reverse. Theoretically any differences could be offset by tariff adjustments, but in practice this is difficult to do and is usually not attempted.

Imports of materials and parts and unfinished goods by registered manufacturers are typically free of tax under the suspension form of tax. With the value-added approach, the tax applies but is credited against the tax due on the sale of the finished product. These imports give rise to few valuation problems.

Evaluation of Manufacturers Tax

The primary advantage of the form of sales tax imposed at the manufacturing level is the relative ease of collection. As suggested above, the number of manufacturers is small, certainly as compared with the number of retailers, and in most countries relative to the number of firms selling at wholesale.[9] In many developing economies there are only a few hundred manufacturers. These are typically large firms, often corporations and foreign owned, and thus easily subject to effective control. Records are good, and the firms are typically subject to audit by public accounting firms, who will detect most outright evasion of tax. The firms are not only large but are often relatively specialized, and therefore exemption of various classes of commodities and rate differentiation are relatively easy. A large portion of the tax is typically collected at importation in conjunction with customs duties, and escape is therefore difficult. These considerations make the tax attractive to countries in which wholesale and retail trade are conducted by large numbers of small firms.

The primary difficulty with taxing at the manufacturing level is the valuation problem, as outlined in previous sections. The tax inevitably encourages changes in business policies and discriminates against firms unable to take steps to lessen tax liability. Adjustments to meet the problem can never be perfect and complicate the operation of the tax. Closely related is the inability to provide equal treatment of imported and domestic goods. Particular difficulties are encountered if a country participates in a common market and the destination principle is employed. Fiscal frontiers must be employed on goods produced in other countries in the common market, and equality of treatment is difficult to attain. This problem can be

9. In Uganda, for example, the number of wholesalers is estimated to be 2,000, compared with 130 registered manufacturers. On the other hand, in Colombia the number of manufacturers is twice the number of wholesalers and the number of retailers is ten times as great.

avoided only if the country of origin collects the tax and remits it to the country of destination, as in the UDAEC countries of West Africa. The origin principle is usable only if the countries use the same sales tax form and rates, since otherwise the producers in the country may find themselves at a competitive disadvantage.

There are several objections to this form of tax from the standpoint of distribution of burden. The most serious, from an economic standpoint, is the variation in the ratio of the tax to consumer expenditures arising from the difference in margins (total value added) between manufacturer and final consumer. The relative tax burden on consumer spending will be high on low margin goods (typically items of everyday usage) and low on luxury goods. This difference can be offset only in very rough fashion by variations in rates.

Another objection is the tendency for the tax to pyramid on the way to the final consumer as merchants apply percentage markups to purchase prices that include tax. The price to the consumer rises by a sum larger than the tax received by the government. Pyramiding occurs in imperfect markets characterized by universal use of percentage markup systems. As long as total demand is not too elastic in a situation in which most prices are being raised, all firms will benefit from the increase, and competition may be very slow to eliminate the excess. On the other hand, some firms may find it difficult to shift the full tax, and the need for shifting through several successive transactions lessens the likelihood of precision. At the same time, separation of the tax from the price, which may be desirable for reasons of price control or consumer awareness of tax, is virtually impossible—partly for bookkeeping reasons, partly because doing so reveals distributor margins to the final consumer, a result merchants dislike.

Even the administrative aspects of the tax are not entirely favorable, apart from the complications created by attempts to solve the valuation problem. As noted, while many manufacturers are large, in most developing countries there are many small artisan producers, who are difficult to reach by taxation. While exemption lessens the administrative problem, it is still serious because of the difficulty of enforcing registration of firms just above the line, and inequity results. The rate is higher with this form of sales tax than with any other; thus the pressure to evade—as well as to alter business practices—is the greatest. In some instances there are administrative complications when exemption depends on the ultimate use and the commodities are sold to a dealer rather than the final user.

Another problem arises from tax rate changes. Merchants will have on hand tax-paid inventory when the rate is changed, and may be able to make additional profit out of the change or may be squeezed severely. Floor stock taxes on inventory (used with excises in the United States) and refunds when the rate falls add materially to the complications. Failure to provide adjustments, however, will result in alteration in buying patterns as firms delay buying in anticipation of rate reductions or stock up in anticipation of increases. The tax-paid inventory feature increases the capital requirements of retailers, who may lack adequate credit, and causes greater losses when goods are damaged or lost or become unsalable.

Despite these rather serious limitations, the tax is a workable one, particularly in earlier years of development when a country has only a few large manufacturing plants. Most of the tax will be collected at importation,[10] while the general nature of the levy avoids unwanted import substitution. The precise valuation refinements are not necessarily serious under the circumstances. The tax is particularly attractive when wholesaling and retailing are small scale and largely family rather than commercial. As development proceeds, however, the scale of wholesaling and retailing increases, and discrimination produced by the manufacturers tax becomes increasingly serious.

The Wholesale and Import Level

A second level for imposition of the sales tax is the last wholesale transaction, that is, the sale to the retailer. This type of levy is usually referred to as a wholesale sales tax or sometimes as a purchase tax.[11] This approach has been suggested for a number of years in various studies of taxation in developing countries, as for example in the Shoup report on taxation in Venezuela.[12] But developing countries have been reluctant to use this type of levy, although several have taxed sales by some wholesalers in the framework of manufacturers sales taxes (Pakistan, for example) and others in the framework of retail sales taxes (Honduras is one). A form of wholesale tax is used in the Indian states of Rajasthan and Madhya Pradesh (basic 6 percent rates). Otherwise, experience with the wholesale form of tax has thus been limited primarily to developed countries: Switzerland, Australia, New Zealand, Great Britain (with limited coverage and high rates), Denmark (1962–1967), and Portugal. The Irish tax has a wholesale element in it.

The Australian tax was introduced in 1930 and that of New Zealand in 1933 to replace declining revenues from customs duties, a decline aggravated by the depression. Australia studied the Canadian experience with the manufacturers tax and chose the wholesale level instead, primarily

10. Even in the Philippines, 299 million pesos were collected at importation in 1968 compared with 138 million pesos from domestic manufacturers.
11. The term "purchase tax" is also used to indicate a sales tax with sharply differentiated rates.
12. C. S. Shoup, *Fiscal System of Venezuela* (Baltimore: Johns Hopkins Press, 1959), chap. 11.

because of the relatively greater importance of imports in the Australian economy. New Zealand essentially copied the Australian tax. The United Kingdom introduced the tax in 1940 because of war revenue needs and the desire to curtail consumption, and Switzerland did so in 1941 to meet rising defense costs. Both countries chose the wholesale instead of the retail level after studying sales taxes elsewhere to avoid having to collect taxes from large numbers of small retailers and, in Great Britain, from a desire to use extensive rate differentiation. The Danish tax was introduced in 1962 as a source of additional revenue.[13] A wholesale tax was recommended in Canada in 1956 to replace the manufacturers tax,[14] but widespread opposition to the change developed, mainly from firms that feared they would be subject to greater taxes than their competitors, and the government did not accept the recommendations. Portugal established the tax in 1966 to diversify its tax structure and increase revenue for military purposes. The same year Eire supplemented its retail sales tax with a wholesale tax on consumer durables to avoid raising the retail tax rate and to place a higher burden on luxury goods.

Structure of Wholesale Taxes

The wholesale tax is applied to the last wholesale transaction through which a commodity passes. Registration of vendors selling at wholesale, but not those selling at retail, serves as the primary basis for delineation of taxable sales. Registration is required of all manufacturers and merchants selling at wholesale, with exceptions subsequently noted. Manufacturers must be registered to enable them to buy materials and parts free of tax and to ensure payment of tax on their sales to retailers or consumers. Retailers are not registered. The tax therefore applies to sales by registered firms (manufacturers or wholesalers) to unregistered buyers (retailers or final consumers), and to imports by unregistered firms (retailers or final consumers) as well.

The tax does not apply to sales by unregistered firms, for example by retailers to consumers, or to sales by one registered firm to another (manufacturer to wholesaler; wholesaler distributor to wholesale jobber), except when the purchaser acquires the goods for a taxable purpose such as for office use. In such instances, the purchaser is usually expected to indicate that he is buying for a taxable purpose and the tax is applied by the seller. If he buys tax free he is required to account for the tax himself. Similarly, registered vendors may import free of tax; the tax then applies in the usual fashion when the goods are sold by the importer. A smaller portion of the tax is collected at importation than under a manufacturers sales tax, since

13. This tax was replaced by a value-added tax on July 3, 1967.
14. *Report of the Sales Tax Committee* (Ottawa, Queens Printer, 1956).

much importing is done by wholesale firms that are registered vendors. Imports could be subjected to tax with subsequent credit, but this procedure would be cumbersome with several domestic transfers prior to sale and is not followed anywhere.

The wholesale tax reflects the same considerations regarding exemptions as other single-stage sales taxes. Purchases of materials and parts becoming physical ingredients of final products are universally exempted. Switzerland limits its exemption to these items. Australia, New Zealand, Great Britain, and Portugal exclude most producers goods, including industrial and agricultural machinery, and Denmark excluded major items. Unprocessed food does not automatically fall outside the scope of the tax as it does with a manufacturers sales tax, although in developing countries much does not pass through the hands of registered wholesalers. Specific exemptions can be provided; all of the wholesale taxes noted above do exempt all or most food products, and the Australian and New Zealand levies also exempt other articles of widespread use.[15] Like the British tax, levies of these two countries are by no means general taxes but resemble extensive excise systems.

Rate differentiation is feasible, and is in fact widely used. The British purchase tax has had a greater degree of differentiation than any sales tax, the top rate at times reaching 100 percent or more. Portugal uses only two rates, 7 percent basic and 20 percent luxury. The Australian and New Zealand rates have ranged from 10 to 40 percent and in some instances higher. The current New Zealand basic rate is 20 percent; the Australian figure is 12.5 percent, with 25 percent on luxuries and a 2.5 percent reduced rate. The Irish rates are 10 and 15 percent. Both Britain and Australia, but not the other countries, have used shifts in rates for fiscal policy purposes relating to inflation control and foreign exchange problems. Switzerland has used a low rate (5.4 percent in recent years) almost solely for revenue.

Since the experience with the tax is limited to the more developed countries (table 4–3), the data of numbers of taxpayers are of limited significance for this study. The Swiss figure is relatively high because of the large number of artisan producers and the volunary registration of larger retailers.

Returns are used for collection. The period is monthly in New Zealand, Australia, and Portugal (with some on a quarterly basis) and quarterly in Switzerland and Great Britain. It was monthly in Denmark, with payment on a quarterly basis.

15. Only about one-sixth of all consumption goods sales are covered by the New Zealand tax. *Taxation in New Zealand: Report of the Taxation Review Committee* (Wellington: Government Printer, 1967).

TABLE 4–3. TAXPAYERS, WHOLESALE SALES TAXES,
BY COUNTRY

Country	Population (millions)	Number of Taxpayers
Australia	11.5	59,000[1]
New Zealand	2.7	4,000
Switzerland	6.0	55,000[2]
United Kingdom	54.7	70,000
Denmark	4.8	40,000
Eire	2.9	6,200

[1] Of these, 37,000 are active.
[2] Consisting of about 10,000 manufacturers, 10,000 wholesalers, 30,000 artisan producers, and 5,000 retailers.

Problems with the Wholesale Tax

Small Firms. The small firm problem is comparable with that for the manufacturers tax, the exact differences determined by the relative numbers of artisan producers and small wholesaling firms and the nature of distribution channels. There are three relevant groups of small firms:

1. The small artisan manufacturer. Exemption of these firms or failure to collect tax from them does not impair operation of the tax, as it does with the manufacturers levy, so long as they sell through registered wholesalers whose sales are subject to the tax. They commonly sell directly to consumers or to small retailers, however, and thus their products, legally or illegally, remain outside the scope of the tax.

2. The wholesale merchant with a small volume of wholesale sales. These are usually not common; a wholesaler usually requires a substantial volume of business for efficient operation. Very small firms will either be exempt or may escape the tax illegally.

3. The retailer with a small total volume of wholesale sales. Especially in developing countries, many retailers make some sales at wholesale, as noted in the next section.

The actual practice is to exempt manufacturers and merchants selling at wholesale with wholesale sales under a specified volume. The Swiss figure is relatively high, the equivalent of about $8,500 annual sales. The Australian, New Zealand, and British figures are identical, amounting to about $1,200 at current exchange rates. The figure under the Danish tax was about $1,450 for manufacturers and $3,500 for wholesale merchants (total wholesale sales). Portugal provides no exemption of small firms.

Dual Firms. Closely related but warranting separate attention is the question of dual firms. Firms frequently conduct both wholesale and retail activity; others are both manufacturers and retailers. The latter situation

causes relatively little difficulty. The tax applies to sales at retail, with valuation adjustments as noted in a subsequent section. But the former creates
complications:

1. If the firm is primarily a wholesaler but makes some incidental retail sales, there is no great difficulty. The firm is registered as a vendor,
makes all purchases tax free, and accounts for its tax on retail sales as well
as those made to retailers.

2. If the firm is primarily a retailer but makes some wholesale sales,
it may be treated solely as a retailer and thus not be registered. The tax
will apply to all purchases, and thus the margin on wholesale sales will
escape the tax. This is usually not too serious a matter if the firm pays the
same amount for the goods it sells at wholesale or retail and makes wholesale sales (to small buyers) at the same prices as it charges consumers. The
wholesale margin escapes, but the tax is no lower than on regular wholesaler-to-retailer transactions. If the firm buys for sale at wholesale more
cheaply than for sale at retail, there is loss of revenue and discrimination.
To allow the firm to buy tax free for sales at wholesale and pay tax when
the goods are resold is troublesome and complicated. Yet this rule must be
used if this type of activity is substantial.

3. If both portions of the business are significant, the solution is more
difficult. The firm can be required to keep records separately for each part
of the business, buying tax free for the wholesale part and paying tax on
sales while buying tax paid for the retail business. But the firm will often
buy goods in one order for both purposes, and it may not know the ultimate purpose at the time of purchase. The separate accounting rule is a
nuisance. The firm may also be regarded exclusively as a retailer or a
wholesaler according to the preponderance of its activity. Most of the countries using the tax employ a 50 percent rule; if more than half the sales are
wholesale (the figure was 10 percent in Denmark) the firm must register
and pay tax on all sales. These firms must distinguish between wholesale
and retail sales in their records or pay tax on the full price of the retail
sales. If the figure is under 50 percent the firm is not registered and the
tax applies to purchase prices, the margin on the wholesale sales escaping
tax.

There is no ideal solution to the problem. The least unsatisfactory
methods are rules 1 and 2 above, plus a requirement for registration if
total sales exceed a certain figure and if more than a specified percentage
consists of wholesale sales.

Valuation Problems. Since the wholesale tax is imposed one step
nearer the sale to the final consumer, variations in distribution of functions
between manufacturer and wholesaler do not affect tax liability as they do
with the manufacturers tax, and producers have no incentive to push dis-

tribution functions to the wholesale level. But differences in allocation of functions between retail and preretail firms do affect liability, with an incentive to shift functions to the retail level.

The primary difficulty, therefore, arises from backward integration by large retailers who buy at low cost from manufacturers, partly because they buy in large quantities and obtain larger quantity discounts and partly because they assume various functions of wholesale distribution, and, with private brands, functions of manufacturing as well. By contrast, any manufacturer or wholesaler who undertakes retailing functions and sells directly to the consumer pays a disproportionately high tax. Accordingly, discrimination and distortion of performance of functions can be avoided only if the price for tax purposes is adjusted to the typical price charged nonintegrated retailers. Thus firms primarily engaged in manufacturing or wholesaling but selling directly to consumers at prices comparable to those charged by retailers would be authorized to discount the actual price for tax purposes to the level at which sales are made to retailers, and firms selling to backward-integrated retailers would be required to apply an uplift to prices for tax purposes.

It is difficult to make these adjustments so as to accomplish the desired results. They complicate the operation of the tax and often produce strong complaints. The result has been a tendency not to provide them. Downward adjustment in price of firms selling at retail is the simplest to make and is more generally allowed. One problem arises with taxable producers goods, normally sold by producer to final user. No adjustment is usually allowed on these transactions, but they are not easily distinguished from the more usual sale through retailers. Switzerland applies a lower rate to these sales.

Serious difficulty arises with any attempt to require backward-integrated retailers to apply uplift. These firms are not so easily identifiable in practice as they are in theory. With modern complex distribution channels, even in the developing economies, retailers may buy at a number of different prices. The differences may reflect in part real economies in selling in large quantities (for which no uplift adjustment should be made) and in part the performance of preretail functions by the retailers. Any attempt to provide complete uniformity of treatment is hopeless and adds greatly to the complexity of the tax. Yet failure to do so favors the large backward-integrated retailer, encourages further integration, and leads to strong complaints from the small retailer. Uplift, in turn, leads to endless complaints from the larger firms when they feel that uplift is unjustifiable or excessive in their particular cases. Great Britain has made the greatest use of uplift, partly because the tax rates have been very high and thus the potential effects serious. But the government encountered all of the problems noted above[16] and eventually reduced substantially the use of uplift. Australia and New Zealand have never used uplift systems; it is generally granted that the result is some discrimination against nonintegrated retailers, but with surprisingly little complaint.[17] Little concern is expressed about the tax advantage enjoyed when goods are sold to a retailer at less than the normal wholesale price (including the growing number of retail brand goods). Portugal also does not require uplift.

Switzerland has followed a completely different route, allowing retailers to register voluntarily and pay tax on their sales at a rate one-third less than the wholesale rate. This provides an escape for retailers who believe that the regular rate discriminates against them. The lower rate is useful only to retailers in fields in which margins are less than one-third. The procedure has reduced criticism of discrimination, even though the adjustment is very rough, but it has resulted in collection of the tax from a larger number of firms. About 5,000 retailers are registered.

Imports. Most imported goods are taxed upon subsequent domestic sale rather than at importation, since they are imported by registered wholesalers. When they are imported by taxable firms, there is a question about the appropriate value for tax purposes because of the varying extent of performance of wholesale functions prior to importation. Australia, under the assumption that the retailer has performed importing and wholesaling functions, adds a 20 percent uplift to represent wholesale margins, and Portugal adds 40 percent—remarkably high figures that undoubtedly discriminate against importation by retailers. Taxation of imports by consumers at the actual prices may be regarded as discriminatory, since essentially a retail price is being paid, but no adjustments are made. On the whole, the problems with imports are much less serious than they are under the manufacturers tax because most enter free of sales tax and are taxed at a subsequent sale. In Australia only about 3 percent of the revenue was collected at importation in 1968.

Evaluation of the Wholesale Tax

The wholesale tax offers definite advantages over the manufacturers tax. First, and perhaps of greatest significance in a developing economy, uniformity of treatment of imports and domestic goods is much easier, since most imported goods will be taxed on subsequent domestic sale—though less of the revenue will be collected at customs and somewhat

16. *Report of the Purchase Tax (Valuation) Committee,* Cmd. 8830 (London: H. M. Stationery Office, 1953).

17. This was confirmed by correspondence with the officials of various retail associations in Australia, reproduced in my article, "Report of the Sales Tax Committee: One Year in Retrospect," *Canadian Tax Journal,* 5 (March–April 1957), 88–107, and by information supplied by the Chief Investigation Officer, Sydney Office, Australian Taxation Department (November 1962).

greater leakage will occur if administrative standards are weak.[18] Valuation problems are also less broad since there is less variation in the location of distribution functions. But the problem of valuation is by no means eliminated, primarily because of the possibility of backward integration by retailers who buy at low prices. And when adjustments are required in such situations—and only Great Britain has seriously attempted them—there is strong resistance, perhaps stronger than against the discounts with the manufacturers tax. The adjustment takes the form of an increase in price rather than a reduction, and therefore the psychological reaction to it appears to be much more adverse even though the net result may be the same.

There is typically no great difference in the number or average size of registered firms between manufacturers taxes and wholesale taxes, and the exact patterns will differ somewhat among various countries. The number of wholesale merchants may be greater or less than the number of manufacturers, depending on the number of small artisan firms and the treatment given them as well as on the nature of wholesaling. In Uganda the government concluded that there were over ten times as many wholesalers as manufacturers subject to tax, whereas in Colombia it has been estimated that there are only half as many wholesalers as there are manufacturers (exclusive of artisan firms).[19] In Taiwan there were reported to be 9,800 wholesalers, 27,700 manufacturers.[20] One of the few systematic studies of distribution channels in a developing economy was undertaken in Zambia (then Northern Rhodesia) in 1962. The number of wholesalers was 284, the number of manufacturers exclusive of small artisans 224.[21]

Regardless of the exact numbers of manufacturers and wholesalers, there are certain to be more taxpaying firms under the wholesale tax, since manufacturers must be registered as well. But this is not likely to be significant; the more important element is the number and size of the wholesale establishments and the extent to which commodities pass through them on the way to retailers. If there are a few large wholesalers and almost all sales pass through their hands, while small manufacturers are numerous, clearly the wholesale tax is advantageous. If many sales are made by manufacturers to retailers, the relative advantage of the wholesale tax is largely lost.

In two other administrative aspects the wholesale tax has an advantage. First, there are likely to be fewer non-arms-length transactions between retailers and their suppliers than there are between manufacturers

18. The tax can, however, be applied at customs and credited against the liability on subsequent sales.
19. Bird, *Sales Taxation in Colombia*, p. 29.
20. Letter from Commission on Taxation Reform, Republic of China, 1968.
21. Republic of Zambia, *Census of Distribution in 1962* (Lusaka: Central Statistical Office, 1965), and Zambia, *Economic Report*, 1967.

and wholesale firms. Second, the handling of exemptions related to end use, for example parts becoming physical ingredients of other goods, is easier. If these goods are sold by manufacturers to wholesale merchants and later sold for exempt use, a refund (or registration of wholesalers) is required under the manufacturers taxes. With the wholesale tax, however, the goods can be exempted when sold by the wholesalers. These sales are rather common; in recent years Canada has processed more than 40,000 refunds a year, arising primarily because of this problem.

In other respects the wholesale tax is likely to be less satisfactory from an administrative standpoint. The dual-firm problem—centering on the combined wholesale-retail establishment—is likely to be much more serious. While manufacturers may sell at retail, application of the tax in such instances causes relatively little problem. But a firm doing substantial wholesale and retail business—as previously discussed—is the source of administrative complexity and potential evasion.

The treatment of other exemptions is likely to be somewhat more troublesome because wholesalers tend to be less specialized than manufacturers.

From the standpoint of equity and economic effects, the wholesale tax offers some advantages primarily arising out of imposition closer to the final sale. Since variation in wholesale margins as a source of difference in ratios of tax to consumer expenditures is eliminated, the ratios should be more uniform than with the manufacturers tax. Accordingly, undesired distortion of resource allocation and discrimination on the basis of consumer preferences should be less. But the difference between the two taxes may not be great, and significant variations in the ratios will still exist; retail margins are usually much larger than wholesale margins. Similar considerations apply to the potential pyramiding of the tax owing to application of percentage markups and to interference with shifting of the tax because of the number of different stages through which it must pass. The wholesale tax encounters less difficulty of this sort but does not escape it.

With the wholesale tax, as with the manufacturers tax, retailers tend to defer purchasing when they anticipate a tax reduction and to increase inventory when they anticipate an increase. Only if refunds are allowed for stocks on hand with a decrease and if a floor stocks tax is used with an increase can this be avoided. While the United States has traditionally followed such policies with its excises, most countries are reluctant to do so for sales taxes.

CONCLUSION

While both manufacturers and wholesale taxes are workable levies in developing economies, they suffer from several common difficulties. The discrimination against certain forms of organization of production and distribution and between domestic and imported goods, with consequent distorting effects and loss in efficiency in the use of resources, is the most serious. The nonuniform distributional effects relative to consumer expenditures produced by variations in margins are objectionable on grounds of both equity and economic efficiency. Both taxes require higher rates than other types and concentrating their impact on one segment of the economy. Both produce fluctuations in merchants' inventories as changes in rate are anticipated and increase retailers' requirements for working capital. Because of these defects, governments have sought other forms of sales tax.[22]

SUPPLEMENTARY REFERENCES

Argentina: Cuello, R. E. "El Impuesto a las Ventas en La Argentina." In Centro Interamericano de Administradores Tributarios, *Documentos y Actas de la Primera Asamblea General* (hereafter referred to as *CIAT Papers*). Buenos Aires: CIAT, 1968. Pp. 523–31.

Canada: Due, J. F. *The General Manufacturers Sales Tax in Canada.* Toronto: Canadian Tax Foundation, 1951.
Report of the Royal Commission on Taxation, vol. 5. Ottawa: Queen's Printer, 1966.
Report of the Sales Tax Committee. Ottawa: Queen's Printer, 1956.

Colombia: Bird, R. M. *Sales Taxation in Colombia: Tax Policy and Development Planning.* Cambridge: Harvard University, Center for International Affairs, 1966.
Isaza Gonzáles, R. "El Impuesto a las Ventas en Colombia." In *CIAT Papers,* 1967.
Levin, J. "The Effects of Economic Development on the Base of a Sales Tax: A Case Study of Colombia. *International Monetary Fund Staff Papers,* 15 (March 1968), 30–101.

Denmark: Shoup, C. S. "Experience with the Value Added Tax in Denmark, and Prospects in Sweden." *Finanzarchiv,* 28 (March 1969), 236–52.
Tait, A., and Due, J. F. "Sales Taxation in Eire, Denmark and Finland." *National Tax Journal,* 18 (September 1965), 292–94.

New Zealand: *Taxation in New Zealand: Report of the Taxation Review Committee.* Wellington: Government Printer, 1967.

Portugal: De Pitta e Cunha, P. "A Wholesale Sales Tax in Portugal." In *Bulletin for International Fiscal Documentation,* 20 (November 1966), 441–46.

United Kingdom: *Report of the Purchase Tax (Valuation) Committee.* Cmd. 8830. London: H. M. Stationery Office, 1953.
Report of the Committee on Turnover Taxation. Cmnd. 2300. London: H. M. Stationery Office, 1964.

General: Due, J. F. *Sales Taxation.* London: Routledge & Kegan Paul, 1957. Chaps. 9, 10.
Lent, George E. "Manufacturers' vs. Wholesalers' Sales Tax Base." *Tax Magazine* (August 1958), pp. 573–601.

22. Carl Shoup reports the principal reasons Denmark abandoned the wholesale tax: (1) the difficulties of excluding producers goods from the tax, (2) the valuation problems, (3) the failure to tax services, (4) the added working capital requirements for retailers, and (5) the desire to raise more revenue with lower tax rates. See "Experience with the Value Added Tax in Denmark, and Prospects in Sweden," *Finanzarchiv,* 28 (March 1969), 237–40.

5.

Retail Sales Taxation

Sales taxation at the retail level is a recent innovation in the financing of developing economies, although it has been perfected in highly developed countries and is widely used in countries in the intermediate years of development. Its use is almost certain to increase as economic development continues and experience with it in less developed economies grows.

DEVELOPMENT AND USE OF THE RETAIL FORM OF TAX

The retail type of sales tax was first used in the subordinate units of federal systems in the United States and Canada. Developed from a low-rate gross receipts business tax, the first state sales tax was imposed by Mississippi in 1932. Eleven states followed the next year; by 1937 22 were using it, and by January 1970 (table 5–3) only 5 states had not imposed it. The first use by a Canadian province came in 1935; the movement was somewhat slower, but by 1969 all except one province (Alberta, ironically the province that had first used the tax but later repealed it) were levying it. Several of the states of India began to impose sales taxes in 1941; in 1968 Orissa and the Punjab were using strictly retail taxes and several others (table 5–5) employed taxes primarily collected at retail.

At the national level the tax came more slowly and at first in more developed countries: Norway in 1940, replacing a turnover tax (chapter 6); Sweden[1] and Iceland in 1960; Eire in 1963. In the 1960s several less developed countries imposed the tax: Honduras, 1964; Rhodesia, 1965; Costa Rica, 1967; Paraguay, 1969. Yugoslavia replaced a manufacturers sales tax with a retail tax in 1965. Other countries, including Guatemala (which imposed the tax and then immediately repealed it because of protests of business groups) and El Salvador, have seriously considered it.

---

1. Replaced by a value-added tax in 1969.

The turnover and value-added taxes of several countries now extend
through the retail level. France used a sales tax at the retail level from
1941 to 1968 as a source of local revenue; the tax was then merged into
the value-added tax. The Swedish tax was replaced by a value-added tax
in 1969 but is included in the discussion in this chapter.

THE BASIC STRUCTURE

The retail sales tax is designed to apply to the retail transaction—the
sale to the final purchaser. This purchaser may be an individual consumer or
a business firm purchasing for its own use rather than for resale or a small
retailer not required to register. The tax applies, technically, to sales at retail (not to sales by retailers per se in the usual sense of that term) whether
made by a retailer, a wholesaler, or a manufacturer. The controlling de-
terminant of tax status is the purpose of the purchase, not the nature of the
vendor. In most jurisdictions (but not in some states of the U.S.) the tax
does not apply to casual sales between individuals but only to sales by
persons engaged in the business of selling.

As with other single-stage taxes, the basis for control is the registration of vendors. All firms, including manufacturing and wholesale establishments, making sales at retail are required to register. In fact, in most
jurisdictions all manufacturing and wholesale establishments are required
to register whether they make retail sales or not to facilitate the exclusion
of their purchases from tax. The tax applies in two types of situations: (1)
when a registered firm sells to a nonregistered buyer—that is, a final consumer—and (2) when a registered firm sells to another registered firm for
taxable use, that is, for use or consumption and not for resale. The liability
for reporting and paying the tax in the second situation may rest upon the
buyer or the seller, both of whom are registered vendors. The tax does not
apply to a sale by one registered vendor to another when the purchase is
made for purposes of resale. Sales for resale are universally defined to include purchases of goods for use as materials or parts in other products
being produced by the firm, under what is known as the physical ingredient
rule. Exceptions are found in the Indian states of Orissa and Jammu and
Kashmir, which tax sales of materials to manufacturers.

Most jurisdictions define other purchases by business firms to be retail sales and thus subject to tax. In the Icelandic, Swedish, and Norwegian
taxes and those of about two-thirds of the states, no additional exemptions
of producers goods are made. Other countries (for example, Eire and Honduras) and several of the states and provinces, however, specifically exclude additional categories, particularly industrial machinery and equipment
used directly in manufacturing, fuel, industrial consumables (articles
directly consumed in the production process but not becoming physical in-

gredients), and agricultural equipment. Other producers goods are almost universally subject to tax.

Exemptions of consumer goods are typically fewer than in nonretail single-stage taxes. The taxes in Eire, Norway, Iceland, and Sweden do not exempt food or other necessities, with minor exceptions; Honduras and Costa Rica limit the exemption to unprocessed foods and a few other basic items. Most unprocessed food cannot be taxed successfully in a developing economy because of sales by very small establishments, and thus outright exemption is particularly desirable. In the United States, only fifteen of the states exempt food, primarily those that have introduced the tax in recent years. Six states provide a credit against income tax liability for sales tax paid on minimum necessary expenditures, with refunds to taxpayers whose credit exceeds their income tax liability.[2] Most of the states now exempt medicines, either in total or on a prescription basis, and a few exempt clothing and some other items. For the most part, however, the coverage of the taxes is very broad. The Canadian provinces provide a greater array of exemptions; food, drugs, and school books are exempt in all provinces and children's clothing in all except two. The Indian levies vary widely in coverage but typically exempt food.

While the retail taxes, like those at manufacturing or wholesale levels, are primarily applied to sales of tangible personal property, they can easily be extended to various consumer services if desired, and there is some tendency to do so. Of the national taxes noted, however, only Eire and Iceland tax a broad range of services, although they exclude professional services. In the United States, two states, Hawaii and New Mexico, tax virtually all services rendered to customers, even including those of doctors, lawyers, and other professionals. Most states still limit taxation of services to hotel and motel accommodations and admissions. But several states have added others, primarily repair of tangible personal property, laundry, dry cleaning, and other services rendered by commercial as distinguished from professional establishments. The provincial taxes applied at first only to tangible personal property. Commencing with Manitoba in 1967, several provinces now tax a limited range of services.

Unlike other single-stage or turnover taxes, retail sales taxes can be quoted separately from the price of the commodity, being added as the person pays his bill. This practice is universal in the states and is required by law in most of them. This rule is designed to satisfy the demands of retail groups, who feared that without separate quotation there would be less assurance of complete shifting of the tax. All Canadian provinces also require separate quotation; Honduras does so unless permission is obtained

2. In 1969 there were seven such states; the Iowa provision was repealed effective in 1970.

to include the tax in the price. By contrast, Norway prohibits separate quotation to lessen popular opposition to the tax. In Eire, while separate quotation is not prohibited it is virtually never encountered. When governments require separate quotation, they frequently prescribe a price bracket system specifying the amount to be collected from the customer on various transactions. These brackets are usually framed to ensure that the vendor will collect roughly the amount that he will pay the government or perhaps slightly more to compensate him for his costs of compliance. A few states and all the Canadian provinces require the vendor to pay the government the exact amount collected from the customer. This rule is of substantial nuisance to vendors and accomplishes little.

RATES

In one group of countries a single rate is applied to all taxable sales (with minor exceptions in some instances).[3] The rates range from 2.5 percent in Ireland and 3 percent in Honduras to 7.5 percent in Iceland, 10 percent in Norway and Sweden (the tax now replaced by a value-added levy), and 12 percent federal plus 2 percent state and 2 to 6 percent local in Yugoslavia. In the United States the state median rate is 3 percent, the range from 2 percent to 6 percent; in Canada the provincial median is 5 percent, with a range from 5 percent to 8 percent. These were rates in force at the end of 1969.

In other countries two or more rates are used, a higher burden being placed on luxury goods. For example, in Nepal the basic rate is 5 percent, the luxury rate 7 percent; in Costa Rica the basic figure is 5 percent, with 10 percent and 25 percent luxury rates. Paraguay applies a 3 percent tax to domestic goods, 5 percent and 10 percent rates to imported goods. The rates of the Indian states using the retail levy range from 1 to 10 percent, frequently with a number of rate classes.

VALUATION

The retail form of tax is free of any significant valuation problems. Since the tax is applied to the final sale to the consumer, the location of the performance of manufacturing and distribution functions has no significance for tax liability, and no incentive to alter the pattern arises. As with other sales taxes, valuation questions arise on non-arms-length transactions, but these situations are rare with retail taxes.

UNTAXED SERVICES

The usual tax-free status of services when separately rendered can lead to some distortion of economic activity. There is an incentive to avoid

3. Excise taxes on particular commodities are typically imposed as separate levies, usually at the manufacturing level.

coupling service with the sale of a good at a single price. This effect can be lessened by extending the tax to various services, but many, including finance and transport, are not regarded as suitable bases for taxation.[4] The most significant problem of this nature arises with real property contract work. Since the labor involved in such contracts is usually not taxable, an incentive is given to fabricate various articles, for example furnace duct work, on the site as a part of the real property contract instead of producing it ahead of time in the shop. Any prefabrication of buildings is discouraged since the tax will be higher.[5] The only complete solution is taxation of real property contracts, but most jurisdictions hesitate to take this step because of their desire to encourage building, to avoid burdening housing, and to avoid collecting taxes from numerous small contractors.

SMALL FIRMS

The major problem is the treatment of small firms—a problem of little consequence in developed economies but of great importance in many developing ones. This problem more than any other has discouraged developing economies from attempting to use the retail sales tax and has, in fact, impeded its use in many developed countries. There are far more retailers than either manufacturers or wholesalers. The exact difference will vary with the country; some estimates are given in table 5–1. When France extended the value-added tax to include retailers, about 1.5 million taxpayers were added. The number of taxpaying firms under the wholesale tax would be approximately the number of manufacturers and wholesalers combined.

The exact relationship of numbers of taxpayers depends on the policies followed in exempting small firms. In Chile, for example, under a tax applying at all stages of production and distribution, the number of registered retailers is about 5 times the number of manufacturers and wholesalers. An estimate of the number of firms that would be registered under the two types of tax, with exemption of small firms of both types, shows a ratio of 1:4. The figures for Eire show 5 times as many retailers as wholesalers, or 9 times the number of firms registered with a manufacturers tax. United States estimates in the early 1950s showed 17 times as many registrants with a retail tax as with a manufacturers tax, 9 times as many as with a wholesale tax. A 1968 estimate, however, shows 7.5 times as many registrants with the retail tax as with a manufacturers tax.[6] In Canada the number of firms registered

4. See chapter 7.
5. Most jurisdictions find that many interpretative problems arise over the exact line between prefabrication and fabrication that is a part of the construction contract.
6. The census data suggest a much smaller number of vendors than the estimate of registered firms based on state data of actual registrants. Part of the difference is attributable to registration of many service establishments. There are wide variations among the states in ratios of registered vendors to population—from roughly 130 to 430 accounts per 10,000 population.

TABLE 5-1. ESTIMATED NUMBERS OF FIRMS AT VARIOUS LEVELS

	Numbers of Firms			Estimated Numbers of Registrants		
Country	Manufac-turers	Wholesalers	Retailers	Manufac-turers Tax	Wholesale Tax	Retail Tax
Eire, 1965	2,500	2,500	40,000	2,500	6,200	29,000
Zambia, 1962	225	284	2,000	225	500	2,500
U.S., 1942	144,000	128,000	2,400,000	144,000	270,000	2,600,000
1968	306,617	308,177	1,707,931	400,000	800,000	3,000,000
Chile, 1967	8,735[1]	1,713[1]	54,623[1]	10,000[2]	12,000[2]	40,000[2]
Canada, 1966	40,000	na	na	40,000	na	320,000
Taiwan	9,816	27,709	114,054			
New Zealand	10,000	3,000	28,000			

Sources:
    Eire: A. Tait and J. F. Due, "Sales Taxation in Eire, Denmark and Finland," *National Tax Journal*, 18 (September 1965), 286–96.
    Zambia: Republic of Zambia, *Census of Distribution in 1962* (Lusaka: Central Statistical Office, 1965).
    United States: 1943: U.S. Treasury, *Considerations Respecting a Federal Retail Sales Tax* (Washington, 1942), p. 1119.
    1968: *Statistical Abstract of the United States, 1968*; estimated registrants based on state registration.
    Chile: Malcolm Gillis, "Sales Taxation in a Developing Economy: The Chilean Case" (Ph.D. diss., University of Illinois, 1968).
    Canada: *Report of the Royal Commission on Taxation*, 1966.
    Taiwan: Information supplied by Commission on Taxation Reform, 1968. Figures were actual current registrants.
    New Zealand: *Taxation in New Zealand: Report of the Taxation Review Committee* (Wellington: Government Printer, 1967).
na = not available.
[1] Actual registrants, present multiple stage tax.
[2] With exemption of small firms.

under the provincial retail sales taxes is about 8 times the number registered under the federal manufacturers sales tax (which includes some wholesalers).

The difference in numbers is actually not too significant, as the task of control and audit of the typical retailer is much simpler than that of the typical manufacturer. The much more important consideration is the nature of retail activity—the smaller size and less adequate records. The published data give some indication of the difference, although they understate it because they do not include the smallest firms. Figures for 1962 for Zambia (then Northern Rhodesia), from one of the few censuses of distribution ever taken in a developing economy, show average sales of manufacturers to be £117,000, wholesalers £152,000, and retailers £31,000. These figures do not reflect the small shopkeepers (numerous in most developing economies),[7] sellers in market and sidewalk stalls or in a room in the home,

7. While Zambia has small shopkeepers, their role is less important than in many developing economies.

and itinerant peddlers. The numbers of these are unknown, but their importance in many countries is unquestioned. These vendors are often illiterate; they keep no records; they have no bank accounts; they have no employees except for members of the family. They may be described as household, as distinguished from commercial, establishments. One must see the vast markets of Kumasi or Kano, the endless tiny establishments of Lagos, and the stores in the rural areas of South America and in the slums surrounding some Latin American cities to realize the magnitude of the problem—one almost nonexistent in most developed countries.

Exemption of Small Firms

Obviously taxes cannot be collected from the smallest vendors. There is justification, therefore, for exempting them outright by law. If they are not registered they cannot buy tax free, and the tax applies to their purchases (so long as they buy from registered vendors). Three principal developing countries that use the retail tax—Honduras, Costa Rica, and Paraguay—provide exemptions, as do the states of India. The approximate exemption figures, shown in table 5–2, are fairly substantial. In Honduras, there are only 1,018 registered firms, in Costa Rica 1,867. By contrast, the developed countries do not provide exemptions of small firms.[8]

The exemption of small firms gives rise to two problems. The first is ensuring that firms above the line are registered. As unregistered firms expand they will cross the line; inspectors must be alert for vendors who appear to be large enough to meet the requirements, and audits of wholesalers must include checks for firms buying enough to put their sales over the minimum. Some firms will shift back and forth across the line; once a firm is registered, it would not be automatically removed if its sales fell below the minimum but only upon application and review by the revenue department. But without question firms that should register will escape doing so.

The more serious consequence is the discrimination in favor of the small vendor. So long as he buys from a registered firm only the margin escapes, but if he buys from an unregistered artisan the entire sale price is free of tax. The result is to discourage the growth of larger-scale retailing. The seriousness of this effect is impossible to determine. Obviously it is a function of the tax rate, and the danger suggests the need for holding retail rates to relatively low figures—perhaps 5 percent. In many countries, the gains from larger-scale retailing are sufficient that a moderate tax differen-

8. Sweden, however, excluded sellers with gross sales of less than about $12 a month from the requirement to register. Eire provides special simplified treatment of small firms, which pay 5s. on the first £50 of monthly sales and 1.25s. on the next £50 of sales. Firms with sales under £750 or less that acquire 90 percent or more of their stock from registered firms and those not meeting the 90 percent requirement but having sales under £250 need not register.

TABLE 5-2. EXEMPTION OF SMALL FIRMS FROM RETAIL SALES TAX

Country	Approximate Exemption Figures (Monthly Sales Converted to U.S. $)
Costa Rica: merchants	3,750
service establishments	2,250
Honduras	2,500
Paraguay	1,200
Indian States:[1]	
Orissa	108
West Bengal	540
Assam	130
Punjab	433
Jammu & Kashmir	108
Delhi	325
Other countries provide no formal exemption.	

[1] Figures of exemptions of retailers under other Indian sales taxes are as follows:

Andhra Pradesh	108	Madras	108
Bihar	163	Maharashtra	325
Gujarat	325	Mysore	108
Kerala	108	Uttar Pradesh	130
Madhya Pradesh	163		

tial will not retard the growth of firms seriously. Frequently the very small retailer will buy from larger retailers at retail prices, and thus the tax is no less than it would be if consumers had bought directly from the larger retailer. If the problem is regarded as serious, various remedies can be considered. One is to apply a higher rate on sales by wholesalers to unregistered retailers to compensate for the failure to tax the retail margin. But this approach creates the serious task for the wholesaler of determining whether a customer is buying for resale or for use. Many of the small firms' purchases come from firms that are primarily retailers and cannot feasibly isolate purchases for resale.

Another alternative is to require the intermediate-sized retailers—those with sales from perhaps $500 to $1,500 a year—to apply for special registration that would not allow them to buy tax free and to pay tax on their margins (value added), so that the combined tax would equal the retail levy. Use of this technique is planned in Honduras. Or, under the procedure used in Finland, and in the state of Louisiana, retailers could be required to calculate the tax on their gross sales and then deduct the tax paid on their purchases.

By these means some tax would of necessity be collected (from the wholesale supplier) on goods passing through these firms along with considerable collection on the margins of the small retailers, even if some evasion occurred. But many of these vendors are illiterate, and it is not certain that enforcement could be made sufficiently effective to make the procedure worthwhile. A final alternative to the problem of small firms is the French *forfait* system whereby small firms are assessed fixed amounts annually based on estimates of probable sales. This approach, noted in chapter 8, is so arbitrary and open to bribery that its use is questionable.

A major problem in any form of sales tax in a developing country is the escape from tax of goods sold by artisan producers directly to final consumers or to small unregistered retailers. According to one estimate, 66 percent of artisan producers in Chile—a country in which artisan production is important despite a relatively high level of economic development—sell exclusively to final consumers.[9] Even so, this problem is no worse with the retail tax than with preretail levies; at least some of the artisan output will be taxed when sold by retailers.[10]

Significance of the Small Firm Problem

Despite the importance of the small shopkeeper in the developing economies, there are few in which a substantial volume of total retail trade is not handled by "commercial" retail stores. A surprisingly high portion of retail sales tax revenue comes from a small number of vendors. In Honduras 12 percent of the registered vendors pay 80 percent of the tax; in Costa Rica 17 percent of the taxpayers pay 71 percent of the tax.[11] The total sales of the larger firms relative to total national income is such as to suggest that a large portion of total retail sales other than nontaxable unprocessed food can be reached. For example, in Zambia in 1962, almost half the total reported retail sales, £20 million out of a total of £44 million, were made by 56 retailers with annual sales in excess of £150,000. Total private consumption, including an estimate of subsistence food produced at home, was about £100 million. Stores with annual sales in excess of £5,000—the ones that could be subjected to control—accounted for £43.2 million of the £43.8 million reported retail sales and undoubtedly a high percentage of total sales other than of unprocessed food. In Chile, in 1964, fewer than 1 percent of the retailers made 39 percent of all retail sales—yet Chile does not have many large department or chain stores. The largest 11 percent of the firms—those with sales in excess of about $15,000 a year—accounted for 78 percent of all reported retail sales. Figures for Colombia show that in the capitals of departments 94 percent

9. S. Malcolm Gillis, "Sales Taxation in a Developing Economy: The Chilean Case" (Ph.D. diss., University of Illinois, 1968), p. 57.

10. To give one specific example: craft producers of furniture in Accra, Ghana, sell a portion of their output directly to consumers and a portion to large retailers. At least the latter portion could be caught by a retail levy.

11. In Honduras 93 percent of the tax revenue is collected in the two major cities Tegucigalpa and San Pedro Sula); in Costa Rica 75 percent is collected in San José.

of the nonfood sales were made through nonfamily stores (those hiring one or more employees) and in the rural areas 72 percent.[12] These countries are not entirely typical; Chile has reached a relatively advanced level of development, and Zambia's retail structure was in a sense imported from the outside. Yet they are likely to be reasonably representative of a large portion of the less developed world except for countries in the very early years of economic development. Increased urbanization sharply increases the percentage of sales handled through "commercial" establishments.[13]

In the Indian states, exemption of small firms (retail and other) has reduced the numbers of registered vendors to manageable numbers. A substantial portion of the total revenue is obtained from the larger vendors; the relative share is increased, of course, by more widespread evasion by smaller firms. Data for three states are given in table 5–3.

IMPORTS AND EXPORTS

Import transactions cause much less difficulty under the retail tax than with any other form, because final consumers do little importing. Most imported goods are therefore taxed in the same fashion as domestic goods at the time of sale within the country. The principal exception is the purchase of taxable equipment or supplies by business firms that are final consumers, but there is usually no significant valuation problem with these transactions.

When sales taxes are used by states within a federal structure, goods imported from outside the country are not taxed at importation but upon subsequent retail sale (or use by a business consumer). Any leakage is limited. The more serious problem is the purchase of goods within the country but outside the state. Taxation of these transactions encounters both constitutional problems of taxing interstate transactions and administrative problems of discovering the transactions, under the usual rule that the state of destination is entitled to the tax revenue. In the United States, use taxes are applied to the initial use within the state of goods purchasd outside. The Canadian provinces apply similar levies. These taxes can be enforced on goods that must be registered, such as motor vehicles, purchases from firms also doing business in the state, and taxable purchases by business firms subject to audit. But they cannot be enforced against typical smaller transactions without establishment of fiscal frontier control, which is usually barred in federal constitutions. Only close cooperation among the states and possible replacement of the destination principle by the origin principle can allow taxation of most interstate transactions. India follows the origin rule; the union government imposes a tax on interstate sales at a

12. Levin, "Effects of Economic Development," p. 92.
13. *Ibid.*

TABLE 5–3. RELATIVE IMPORTANCE OF VENDORS CLASSIFIED BY SALES VOLUME, STATES OF
MADRAS, ANDHRA PRADESH, AND GUJARAT

State	Population (millions, 1961)	Total No. Registered Vendors[1]	Distribution (%) of Vendors by Annual Sales Volume (rupees)			Distribution (%) of Tax Collections by Vendors by Annual Sales Volume (rupees)		
			Under 50,000	50,000– 1 million	Over 1 million	Under 50,000	50,000– 1 million	Over 1 million
Madras	33	53,407	75	25[2]	na	14	86[2]	
Andhra Pradesh	36	51,441	71	12	17	10	7	83
Gujarat	21	65,483	37	58	5	5	31	54

Source: Derived from tables in W. R. Mahler, "Sales and Excise Taxation in India" (Ph.D. diss., Syracuse University, 1969). The Mahler tables were derived from published studies of the tax structures in the three states.
na = not available separately.
[1] Figures for Madras are for 1956–57; for Andhra Pradesh, 1959–60; for Gujarat, 1965–66.
[2] Including those with sales over 1 million rupees.

uniform rate on most goods, the rate of the state of origin on others. The state of origin collects the tax and retains the revenue.

Export sales create virtually no difficulty, since they are exempt and commodities will rarely be taxed before the export transaction.

EXEMPTIONS AND RATE DIFFERENTIATION

Both exemption and rate differentiation create complications for administration and compliance that are more serious than with preretail taxes. With usual exemptions and differentiation, many retailers will sell both taxable and exempt goods and goods in more than one rate bracket. The typical retailer encounters several problems. One is to ascertain whether certain goods are taxable or exempt and to ensure that his clerks, who are typically without much education or training, apply the tax correctly. Another is to maintain accurate records of sales in various rate categories. Retailers do not ordinarily keep records by type of commodity and cannot easily be induced to do so. Thus records of sales by various rate categories are not likely to be accurate, even if the retailer makes a serious effort. The tendency is inevitably toward overstatement of sales of exempt or low-rate commodities. Auditing is more time consuming and costly.[14] Most retailers can cope reasonably well with a very limited number of clearly defined exemptions, such as unprocessed food or prescription drugs. Exemption of the former is almost imperative anyway, since in a developing economy much food is sold through small vendors who cannot possibly be subjected to tax. But to add a number of complex exemptions such as

14. State sales tax administrators in the United States regard exemptions as the chief source of administrative difficulty.

children's clothing is certain to impair the functioning of the tax. Similar considerations apply to rate differentiation. Application of a higher rate to a few categories of high per unit value sold by specialized vendors, such as motor vehicles or television sets, is workable, although some complications will result. But to use several rates, with different figures applying to goods such as cosmetics widely sold by retailers handling other goods as well, is to create grave problems. Most Indian sales taxes are characterized by numerous exemptions and extensive differentiation, which makes effective operation virtually impossible. There are 33 exempt classes in West Bengal, for example, and 32 in Orissa, and there are 37 rate classes in the tax in Maharashtra.

EVALUATION OF RETAIL SALES TAX

The retail form of sales tax is in many respects the most satisfactory form of single-stage tax. Because all distribution margins are included, the base of the tax is larger than that of the preretail taxes, and the rate necessary to yield a given revenue is lower. The lower the rate, the less the immediate incentive given vendors to evade the tax and the weaker the popular opposition. Services can more easily be integrated into the base of this tax than others because they are essentially retail activity and because many firms combine sales and service activity.

The inclusion of all distribution activities within the scope of the tax also eliminates the valuation problem and the incentive to shift activities forward beyond the point of the tax, and therefore the major disadvantages of the wholesale and manufacturers tax are avoided. The tax can be applied to actual selling prices without adverse effects. A few non-arms-length transactions may be encountered, but they are much less frequent because ownership of consuming units by vendors is much less common than ownership of retailers by wholesalers or manufacturers or of wholesalers by manufacturers.

The retail tax minimizes the dangers of distortion of resource allocation and of discrimination against various people because of relative preferences, compared with preretail single-stage taxes. Since the tax must be shifted only once, it is reasonable to conclude that exact shifting will be more likely to occur, and the danger of pyramiding through percentage markups is avoided. With complete shifting and no pyramiding, the tax will bear a uniform relationship (or a desired pattern of nonuniformity) to consumer expenditures on various goods, since differences in margins will no longer be significant for relative burdens. Separate quotation of the tax from the price can be required. In general, the retail tax is a simple levy compared with any other form of sales tax; it is easily understood by vendors and the public alike, even in countries in which economic development is not far advanced.

The basic limitation to the retail tax is the large number of retailers and the very small size of many retail sellers in developing economies. The typical seller in a market or roadside stand or the itinerant peddler cannot be controlled for purposes of sales tax collection. If these vendors dominate retailing in a country, a retail sales tax is obviously impossible, regardless of its other merits. But in many countries, some with very limited development, commercial establishments capable of being controlled for tax purposes handle a substantial portion of total retail trade, and the tax can be employed provided the typical small vendor is exempted and the tax applied to his purchases from a supplier, as in Costa Rica and Honduras. Such an exemption reduces the number of taxpayers to a manageable number and eliminates the most troublesome firms.

A second limitation is the inability to collect substantial amounts of tax at the time of importation. Application of tax to sales rather than to importation is advantageous in many ways, as noted above, but the danger of loss of revenue from evasion is increased.

The remaining limitation is the difficulty created by exemptions and rate differentiation. Exemption must be limited to a few categories, and differentiation must be avoided or severely restricted if the tax is to function effectively. Any extensive differentiation—if desired for distributional or other reasons—must be introduced by other elements in the tax structure. If higher rates on luxuries are regarded as essential for distributional or foreign exchange reasons, they must be confined to a few items of high unit value over which control is possible. The retail tax may be supplemented by luxury excises collected from the manufacturer or importer.

TABLE 5–4. INDIAN RETAIL SALES TAXES

State	Rate, %	Exceptions to Retail Bases	Exemptions	% of State Tax Revenue, 1967–68
Assam	5	On first sale[1] of 8 classes of goods, rate 2 to 10	41 categories	20
Delhi	0.5 to 10; basic 5	First sale on 6 classes of goods	na	na
Jammu & Kashmir	1 to 10; basic 5	Some goods taxed on first sale	na	6
Orissa	1 to 7; basic 5	Solely retail	33 categories	49
Punjab	0.5 to 10; basic 6	Solely retail	46 categories	33
West Bengal	6	First sale on 16 commodities	35 categories	47

Source: Based on data in J. K. Godha, "The Working and Administration of Sales Tax in Bombay/Maharashtra State" (Ph.D. diss., University of Poona, 1969); W. R. Mahler, "Sales and Excise Taxation in India" (Ph. D. diss., Syracuse University, 1969).
na = not available.
[1] That is, sale by manufacturer, wholesaler, or importer.

TABLE 5–5. U.S. STATE SALES TAXES, JANUARY, 1970

State	State Sales Tax Rate (%)	Sales Tax Revenue as % of Total State Tax Revenue, 1969	Sales Tax Revenue as % of Personal Income, 1969	Food Exemption	Year of Introduction	Major Characteristics	Municipal Sales Tax Rates, % (Typical)
Alabama	4	34.3	2.4		1937	Extensive municipal sales taxes	1–2
Arizona	3	35.9	2.9		1933	Supplemental taxes on utilities, mining	0.5–1
Arkansas	3	32.7	2.2		1935		([4])
California	4	32.1	2.2	x	1933	Municipal taxes universal	1
Colorado	3	30.2	1.8		1935	Income tax credit	1–2
Connecticut	5	32.2	1.4	x	1947		
Florida	4	45.2	2.9	x	1949		
Georgia	3	37.2	2.4		1951		
Hawaii	4	47.4	5.1		1933	Extensive supplemental taxes on nonretail activities; income tax credit	
Idaho	3	25.5	2.0		1965[1]		
Illinois	4	51.4	2.3		1933	No commodity exemptions	1
Indiana	2	22.6	1.2		1963	Broad base; income tax credit	
Iowa	3	35.1	2.3		1934	Taxation of numerous services	
Kansas	3	35.7	1.8		1937		
Kentucky	5	37.8	2.9		1960[1]		
Louisiana	2	20.6	1.6		1936	Some precollection at whole-sale level	1–2
Maine	5	44.5	2.6	x	1951		
Maryland	4[2]	17.7	1.2	x	1947[1]		
Massachusetts	3	12.8	.8	x	1966	Numerous exemptions; income tax credit	
Michigan	4	35.3	2.5		1933	Broad exemption of producers goods	
Minnesota	3	19.0	1.4	x	1967		
Mississippi	5	43.3	3.6		1932		
Missouri	3	41.6	2.0		1934		0.5–1
Nebraska	2.5	32.4	1.5		1967	Broad base; income tax credit	0.5–1
Nevada	3	35.2	2.5		1955		0.5
New Jersey	3	22.4	1.0	x	1961[1]	Numerous exemptions	
New Mexico	4	34.8	3.1		1934	Taxation of virtually all services	
New York	3	13.1	.9	x	1965	Widespread municipal sales taxes	1–3
North Carolina	3	23.7	1.8		1933		1[3]
North Dakota	4	33.8	2.1		1935	Limited food exemption	
Ohio	4	40.3	1.7	x	1935	Broad exemption of producers goods	([5])
Oklahoma	2	18.4	1.2		1933	Widespread municipal sales taxes	1
Pennsylvania	6	39.3	2.2	x	1956[1]	Numerous exemptions	
Rhode Island	5	36.3	2.2	x	1947		
South Carolina	4	29.6	2.2		1951		
South Dakota	4	37.8	1.8		1933		0.5
Tennessee	3	35.4	2.2		1947	Taxation of some services; extensive municipal taxes	1
Texas	3.25	25.8	1.3	x	1961	Extensive municipal taxes	1
Utah	4	32.1	2.3		1933	Taxation of some services; municipal taxes	0.5
Vermont[6]	3	..	..	x	1969	Income tax credit	
Virginia	3	20.0	1.3		1966	Broad base	1

TABLE 5–5 (*continued*)

State	State Sales Tax Rate (%)	Sales Tax Revenue as % of Total State Revenue, 1969	Sales Tax Revenue as % of Personal Income, 1969	Food Ex-emp-tion	Year of Intro-ducton	Major Characteristics	Municpal Sales Tax Rates, % (Typical)
Washington[7]	4.5	43.2	3.5		1935	Supplemental gross receipts tax	
West Virginia[7]	3	19.5	1.5		1933	Supplemental gross receipts tax	
Wisconsin	4	10.7	.8	x	1962		([5])
Wyoming	3	37.9	3.0		1935	Taxation of some services	

Source of Revenue Data: U.S. Bureau of the Census, *State Government Finances in 1969.*
[1] Used briefly in 1930s but allowed to expire (Pennsylvania 1932–33, New York 1933–34, Kentucky 1934–35, New Jersey 1934–35, Idaho 1935–36, Maryland 1935–36).
[2] On farm and industrial machinery and equipment, 2 percent.
[3] County levy.
[4] One city only.
[5] Tax of 0.5 percent authorized for counties.
[6] Not in operation in 1969.
[7] Excluding gross receipts business tax.

TABLE 5–6. CANADIAN PROVINCIAL RETAIL SALES TAXES, 1969

Province	Designation of Tax	Date Tax Effective	Rate (%) July 1, 1969	% of Net General Revenue, 1968	Special Features
British Columbia	Social services tax	1948	5	23	
Manitoba	Revenue tax	1967	5	12	Some services taxed; industrial machinery exempt
New Brunswick	Social services and education tax	1950	8	16	Some services taxed; industrial machinery exempt
Newfoundland	Social security assessment	1950	7	17	Limited exemptions
Nova Scotia	Hospital tax	1959	7	12	Industrial machinery exempt
Ontario	Retail sales tax	1961	5	19	10% rate on meals, liquor
Prince Edward Island	Revenue tax	1960	7	11	Some services taxed: industrial machinery exempt
Quebec	Taxe de vente	1940	8	22	Producers goods exemption related to sales outside the province
Saskatchewan	Education and health tax	1937	5	16	

Note: Only Alberta does not impose a sales tax. All provinces exempt food and medicine; most exempt children's clothing.

SUPPLEMENTARY REFERENCES

Canada: Due, J. F. *Provincial Sales Taxes.* Rev. ed. Toronto: Canadian Tax
    Foundation, 1964.
    Report of the Ontario Committee on Taxation. Chap. 29. Toronto:
    Queen's Printer, 1967.
    Rapport de la Commission royale d'Enquête sur la Fiscalité, chap. 6. Que-
    bec: Government of Quebec, 1965.
Honduras: Suazo, J. Efraín. "El Impuesto sobre Las Ventas en Honduras."
    CIAT Papers, 1968. Pp. 459-520.
    Due, J. F. "The Retail Sales Tax in Honduras." *Inter-American Economic
    Affairs,* 20 (Winter 1966), 55-67.
United States: Due, J. F. *State Sales Tax Administration.* Chicago: Public Ad-
    ministration Service, 1963.
    Morgan, D. C., *Retail Sales Tax.* Madison: University of Wisconsin Press,
    1964.

6.

Turnover and Value-Added Taxes

All single-stage sales taxes suffer from two limitations. First, their character requires a demarcation of the taxable stage from nontaxable stages and identification of the taypaying firms. This is not an insurmountable task, but it may appear difficult to a government in a developing economy, particularly since many enterprises carry on activity at more than one stage. The second limitation is the rate required for a given revenue and the related concentration of impact on a single set of firms. Both considerations provide strong incentives to developing countries to extend the tax beyond one stage, either when the tax is imposed or later when additional revenue is required.

Application of taxes to all transactions appears to be very simple and to maximize revenue at a given rate; accordingly it has a siren-like appeal to governments, which have frequently followed this path to disaster. Once they come to rely on the tax, escape from it is difficult because any change to a single-stage levy requires a much higher rate, a difficult step to take politically and perhaps administratively. There are few more persistent errors in the tax field than to become trapped in the web of the hopelessly objectionable multiple-stage sales tax.[1] At last, development of the value-added tax has provided an escape that, while not eliminating the high-rate problem, does avoid the necessity of concentrating the entire tax burden at one stage in production and distribution.

The Turnover Tax

A general multiple-stage or multipoint sales tax, applying to sales at all stages of production and distribution, is generally known as a turnover,[2]

1. The support given this tax by a few writers on the question—e.g., R. J. Chelliah, *Fiscal Policy in Underdeveloped Countries* (London: George Allen & Unwin, 1960)—is most unfortunate.
2. This term is still used occasionally to refer to all sales taxes.

or transactions tax (in Germany, one of the pioneer users, *umsatzsteuer*), or cascade tax. This is the *alcabala* of medieval Spain, first imposed on a nationwide continuing basis in 1342 and long a major source of revenue in Spain and the Spanish colonies. Rates reached as high as 10 percent on all transactions. Adam Smith and other economists blamed the tax for the economic decline of Spain, and it fell into general disfavor, although it was not completely eliminated in Spain till the present century. Its modern use began in the Philippines with a low-rate tax imposed in 1904 on all transactions. At first it was a business occupation tax, but gradually it evolved into a sales tax.[3] The first major use of the tax began in Germany at a fractional rate in 1918 and at a higher figure in 1919. Despite long criticism, it continued as the major indirect tax in the German system until January 1, 1968. The turnover tax spread to the other countries now making up the European Common Market. France imposed it in 1920, eliminated it in 1936, reinstated it in 1939, and finally abandoned it in 1955; Italy, Belgium, Luxembourg, and the Netherlands all introduced it, as well as Austria. It was used in Canada from 1920 to 1923, when it was replaced by the present manufacturers sales tax. It has also been used by Ceylon, Taiwan, Indonesia, and Korea; by Latin American countries, including Mexico, Chile, Peru, and the states of Brazil and Argentina; and by several states of India. Some use is made in the west and equatorial African states that were French colonies, for example Chad and the Central African Republic. Spain, the originator of the tax, reintroduced it in 1964, with a 1.5 percent national and 3 percent provincial rate.

Unlike the single-stage taxes, the turnover tax constitutes a supplement to prices at every transaction: on materials, partly finished goods, final products. Services are frequently taxed as well as commodities. This discussion assumes that each tax element shifts forward ultimately into the price of the final product, although admittedly the differential burden may make complete shifting even less likely than with other forms of sales taxes.

An Example: The Chilean Tax

The experience of Chile provides a useful example of the development and problems of turnover taxation.[4] The turnover tax was imposed in 1954 to replace a manufacturers sales tax in order to obtain more revenue without a higher rate. The tax applies to all commodities except for a few basic unprocessed foods and to most services except those of professional nature and most freight transport. The basic tax rate gradually increased from 3 percent to 8 percent by 1969. There are more than 20 different rates

3. J. S. Hord, *Internal Taxation in the Philippines* (Baltimore: Johns Hopkins Press, 1907).
4. Gillis, "Sales Taxation."

on various commodities and services. A reduced 1.4 percent rate applies to certain seminecessities, and rates of 14 and 23 percent are exacted at each transaction on a wide range of commodities regarded as luxuries. Special production taxes (excises) apply to a number of commodities, most of them in addition to the sales tax. The basic rate on services is also 8 percent, but many are subject to special rates. There are about 95,000 firms filing returns; many small firms do not in fact pay, although there is no formal exemption of small vendors. There is little effective sales tax audit despite a good program of income tax auditing; heavy reliance is placed on a lottery (*sorteo*) system, discussed in more detail in chapter 8, which is designed to encourage sellers to issue receipts. Despite the limited control, the tax is highly productive of revenue, yielding from 25 to 30 percent of governmental tax revenue. The yield constitutes about 4.4 percent of gross domestic product. The tax has undergone increasing criticism on the basis of economic effects and complexity, and the government is now committed to a program of reform.

Other Examples

The Mexican tax is similar but with a lower rate (1.8 percent federal, 1.2 percent state) yielding only about 11 percent of the federal revenues.[5] Many services are included in the tax. Exemptions are limited to a few basic necessities. Like the Chilean tax, Mexico's has no significant provisions to lessen the "cascade" effects, although a few commodities are subject to a single special rate at the production stage. By contrast, the German and other European turnover taxes contained a number of provisions to minimize the "cascade" influence. Wholesale merchants, for example, were subject to a much lower tax rate (in Germany, 1 percent instead of 4). In Belgium and Austria a number of commodities are subjected to a single levy at one stage in production or distribution (usually manufacturing) in lieu of the regular tax.[6]

Several of the West African levies are very heavy. The Chad figures are 15 percent on production, 12 percent on services, 6 percent on transport; those of the Central African Republic 7 percent on goods at all stages, 10 percent on services, 5 percent on rentals; of Cameroon, 6 percent.

The rates of the Indian multiple stage taxes are shown in table 6–1. As the table indicates, the basic rate is 3 percent in all the states except Bihar, which uses a basic figure of 1 percent on all sales except those at retail, where the rate is 4 percent. All of the states substitute single-stage

5. A. Gutiérrez Kirchner, "Estudio sobre el Impuesto a las Ventas en Mexico," in *CIAT Papers*, pp. 549–58.
6. Known as *Phasenpauschalierung* in Austria, *forfaitaire* collection in Belgium. Neither of these terms is directly translatable into meaningful English.

TABLE 6-1. TURNOVER TAXES IN INDIA

State	Year Tax Established	Basic Rate, 1968 (%)	Sales Tax Revenue as % of Total Tax Revenue, 1967–68	Tax on First Stage Only in Lieu of Turnover Tax (%)[1]
Andhra Pradesh	1951[2]	3	45	0.5–10, specified goods
Bihar	1944	1; 4 on last sale	37	7 –10, 50 commodities
Kerala	1963[2]	3	40	1 –12, specified goods
Madras	1939	3	48	1 –12, on many goods
Mysore	1948	3 (1.5 on some)	43	1 –11, on some goods
Uttar Pradesh	1948	2(0.5–10)	30	1 –10, specified goods

[1] In some instances on later sales. In Bihar the single-stage tax is imposed on some goods in addition to the turnover tax.
[2] Carried over when state formed.

levies at higher rates, usually at the first sale in the state (by manufacturer or importer), on a number of goods.

The turnover form of sales tax has been widely defended in India on the usual grounds of simplicity, spread of the direct impact over many vendors, and reduced evasion. In practice, because of the exceptions and single-stage levies on many goods, the taxes are not simple but hopelessly complex. As a result there has been strong support for replacing them by single-stage levies. Little attention has been given their encouragement of integration; in fact some economists in India have regarded such effects as advantageous because "the middleman is eliminated."[7]

Evaluation of Turnover Tax

As suggested above, the turnover tax offers two advantages. So long as a uniform rate is applied, no delimiting of particular stages and identification of sellers in them is necessary, since the uniform rate applies to all business firms. Secondly, revenue is maximized at a given tax rate, since all transactions are taxable.

On the other hand, the tax has so many disadvantages that continued use of it, at least at rates that will raise substantial revenue, is intolerable in terms of efficiency, optimal economic development, and equity. The undesirable effects have become obvious wherever the tax has been used:

1. Distorting effect on organization of production and distribution. Since the turnover tax provides a strong incentive to short-circuit links in production and distribution channels, it artificially promotes integration. Subcontracting in manufacturing becomes almost prohibitive; firms pro-

7. The taxes are discussed at length in Mahler, "Taxation in India." The question of the relative merits of the turnover tax was reviewed in detail in the *Report of the Taxation Enquiry Committee* (New Delhi: Ministry of Finance, 1955) and in similar reports in various states.

duce their own materials and parts, and specialization is hampered. Many independent wholesale merchants are eliminated, since manufacturers sell to retailers (or consumers). Or the merchants become merely consignment selling agents. In Chile the tax has caused a great increase in consignment selling; estimates of the portion of wholesale sales on a consignment basis range from 45 to 90 percent, whereas this method of selling was uncommon before the tax.

2. Discrimination. The tax discriminates severely against firms not in a position to integrate when their competitors are doing so. The discrimination is particularly severe against smaller firms, which are virtually forced to evade the tax or go out of business.

3. Complications to mitigate integrative effects. If countries seek to lessen the effect on integration, as the European but not the Latin American countries have done, simplicity is lost and operation of the tax becomes highly complex. Identification of taxpayers at various stages becomes necessary, as with a single-stage tax.

4. Tax treatment of imports and exports. The usual goal of tax policy is to tax imported goods on the same basis as domestic goods and to free exports completely from tax. This result is impossible to attain with a turnover tax. There is an inherent tendency to favor imported over domestic goods since the former pass through fewer taxable stages within the country, especially when they are imported in finished form. Attempts to compensate by the use of higher customs duties are not satisfactory because of the number of possible stages at which goods may be imported. On exports, refund of the exact amount of tax at the time of exportation is impossible because the cumulated amount cannot be ascertained. As a consequence there is great danger of underrebating, with harm to the domestic industry selling in foreign markets, or overrebating (as Chile apparently has consistently done), with danger of retaliation since an excessive rebate is in effect an export subsidy.

TABLE 6–2. TURNOVER TAXES IN ASIA

Country	Present Tax Established	Rates (%)	Coverage
Ceylon	1963	5 basic on manufacturers, 1 on other businesses	Almost universal, including services, professions
Taiwan	na	0.6–6, various types of businesses	Broad coverage
Indonesia	1960	10, 20	Many exclusions to reduce cascade effect
Korea	na	0.03–2	Regarded as business activity tax
Thailand	1961	5 basic; range 1.5–25	Retailers not subject; most tax collected from manufacturer and importer. Limited cascade element.

na = not available.

5. Resource allocation. Different commodities pass through varying numbers of transactions on the way from initial production to sale to final consumer. Accordingly, even with exact forward shifting, the ratio of the tax to consumption expenditure will vary among different goods, with consequent reallocation of resources and potential excess burden.

6. Distributional effects. An unfortunate consequence of the tax is the inability to ascertain the distributional patterns, because with multiple application of the tax and taxation of all producers goods as well as consumer goods, the tax element in the final price cannot be calculated. But almost certainly the burden will not be uniform relative to consumer spending. This nonuniformity not only distorts resource allocation but also produces undesired distributional effects, with discrimination against consumers with strong preferences for high-tax goods. There is no necessary relation between the effective tax and the distribution of expenditures by income group. Items of wide usage may have relatively heavy burdens compared with items purchased primarily in the higher income groups.

Undesired distributional effects are also produced by pyramiding through use of percentage markups and by uneven shifting. Some firms will find difficulty in shifting the tax because their relative burdens are heavier than those of competitors.

7. Problems with differentiation and exemptions. If a country seeks to improve the distributional pattern by rate variation, the complications are greater than with other taxes. If the differentiation is limited to certain stages these must be identified, and one of the few advantages of the tax is lost. If differentiation is carried through production and distributional channels, a host of problems ensue, particularly those of applying different rates at the retail level. Exemptions create similar problems; complete exemption of any commodity (except perhaps certain unprocessed foods) is impossible because the tax will apply to supplies, equipment, and materials used in its production unless complex measures are taken to prevent it.

In the Latin American countries, and to some extent even in Europe, the measures taken to provide a more acceptable pattern of income distribution and to lessen distorting effects have resulted in almost hopeless complications in rate structures that have aggravated the problems of operation.

8. Hidden nature of the tax. The tax cannot possibly be kept separate from the prices of the products, in view of the cumulative application.

9. Number of taxpayers. The number of taxpaying firms is larger than with any single-stage tax unless the turnover tax is not applied at the retail level.[8] If it is not, a substantial portion of the tax base is lost, and taxpay-

8. In Germany, with about 60 million people, there were about 3 million taxpayers. In Ceylon, firms with sales under 100,000 rupees annually (about $11,000) are exempt. As a consequence most retailers are not covered, and there are only about 10,000 taxpayers.

ing firms must be delimited from retailers. With single-stage taxes, farmers' and artisans' products will be reached at some stage (unless they are sold directly to final consumers or through very small retail vendors) without registration of farmers and artisans. With the multiple-stage tax, even if the goods are reached at a later stage a net loss of revenue occurs because of failure to tax at the earlier stage.

As suggested above, these defects are so serious and lead to so many complaints that the tax is completely unacceptable as a revenue source for any country. The great danger lies in its appeal to the unwary and the realization that at low rates its defects are not serious. Thus a country may adopt the tax at a low rate, perhaps initially regarding it as a business occupation levy, and then gradually increase reliance on it and greatly aggravate the undesirable features and the complaints. At the same time it will find that reform becomes increasingly difficult because of the high rate required for any substitute levy. To replace the revenue of the 8 percent Chilean tax, for example, would require roughly a 20 percent tax at the retail level or a 30 percent tax at the manufacturers level. Such rates are regarded as intolerable, partly because of the concentrated impact on a single group of firms. Thus escape is very difficult politically without a hybrid type of tax that will eliminate the evils of the turnover tax but avoid a high rate concentrated on one stage in production and distribution channels. There are two alternatives: a combination of two of the single-stage taxes and a value-added tax.

DUAL LEVIES

A few countries have utilized or considered a dual system, involving single-stage taxes at more than one level. The Finnish tax for a time was a hybrid of the manufacturers and retail taxes, and in more recent years of the wholesale and retail taxes with a value-added feature. Two of the Indian states use dual levies,[9] and in a sense such a system is employed in Canada, with a manufacturers tax at the federal level and retail taxes at the provincial level. In 1966 Ireland added a wholesale tax on consumer durables to its retail sales tax system to produce a partial dual levy.

A dual system avoids the evils of the turnover tax because each commodity is subject to tax the same number of times as it passes through production and distribution channels. The only distorting effects are those characteristic of wholesale and manufacturers sales taxes, and these are minor compared to those of a turnover tax. At the same time the dual sys-

9. The taxes of the two, Maharashtra and Gujarat, are very similar. A tax is applied at rates ranging from 1 to 45 percent to the sale by the manufacturer, or 2 to 6 percent on the sale to the retailer, or to both sales at rates from 0.25 to 10 percent on the first sale and 0.25 to 3 percent on the last sale. To this is added a general 0.25 percent levy on all retail sales.

tem allows a substantially lower rate than a single-stage tax because of the dual base. There are several other advantages as well. The undesirable features of the manufacturers tax are lessened because of the reduced rate, while the advantages of collecting taxes at preretail levels are partly attained. The lower burden at retail compared with that for a single-stage retail tax reduces potential evasion and loss of revenue from exempting small retailers. A significant advantage is the ability to obtain rate differentiation by varying rates at the manufacturing level. In a federal structure the dual system permits each level of government to have autonomy in the sales tax field.

The dual levy retains, in part, the inherent disadvantages of the wholesale or manufacturers taxes, explained in chapter 4, and adds to administrative problems. The number of registered vendors will not be much greater than with a retail levy, but questions of identification of taxpayers and taxable sales, interpretation, and enforcement arise with each of the two elements in the tax. If a country can raise desired revenues with a single-stage retail tax with small retailers excluded, there is little merit in using the dual system, which is primarily a device to escape the heavy burdens at a single stage. If it cannot, the dual system is far superior to the turnover tax and simpler than a value-added tax, although it does not have all advantages of the latter. Even in a federal structure the dual tax results in duplicate collection and audit activity, and partly for this reason the Canadian Royal Commission recommended a shift of the federal tax to the retail level. This proposal encountered a major political obstacle: fear of public reactions to the 15 to 18 percent rate that would be necessary.

THE VALUE-ADDED TAX

The retail price of a commodity is the sum of the values added by the sequence of firms in the production and distribution channels: the differences between selling prices and costs of purchased goods and materials. Thus another possible form of sales tax is one that applies to each firm at each level of production and distribution, but that taxes the value added rather than total receipts. The total yield of such a tax[10] would equal the yield of a retail sales tax with the same rate, since the bases are identical in magnitude.[11] Such a levy, known as a value-added tax (TVA or VAT), is the newest of the major forms of sales tax. The idea dates back at least to

10. With imports taxed and exports free of tax, this magnitude is not exactly equal to the total value added in the economy.
11. An attempt by W. H. Oakland to demonstrate that the value-added tax is not identical to a retail sales tax ("The Theory of the Value Added Tax," *National Tax Journal,* 20 [June and September 1967], 119–36, 270–81) would appear to be unsuccessful, as shown by C. S. Shoup, "Consumption Tax, and Wages Type and Consumption Type of Value Added Tax," *National Tax Journal,* 21 (June 1968), 153-61.

1918, when the tax was recommended to the German government by von Siemens as a substitute for the turnover tax.[12] The manufacturers sales taxes of several countries eventually gained partial value-added elements—for example, Argentina in 1935, and France in 1948. The tax, instead of applying only to sales of finished products, as in Canada, was imposed on all sales by manufacturers, but each manufacturer could deduct amounts paid for materials and parts from sales in calculating his tax. From this form of levy it was a simple step to extend the value-added principle into distribution channels and to broaden the deductible categories of purchases to cover most producers goods. France extended the tax into wholesale channels and broadened the producers goods deductions in 1954[13] and in 1968 extended it to the retail level. Finland introduced the value-added element at the retail level in 1964. Wholesalers pay tax on their entire sales, retailers only on value added.[14] In 1962 the value-added tax was recommended for member countries by the fiscal (Neumark) committee of the European Economic Community (EEC)[15] and was later approved by the EEC Council of Ministers. Germany made the change January 1, 1968, Belgium and the Netherlands on the same date in 1969; and Luxembourg in 1970. Italy is expected to follow in the next two years. These taxes extend through the retail level, as do those of Denmark, introduced in 1967, and Sweden, 1969. Norway introduced a 20 percent value added tax in 1970. Meanwhile the tax was considered in the larger Latin American countries and adopted by Brazil (states) in 1965 and Uruguay in 1968, replacing turnover and manufacturers sales taxes respectively. Its introduction was planned in Mexico and Argentina in 1970. A value-added tax proposal was submitted to the legislative body in Chile in 1969. The Ivory Coast has adopted a value-added tax of the French variety. In 1965 the state of Louisiana modified its retail sales tax to extend it to the wholesale suppliers of retailers with a value-added feature.

Types of Value-Added Tax

Value-added taxes may be classified in several ways. One is on the basis of coverage of stages. The taxes may apply throughout the production

12. The history of value-added tax proposals is summarized in J. F. Due, "Value Added Tax Proposals in the United States," in P. L. Kleinsorge, ed., *Public Finance and Welfare: Essays in Honor of C. Ward Macy* (Eugene: University of Oregon Press, 1966), pp. 111–26.

13. Clara Sullivan, *The Tax on Value Added* (New York: Columbia University Press, 1965).

14. A. Tait and J. F. Due, "Sales Taxation in Eire, Denmark and Finland," *National Tax Journal*, 18 (September 1965), 286–96.

15. International Bureau of Fiscal Documentation, *The EEC Reports on Tax Harmonization, The Report of the Fiscal and Financial Committee* (Amsterdam, 1963).

and distribution stages, or they may be confined to limited stages—manufacturing plus wholesale, or wholesale plus retail.[16]

A second classification is made on the basis of the method of calculation. Under the tax credit form, the most common, a firm calculates its tax liability by applying the tax rate to total sales and subtracting the tax paid on purchases during the period (or, as in France, during the preceding period). Another plan calls for the firm to apply the tax to a calculated figure of value added. This figure is ascertained either by subtracting from total sales the amounts paid during the period for produced goods or specified categories of them (subtraction method) or by adding the various payments that comprise value added: wages paid, interest paid, net profits, and so on (addition method). The tax credit method is widely regarded as the best. It is simple for the firm to operate and for the government to audit. It avoids (or at least obscures) some troublesome questions that arise in the calculation of value added (such as treatment of contributions to charity). It facilitates the handling of rate differentiation and exemptions, and, most importantly, it provides a cross check among firms. Tax paid by one firm appears as a deduction by another, as is subsequently explained. The other methods have no significant advantages except possibly when the tax is used by a subordinate unit of government.

A third classification is based upon the tax treatment of final-product capital goods such as machinery, equipment, and supplies.[17] Three options are available. First, with the *consumption* form (France and ultimately all EEC countries), taxes on all goods purchased for business use may be deducted on a current basis. The coverage of this form is the same as that of a retail sales tax confined to consumption goods and thus to consumer expenditures. Second, with the *income* form (as proposed in Mexico), deduction of taxes on durable capital goods is permitted but only on a depreciation basis rather than when the equipment is purchased. Tax on nondurable producers goods is deductible in the period of purchase. The effect is to delay deduction, add to the working capital requirements, and tax an expanding firm more than under the consumption form. The total base is equal to total personal income. Third, deductions may be limited to materials and parts becoming physical ingredients of produced goods, with other producers goods, including capital equipment, not deductible on either current or depreciation bases. This *product* variety, as proposed in Chile, is equivalent to a retail sales tax on all final products, both consumption goods and final-product capital goods.

16. A tax using the value-added principle at one stage only (usually manufacturing) is not commonly designated a value-added tax.

17. The classification of value-added taxes into the three forms was first developed by C. S. Shoup, "Theory and Background of the Value Added Tax," *Proceedings of the National Tax Association for 1955*, pp. 7–19.

The choice among these forms must be based on the same considerations that are used to determine whether producers goods should be exempt from sales taxes generally, as explained in chapter 7. The most obvious argument for the consumption form is the maximum stimulus it provides for new investment—a primary objective of France, Sweden, Denmark, and other countries in shifting to the value-added form.

Summary of Current and Proposed Value Added Taxes

Table 6–3 outlines the features of several existing and proposed value added taxes.

The European taxes[18] are all basically similar in design. Those of the Common Market countries were developed or modified in conformity with EEC directives, and the Scandinavian countries followed closely, differing mainly in the use of a single rate instead of several. The exact coverage, particularly of services, varies somewhat, as does the treatment of small firms. The French tax is much heavier than the others. All European levies provide for deduction of taxes on all business purchases, with minor exceptions, partly because of emphasis on export markets. The tax of the Ivory Coast is quite similar to the French. The Latin American taxes, on the other hand, restrict deductibility of taxes on producers goods much more severely, partly to avoid any incentive for excessive capital intensity. They are also less complete in coverage, typically not extending through the retail level. The federal tax in Brazil applies only to the manufacturing sector, the state taxes to the distribution sector.

All of the present taxes employ the destination principle. Imports are subject to tax and exports are exempted, with full credit at export for taxes paid at various stages of production and distribution. The EEC countries plan eventually to use the origin principle to minimize problems of collection on intercountry sales, with greater uniformity of taxes than now prevails. All taxes use the tax deduction method of calculation except the state taxes in Brazil, to some extent, and the proposed levy in Argentina.

Merits of the Value-Added Tax

The value-added form of sales tax offers the great advantage of economic neutrality. It avoids the adverse economic effects of the turnover tax without concentrating the burden at a single stage. Since the tax applies only to the value added by each firm—not to gross receipts—the organization of production, the degree of integration, and the location of particular functions do not affect the overall tax liability so long as all sectors, including retailing, are covered. A highly integrated firm will pay the same tax as the sum of the tax paid by the several independent links in a competing

18. Excluding the Finnish tax, regarded as a dual levy with a value-added feature.

TABLE 6-3. CURRENT AND PROPOSED VALUE-ADDED TAXES JANUARY 1970

Europe

	France	Germany	Denmark	Sweden	Netherlands
Year introduced	1953-54	1968	1967	1969	1969
Method	Tax credit	Tax credit	Tax credit	Tax credit	Tax credit
Major exemptions	Basic foods	Very limited	Very limited; some foods	Basic necessities	Basic foods, medicine
Services coverage	Originally separate tax; most now covered, except professions, banks, insurance	All, with few exceptions (banking, communications, some professions)	Specified services taxed; many covered	Many specified services covered	Most covered except professions, insurance
Treatment of farmers	Exempt	Covered	Covered	Covered	Exempt
Treatment of retailers	Now included; initially not	Covered	Covered	Covered	Covered
Treatment of artisans	Exempt	Covered	Covered	Covered	Covered
Small firms generally	Exempt or *forfait* collection	Under $5,000 annual sales exempt	Under $667 annual sales exempt	Very small firms exempt	Under $300 annual sales[1]
Tax on capital goods	Deductible except on personal vehicles	Fully deductible, but offset until 1973[2]	All deductible	All deductible	Ultimately fully deductible; partially in transition period
Rates (%):					
Basic	25	11	12.5	11.1	12
Reduced	7.53, 17.65	5.5	....	....	4
Luxury	33	....	....	....	..

Supplementary Note: The value-added tax was introduced in Luxembourg in January 1970. The basic rate is 8 percent, the reduced rate 4 percent. The structure is very similar to the German tax.

Latin America

	Uruguay	Brazil	Mexico	Chile	Argentina
Year introduced	1968	1965 (state)	Proposed 1970	Proposed	Proposed
Method	Tax credit	Tax credit[3]	Tax credit	Tax credit	Calculation of value added by deduction
Major exemptions	Basic necessities	Basic necessities	Basic necessities	Unprocessed food, few other items	Basic foods, books, farm machinery
Services coverage	Some covered	Not covered	Most covered	Separate tax on most; not professional	Most covered
Treatment of farmers	Exempt	Covered	Exempt	Exempt	Not exempt per se, most not covered
Treatment of retailers	Exempt	State levies: covered; federal: manufacturers only	Covered	Exempt[4]	Covered
Treatment of artisans	Covered	Covered	Covered	Small exempt	Small exempt

	Uruguay	Brazil	Mexico	Chile	Argentina
Small firms generally	Under $8,000 annual sales exempted	Covered	Covered; simplified collection	Exempt under certain sales	Small exempt[5]
Tax on capital goods	Partially deductible	Only tax on raw materials and parts deductible	Depreciation basis for capital equipment; others current	Parts and materials only	Depreciation basis for capital equipment; others current
Rates (%):					
Basic	10	See footnote 6	5	20	6
Reduced	..		..	..	2
Luxury	..		10	35	10, 15, 20

Africa

	Ivory Coast
Year introduced	1960
Method	Tax credit
Major exemptions	Foods, drugs; only industrial and imported goods taxed
Services coverage	Separate tax
Treatment of farmers	Not covered
Treatment of retailers	Not covered
Treatment of artisans	Small not covered
Small firms generally	*Forfait* collection, firms under $60,000 annual sales
Tax on capital goods	Raw materials, parts, equipment deductible
Rates (%):	
Basic	17.64
Reduced	....
Luxury	43

[1] May request exemption.
[2] Reduction offset initially by special investment tax, which declines in steps until elimination in 1973.
[3] Except in part for state levies.
[4] Subject to separate retail sales tax.
[5] Producers under $17,000 annual sales, retailers under $68,000.
[6] Federal: variety of rates, most 4–10 percent; state: 17 percent central and south, 18 percent other, 15 percent interstate.

nonintegrated distribution system. Shifting functions forward will reduce the tax liability of a particular firm but will increase that due at later levels, with no net change. A value-added tax extended only through the wholesale level will have the same distorting effects as a single-stage wholesale tax by encouraging firms to push activities forward to the retail level.

The value-added tax extending through the retail level can attain most of the advantages of the retail tax. Under the assumption of forward shifting, the tax will constitute a uniform percentage (or a desired pattern of nonuniformity) of consumer expenditures on various goods. Exports can be freed of tax without difficulty and imports taxed on the same basis as domestic goods. If goods are imported by final consumers, for example, the full value added will be taxed at importation. Pyramiding will at least be less than with preretail taxes and will perhaps be avoided entirely, because the tax credit technique requires separation of tax from selling price at each transaction. Services can easily be covered.

At the same time, a substantial portion of the tax will be collected at preretail levels—70 percent, for example, if retail margins (the value added at retail) constitute 30 percent of the final selling prices. Much of this income will be collected at the import stage in the earliest years of development. Thus a government is assured of a large portion of the total revenue even if there is considerable evasion at retail, and such evasion will create less competitive disturbance since only the tax on the margin is involved.

A significant advantage of the value-added form of sales tax compared with all other forms is the built-in cross-check feature. The tax paid by one firm is reported by firms purchasing from this vendor as a credit against their own tax liability. Therefore any underreporting of tax by the first firm is likely to be discovered, and firms will become aware of this danger. The buyer has no incentive to buy tax free from his supplier (so long as he cannot escape tax on his sales), because if he does he will simply have less tax credit to deduct and will owe more tax on his own sales. This cross check does not function on the final sales to the consumer, but it does at all previous transactions. While the advantage is without question significant, it can be exaggerated; the cross check does not occur automatically, and audits are required if firms are to fear discovery of underreporting. Similar cross checks are possible (and commonly employed) with other types of sales tax. But the potential for cross audit is more obvious with the value-added tax and encourages more correct reporting, and auditors have contact with firms at all levels, which they may not have, or may have only nominally, with single-stage taxes.

Another potential advantage of the value-added tax is the possibly greater ease of excluding producers goods from coverage.[19] This was the primary reason why Denmark and Sweden shifted from single-stage to value-added taxes; they were particularly interested in eliminating all tax elements from export producers.[20] Deduction can be limited to taxes paid on materials, parts, and other physical ingredients or can be extended to include tax paid on all purchases for business use or all except certain cate-

19. This consideration is stressed by Ann F. Friedlaender, "Indirect Taxes and Relative Prices," *Quarterly Journal of Economics,* 81 (February 1967), pp. 125–39.
20. Shoup, "Experience with the Value Added Tax."

gories. Control of the deduction would appear to be somewhat simpler than with exemption from tax of sales for production purposes. The control is exercised over the deductions of the firms purchasing the goods rather than those of the suppliers, who do not necessarily know the final use. This conclusion was reached by Danish officials after experience with both forms of tax.[21] But this advantage can also be exaggerated. A firm's accounts do not necessarily show accurately whether items have been purchased for business use or the owners' personal use (especially in smaller businesses), and as with other sales taxes it is necessary to inquire into actual use. But at least the inquiry is somewhat easier to make, and vendors are not required to segregate sales into taxable and tax-exempt categories.

This advantage is significant only when the purchases are made by firms subject to value-added tax, as explained in the next section.

Limitations

The value-added tax is not without limitations;[22] its advantages have been overstressed by some of its supporters. The most serious objection to the tax is the greater overall complexity compared with the other forms of sales tax, although the tasks for some vendors are simplified. The concept of the tax is much more difficult to make clearly understood, particularly in a developing economy. The number of active taxpayers is greater than with any single-stage tax; in Great Britain the estimate is 2 million firms, compared with 65,000 with the wholesale tax. While the number of registered firms will not differ greatly from that for a retail sales tax with comparable coverage, many of the nonretail firms registered under the latter have little or no liability. The task of record keeping is somewhat greater, since taxes paid on purchases must be compiled and cumulated in addition to data on sales. This is not a difficult task for most firms, but it does require time and effort. The complexity argument is difficult to evaluate; it is clearly of some significance but likewise can be overstated.

Another major problem is the necessity to avoid or minimize exemptions and rate differentiation if the tax is to function satisfactorily in a developing economy, or perhaps in any country. Most of the problems in France have centered around nonuniformity.[23] To achieve the desired effects, differentiated rates must be carried throughout the system or used

21. *Ibid.*

22. W. Missorten, "Some Problems in Implementing a Tax on Value Added," *National Tax Journal*, 21 (December 1968), 396–411; F. Forte, "On the Feasibility of a Truly General Value Added Tax," *National Tax Journal*, 19 (December 1966), 337–61; T. M. Rybczynski, ed., *The Value Added Tax* (Oxford: Basil Blackwell, 1969).

23. See, for example, Georges Egret, "The Value Added Tax in France," in Rybczynski, ed., *Value Added Tax*, pp. 20–29.

exclusively on the final retail sales. If varying rates are used at early stages but not at later ones, the tax credit feature will eliminate the effects. Differentiation throughout increases the tasks of taxpayers at all stages; its application only at retail concentrates the task on the firms least capable of performing it and requires the demarcation of retail sales, which can otherwise be avoided. In part the same considerations apply to commodity exemptions. These must likewise be carried through all stages if they are to be effective, or a full refund must be given at the final stage for all taxes paid up to then, as provided for exports. Either approach is workable, although troublesome, so long as a few well-defined categories of commodities are involved. It is almost unworkable for a large number of items, particularly at the retail level.

Similar problems arise with the exemption of groups of firms. If a particular set—for example, farmers—is exempted outright, sales to it become taxable, and there is no simple mechanism for deducting the tax paid on purchases from subsequent taxes payable on the goods. One solution is to exempt sales to these groups, but this creates serious problems except when limited to a few major categories (such as seed, livestock feed, and fertilizer). An alternative is to allow the tax paid by farmers on their purchases to be carried forward for credit beyond the farm stage. This is even more troublesome if attempted in any precise way. The Netherlands uses a variant of this technique; 4 percent of the prices of goods purchased from farmers is assumed to reflect the tax paid by farmers on their purchases and is deductible. Yet taxation of large numbers of small firms, particularly farmers, is virtually impossible administratively. Furthermore, since farmers sell in relatively perfect markets, immediate shifting of the tax is impossible and the tax would rest inequitably upon the farm operators.

It is possible to exclude retailers from the tax and thus confine it to preretail channels, as was the policy in France until recently and is proposed in Chile. Such a tax provides the advantages of the value-added principle, particularly cross check in audit, at preretail levels; lessens distortion of the location of distribution functions as well as valuation problems at the preretail levels; and greatly reduces the number of taxpaying firms, particularly smaller ones. In countries in which most retailing is small in scale, limiting the complex value-added tax to the nonretail levels is particularly attractive. But doing so eliminates much of the advantage of the value added principle. Retailers must be distinguished from other types of firms, and special rules must be devised for firms engaged in both retail and wholesale activity. The inherent advantages of a tax through the retail level—uniformity, neutrality for allocation of distribution functions, ease of tax treatment of exports and imports—are partly lost. The exclusion from tax of producers goods used by retailers, if desired, is difficult to implement. The tax rate must be higher to gain a given revenue.[24] Retailers may lose the trade of customers authorized to credit taxes on purchases. Nevertheless, at least as a transitional step toward a complete value-added tax, exclusion of retailers may be the wisest policy.

The Value-Added Tax as an Aid to Export Industries

The typical effort of a developing country to aid industrial development by the use of protective tariffs can easily result in many small-scale, inefficient protected industries with limited domestic markets. A more satisfactory approach to industrialization for some countries is to concentrate on a few export industries, ones for which the country has the greatest relative advantage. One method is to eliminate customs duties and replace other taxes on business firms by a value-added tax applying to imports as well as to domestic sales.[25] A full refund of the tax paid would be given on exports, while elimination of other taxes would improve the position of home industries in world markets. Furthermore, industries that the government particularly wishes to encourage could be freed from liability on domestic value added and given a credit on exports not only for tax paid on imports but also for phantom tax on domestic value added even though not actually paid. Firms would thus be encouraged to increase domestic value added and reduce imports of partly finished goods.

The objective of this plan—to stimulate large-scale export industries to compete in world markets instead of many inefficient local industries—obviously has merit. The approach is not without problems, however.[26] Elimination of all taxes on corporate income would break down the progressivity of the income tax structure, and it would artificially encourage the use of the corporate form of organization and retention of earnings within the business. This result would aid development to some extent, but at a substantial cost in terms of the objectives of the tax structure. The value-added form of tax is not actually necessary for the key elements in the proposal; a wholesale sales tax would serve about as well. The refund of a phantom tax is such an obvious export subsidy that retaliation would be almost inevitable. Subsidization of exports can lead to inefficiency in the use of resources just as effectively as can protective tariffs and is not likely to be permanently successful.

24. As proposed in Chile, a retail sales tax can be used together with a value-added tax extended through the wholesale level to lessen the required value-added tax rate.

25. R. I. McKinnon, "Export Expansion through Tax Policy," *Malayan Economic Review*, 11 (October 1966), 1–27.

26. R. M. Bird, "A Value Added Tax for Singapore," *Malayan Economic Review*, 12 (April 1967), 39–41; C. T. Edwards, "A Value Added Tax?", *Malayan Economic Review*, 13 (October 1968), 22–49; Wu Ta-Yeh, "McKinnon's Value Added Tax and Industrial Development in Singapore," *Malayan Economic Review*, 13 (October 1968), 50–63.

Tax Shifting Problems and Distributional Effects

Thus far we have assumed that the value-added tax will shift forward in exact amounts and thus produce an overall distributional pattern identical with that of a fully shifted retail sales tax, provided the tax extends through the retail level. The requirement that the tax be kept separate from the price of the product because of the tax credit feature facilitates forward shifting and discourages pyramiding. When a government establishes a value-added tax with the clear intent that it be shifted forward, it is reasonable to assume that monetary policy will permit an increase in the general price level to reflect the tax. Apart from the usual obstacles to precise shifting, such as the existence of increasing cost conditions with a net decline in the sales of the product, in the typical imperfect market the policy of the firms toward the tax will influence the actual shifting. If all raise prices by the amount calculated by applying the tax rate to the sale price, the tax will shift forward exactly. But this policy involves disregard by the firms of deductibility of tax paid on purchases other than goods acquired for resale. The actual net liability of a firm will be zero in a particular period if the tax credit on purchases of producers goods equals tax due on sales. If such a firm considers its net tax position and does not raise price at all the competing firms may find shifting difficult or impossible. The deviations from shifting may be particularly significant at the retail level, where the requirement of separate quotation of prices is likely to be relaxed.[27]

When markets are perfectly competitive, immediate shifting is virtually impossible. Individual firms have no control over prices and cannot "add" the tax to the prices; price, including tax, will rise only as supply falls. This may require a substantial period of time.

There are also questions about the distributional effects of a value-added tax that does not allow credit on purchases of producers goods other than parts and materials. The base of such a tax is identical to that of a retail sales tax applying to all final-product capital and consumption goods and thus to total personal income plus depreciation. If the income form is used, with the tax deducted on a depreciation basis, the base is equal to personal income. In perfectly competitive markets it may be argued that such a tax—retail or value-added—has the same distributional effects as a proportional income tax, the tax on capital goods being equivalent to a tax on savings.[28] But with imperfect markets this conclusion no longer follows. The firms are likely to regard the tax paid on purchases of producers goods as elements in the cost of the goods and either to treat them as current operating expenses or to include them in the capital cost figures that serve

27. J. F. Due, "The Value Added Tax," *Western Economic Journal,* 3 (Spring 1965), 165–71.
28. P. M. Mieszkowski, "On the Theory of Tax Incidence," *Journal of Political Economy,* 75 (June 1967), 250–62. Mieszkowski extends his conclusions to imperfect markets.

as the basis for depreciation. As a consequence, the portion of the tax on producers goods will be reflected in the prices of the consumption goods made with them and thus be distributed in relation to consumer expenditures, with some nonuniformity owing to varying capital intensity in production processes.

The Question of Labor Intensiveness

The major complaint against the principle of the value added tax is that with tax on producers goods deductible, and even to some degree without, the tax discriminates against labor intensive firms and industries because the value added represents a higher percentage of the selling price than it does in more capital intensive activities. Thus, it is argued, the tax will encourage firms to increase capital intensiveness to reduce the tax they actually pay, a result particularly undesirable in a country with a relative surplus of labor.

Basically this argument is fallacious. If a firm uses additional capital equipment and less labor, it reduces the amount of tax that it pays directly, but more tax per unit of product is shifted forward to it. The ratio of total tax to selling price is the same, provided the tax on capital goods is fully deductible when the purchase is made. If it is not deductible at all (product form), the relative cost of using capital equipment is increased and labor intensive techniques are favored artificially. With the income form (tax deductible on a depreciation basis), the cost of using capital equipment is increased by the amount of the interest cost on the capital required for the tax on capital equipment.

One difference between value-added taxation and other forms is that if it is applied to professions and other services, the taxes paid by the service establishments will be a relatively high fraction of their total receipts compared with those of other firms, since their tax deductions are relatively small. But the overall tax, expressed as a percentage of price, is not heavier, of course; nonservice firms have more tax passed forward to them from their suppliers. If a country shifts from a turnover or single-stage tax on commodities to a value-added tax that includes services, the service industries, which were previously favored, will bear a heavier burden, and the consequences for resource allocation may not be desired. In addition, service firms selling in markets where forward shifting is difficult or demand is very elastic (such as passenger transport) will suffer. But these effects are not attributable to the value-added tax per se but to the discrimination, deliberate or not, in favor of services under the other types of tax.[29]

29. Henry Aaron, "The Differential Price Effects of a Value Added Tax," *National Tax Journal*, 21 (June 1968), 162–75, shows the relative shift in tax impact by industry that would occur if the U.S. corporate income tax were replaced by a value-added tax.

In some respects taxation of services is more satisfactory with a value-added tax than with other forms of sales tax because of the tax credit feature. Under the usual single-stage tax it is difficult to confine the tax to consumer services. Taxation of services rendered to business firms encourages the firms to provide the services themselves. With a value-added tax, deductibility of the tax on such services (which can be granted even if taxes on capital equipment are not deductible) avoids this adverse consequence. Unlike commodity exemptions, an exclusion of some services from the value-added tax while others are taxed raises few administrative difficulties because of the specialized nature of most service establishments.

One group of services, however, is particularly troublesome for value-added taxation—those of financial intermediaries such as banks and insurance companies. A determination of what may legitimately be regarded as "value added" is complicated because a large portion of the receipts consists of interest, which often does not constitute value added and is not subject to tax. Complete exemption of such institutions may be the only suitable approach.

Somewhat similar questions arise with capital gains. Should gains from the sale of land or capital assets be included in a firm's taxable sales figures? In terms of the general intent of sales taxation, the answer would appear to be negative, since these items do not reflect consumption expenditures. Closely related is the question of the sale of secondhand goods. It may be argued that if their prices reflect the tax originally paid on them, they should not be taxed again. But as a practical administrative matter it is far simpler to include them, and exclusion encourages the converting of new goods into used ones for tax purposes.

CONCLUSION

It is difficult to assess precisely the potential of the value-added form of tax compared with single-stage alternatives for developing economies because of a lack of adequate experience. Clearly the value-added tax is superior in many respects to the turnover tax and represents a fruitful avenue of reform for a country that is making extensive use of the latter and is unwilling to risk the high rate and limited impact of a single-stage tax. But for a country that is using or is contemplating a single-stage tax and that seeks somewhat modest revenues at least at first, it is doubtful that the spreading of the impact and the cross-audit features of the value-added tax more than compensate for the loss of the simplicity of the other form. This is a question that can be answered only in the context of a particular situation and even then only tentatively. The evidence does strongly suggest that if a value-added tax is used, universal coverage and uniformity of rate are highly important for satisfactory operation.

SUPPLEMENTARY REFERENCES

The literature on value-added taxation has become very extensive in recent years; only major references are noted below.

Border Tax Adjustments and Tax Structures in OECD Member Countries. Paris: Organization for Economic Cooperation and Development, 1968.

Centro Americano de Administradores Tributarios, *Estado Actual de la Legislacion Comparada Relativa al Impuesto sobre las Ventas.* Panama: CIAT, 1970.

"The Common System of Tax on Value Added." *European Taxation,* 7 (July–August 1967), 146–207.

Due, J. F. *Sales Taxation.* London: Routledge & Kegan Paul, 1957. Chaps. 4–7.

Investigacion Fiscal (Mexico), January 1969.

McKinnon, R. I. "Export Expansion through Tax Policy: The Case for a Value Added Tax in Singapore." *Malayan Economic Review,* 11 (October 1966), 1–24.

Norr, M., and Hornhammer, N. G. "The Value Added Tax in Sweden," *Columbia Law Review,* 70 (March 1970), 380–422.

Ojha, P. D., and Lent, G. E. "Sales Taxes in Countries of the Far East," *International Monetary Fund Staff Papers,* 16 (November 1969), 529–79.

Reig, E. J. "Problemas en la Estructuración de un Proyecto de Ley de Impuesto al Valor Agregado." *CIAT Papers,* 1967. Pp. 533–46.

Report of the Committee on Turnover Taxation [Richardson Committee]. Cmnd. 2300. London: H. M. Stationery Office, 1964.

Report of the Taxation Inquiry Committee. Colombo, Ceylon: Government Press, 1968. (On turnover tax.)

Rybczynski, T. M., ed. *The Value Added Tax.* Oxford: Basil Blackwell, 1969.

Shoup, C. S. "Experience with the Value Added Tax in Denmark, and Prospects in Sweden." *Finanzarchiv,* 28 (March 1969), 236–52.

_____. *Public Finance.* Chicago: Aldine, 1969. Chaps. 8, 9.

Sullivan, Clara. *The Tax on Value Added.* New York: Columbia University Press, 1965.

"The Turnover Tax on Value Added in Europe." *European Taxation,* 8 (November–December 1968), 239–310.

7.

Structural Aspects of Sales Taxes

Regardless of the general form of sales tax chosen, the success of the tax in attaining the objectives in a developing economy will be influenced by its exact structure, particularly the treatment of producers goods and the coverage of consumption goods.

THE TAX TREATMENT OF PRODUCERS GOODS

The production of a good or service requires various inputs: labor, entrepreneurial activity, raw materials, capital equipment, land, money capital. Uniform taxation of all inputs at one stage in production or distribution would produce the same pattern of tax as a levy on the sales of that stage. A tax on inputs at all stages would produce the same result as a general turnover tax. Taxation at each stage of inputs other than produced goods already taxed at an earlier stage would have the same impact as a value-added tax.

But taxation of the purchase of some inputs and not others produces a number of undesirable consequences. The usual sales tax does not apply to services rendered by employees, interest, rent, or profits, per se, but frequently does to inputs that consist of produced goods—those purchased for resale, materials and parts, fuel and other goods consumed directly or in a short period in the production process, and durable capital equipment—and to some services acquired from other firms rather than from employees.

Undesirable Consequences of Taxing Particular Inputs

Taxation of particular types of inputs, particularly produced goods, prevents attainment of a truly single-stage character and so interferes with the attainment of the desired goals of the tax in several ways. The disadvantages are similar to those of a turnover tax, although in lesser degree:

139

1. Factor combinations are altered. Different combinations of factors result in different amounts of tax, and thus the most profitable combination is no longer—except by accident—the one that is optimal for economic efficiency. Taxation of materials but not labor encourages the use of additional labor to utilize materials better. If capital goods are taxed and labor is not, firms are encouraged to use more labor intensive methods.

2. Firms are given an incentive to produce goods themselves rather than purchase them, since this eliminates the gross margins (value added) of the suppliers from the tax base. The advantage is particularly great with services if they are taxable when acquired from a separate firm but are tax free when produced by a firm's own employees. When the tax treatment encourages firms to produce goods, especially capital equipment, instead of purchasing them, the potential advantages of specialization and large-scale production in the capital equipment industries are lost—a consequence of particular severity in a developing economy with a limited market for these industries.

3. The distributional effects of the tax may be less acceptable. Because of differences in production techniques, some firms are subjected to higher taxes on inputs than competing firms and may have difficulty in shifting the entire tax. The tax element in the prices of various consumer goods are not uniform because of varying ratios of tax on inputs to selling prices, depending in part on the capital intensity of production. Desired deviations from uniformity cannot be attained. Exempted commodities, for example, cannot be completely excluded from tax because some inputs used in their production are taxed. The final burden on expenditures for various commodities cannot even be known, and the overall distributional effects of the tax cannot be ascertained.

4. Taxation of inputs makes it impossible to free exports completely from tax and to ensure that imports are subject to the same tax as equivalent domestic goods. Since the total tax on inputs used to produce goods for export cannot be ascertained it cannot easily be rebated at export, and exports are likely to be restricted to some extent with given exchange rates. Even with flexible exchange rates, the distortion of relative prices of exported goods impedes optimal export production. Imports are favored compared to domestic goods because inputs of the latter are taxed while those of the former are not.

Capital Equipment

Taxation of purchases of durable capital equipment has two particularly significant effects: the equipment is made more costly, increasing both the amount of depreciation that must be earned over its life and interest costs on the greater money capital that must be invested. Even taxation of materials and other current inputs has some effect on capital requirements, since working capital must be larger, but the effect of the taxation of capital equipment is much greater. One consequence is a reduction in the amount of real capital equipment that can be acquired with a given amount of money capital, with consequent lower level of real investment, to the detriment of economic development. The original volume of investment can be restored by a reduction in the interest rate, if investment is adequately interest-elastic, but the price structure is distorted in the process.

Exclusion of Producers Goods

There are several obstacles to complete exclusion of all inputs from a sales tax. The first is identification of sales of inputs and those of final products. Many commodities and services can be used for either purpose. Accordingly, unconditional exemption by type of commodity is not universally possible, though some goods and services rendered primarily for business use, such as freight transport, can be excluded this way. Exclusion must usually take the conditional form, determined by the use made in the particular case. But it may be difficult for the seller to determine the ultimate use at the time of sale, particularly with a preretail tax when the buyer is purchasing for resale. Checks upon ultimate use at the time of audit are difficult and costly.

Partly—but not entirely—because of this problem, governments often limit the exclusion of producers goods to categories that can easily be controlled. Almost universally, except under a turnover tax that makes no attempt to exclude inputs, purchases of goods for resale and materials and parts that become physical ingredients of produced goods are excluded. Under a retail tax they are typically excluded through definition of a taxable sale as sale for use or consumption and not for resale. Many sales taxes confine the exclusion of producers goods to this category. Others add additional ones, particularly (1) fuel and other consumables, goods used up in the production process but not becoming physical ingredients; (2) agricultural feed, seed, fertilizer, and machinery; and (3) industrial machinery and equipment, the major items of real investment. Building materials, office equipment and supplies, equipment used in distribution, and motor vehicles—to name only the major categories—remain taxable. Not infrequently 20 to 25 percent of the yield of a sales tax comes from sales of inputs.

In addition to the administrative and compliance considerations, there are other reasons why many inputs remain taxable. Some governments prefer to tax various inputs rather than to use a higher tax rate on consumption goods. In part this represents a desire to spread the impact of the tax, in part it reflects the political appeal of making the tax apply to purchases by business firms rather than individuals. Such a procedure has a strong popular appeal because the ultimate shifting of this element of the tax to the final consumer (often with a markup) is not recognized.

Sales tax laws are also frequently drafted by persons who have little knowledge of the functioning of the economic system. To them the notion that a sales tax should apply to all final products seems logical; they fail to see the undesirable effects of taxing inputs.

With the introduction of the value-added tax in Europe, the exclusion of producers goods has been broadened to include virtually all inputs. The Swedish and Danish taxes provide complete exclusion, the French tax now does except for personal motor vehicles, and the German and Dutch taxes will do so after a transitional period. Exclusion of additional producers goods was a primary objective of the shift to the value-added form, at least in France, Sweden, and Denmark.

Exclusion of Capital Equipment

While the principle that inputs should not be taxed is now widely accepted in theory and to an increasing extent in practice in the developing economies, in recent years two economic arguments have developed against the exemption of durable capital goods in such countries. The first is based on a deliberate intent to decrease industrial capital intensity. Many developing economies suffer from a relative labor surplus and a severe capital shortage, in the sense that the marginal productivity of labor is low compared with that in developed economies whereas the marginal productivity of capital is high (at least if risk is ignored). There are numerous underemployed and in some instances unemployed, as the total capital is not adequate to allow employment of all available workers at tasks that allow a subsistence wage. Accordingly, goes the argument, development will be aided by tax and other measures that encourage the use of more labor intensive techniques than firms might otherwise find advantageous.

This argument is criticized on the grounds that artificial encouragement of less efficient methods restricts the ability of the economy to export and reduces potential output levels. The primary difficulty is not overintensivity of capital relative to the optimum but rather the low productivity of unskilled workers. This argument cannot be resolved within the framework of this study. A reasonable conclusion appears to be that (1) some capital intensive industries and methods aid development so greatly that they should not be discouraged or forced to lose efficiency through artificial incentives to greater use of labor; (2) when more labor intensive methods can be used with little loss in efficiency, optimal development justifies governmental action to bring about this result; and (3) general taxation of capital equipment is not likely to produce the desired results because it retards all investment rather than selected types.

A related argument defends taxation of capital goods as an offset for various influences that may make labor artificially expensive and capital artificially cheap; in other words, prices determined by market forces may not reflect relative real costs. There are several possible causes:

1. Wage rates may be pushed to artificially high levels.[1] A basic problem facing many developing economies is a high level of wages in the modern sector compared with subsistence incomes in the traditional sector. A few industries capable of paying high wages develop. Commonly they are foreign owned and their managers are influenced by wage rates abroad. Many of the skilled personnel initially are from abroad, and nationals who replace them receive comparable wages. Unions soon develop among these workers and push wages still higher. Other sectors of the economy cannot pay equivalent wages. Serious consequences result—a reduction in the real income of persons in the lowest income sectors, especially the traditional one, and conversion of underemployment into unemployment. The high wages produce excessive capital intensivity.

2. Payroll taxes, often used to finance social security programs after the example of developed countries, artificially increase labor costs.

3. Money capital may be artificially cheap, especially for subsidiaries of foreign companies, the government, and joint government-private undertakings. Money is available to these users at near world interest rates or even less as a result of foreign aid and lending by international agencies. The consequence is to encourage excessive capital intensity and the use of excessively long-range labor-saving techniques. At the same time, money capital is very expensive or unavailable to small-scale labor intensive entrepreneurs because of greater risks and imperfections in the capital market.

4. In some countries, capital equipment, which is mostly imported, is artificially cheap because the exchange rate is held artificially high by exchange controls. This is apparently a major consideration in Colombia, for example.

5. Noneconomic influences may distort investment decisions. Large foreign-owned enterprises may adopt the same production techniques that they use at home without consideration of relative labor and capital costs. Use of the most "efficient," modern techniques is deeply ingrained in the thinking of many business executives. Frequently modern labor intensive techniques are not available, since research in developed economies is directed to the capital intensive methods. Governments are also guilty of using the most modern techniques to impress observers, internal and external.

1. W. Arthur Lewis, *Development Planning* (London: George Allen & Unwin, 1966), part II-5.

Certainly these influences distort the choice of methods and should be considered in the decisions about the tax treatment of capital goods. Some factors are relevant in some countries, some in others. The chief dangers in the taxation of capital goods to offset these influences are the unnecessary restriction of total investment and the inability by tax methods to distinguish between investments that contribute greatly or little to economic development. Other planning techniques may be far more effective in terms of the goals.

In summary: the general case for excluding all producers goods, at least all except durable capital goods, from the sales tax is very strong. But administrative considerations require that the exclusion be somewhat restricted in scope except with the value-added tax, and perhaps with that as well.[2] The tax treatment of durable capital goods is subject to conflicting considerations. The weight of the evidence appears to favor exemption except when taxation is justified by special circumstances that artificially increase the cost of labor compared with capital throughout industry. Even in these instances other techniques may be preferable to taxation of capital goods.

THE COVERAGE OF CONSUMPTION GOODS

By the inherent character of sales taxation, as distinguished from excise taxes, there is a strong case for broad coverage of consumption goods, both tangible commodities and services. First, only a general tax can avoid the undesirable features of any consumption tax of limited scope: the discrimination among individuals according to their relative preferences for various goods and the reallocation of resources, with potential excess burden. Any exemption inevitably favors those persons with high preferences for the exempted goods and leads to a shift of resources to the production of these goods.

Second, exemptions complicate the application of the tax, the record keeping of the taxpayers, and the audit of returns, and pave the way for evasion. Experience universally demonstrates that exemptions greatly reduce the effective operation of a sales tax. Questions of interpretation constantly arise, particularly with the development of new products; vendors have difficulty in ensuring that their clerks apply the tax correctly; sales of exempt and taxable commodities must be distinguished in the records; vendors have a tendency to overstate exempt sales; and audit is made much more difficult. Finally, exemptions inevitably reduce revenue, so the tax rate must be higher to obtain a given amount of money.

2. A major problem with the value-added tax is the exclusion of inputs of firms that are not liable for payment of tax (e.g., farmers), but that produce goods purchased as inputs by taxpaying firms.

Thus the case for broad coverage, with exemption only with specific justification, is very strong. This rule applies to services as well as to tangible commodities; the long-standing tendency to tax commodities but not services, particularly in English-speaking countries, has little justification in terms of the potential objectives of the tax. Services satisfy personal wants in the same fashion as commodities. Since they are frequently rendered in conjunction with the sale of goods by the same vendors, taxation of the service element simplifies the application of the tax. Failure to tax the services when separately rendered while taxing them when performed as an element in the sale of the goods, as is common, encourages separate provision. For example, if services involved in building construction are not taxable, firms are encouraged to fabricate on the site as part of the building contract rather than on a large-scale basis in the shop. Various studies suggest that expenditures on many services rise more rapidly than those on commodities, and thus the distribution of the burden will be less regressive with services taxed.

Justification for Exemptions

In any economy, but especially in one in the earlier years of economic development, one segment of the population is barely able to maintain a subsistence level and by usual standards has no taxpaying ability. To apply a sales tax of any magnitude to the purchases of these people is contrary to universal standards of equity, and by pushing their living levels still lower it will lessen productivity and retard economic development. Accordingly, exemption of the major items of consumption of the lowest income groups is essential. Such exemptions must be determined by examination of family spending patterns in these income levels. In practice this has seldom been done, although in most developing economies the primary patterns are obvious: most of the expenditures are for unprocessed food,[3] plus a little clothing. Since with a few exceptions, varying with the country, the lowest income groups buy unprocessed food, exemption of such food has particular merit. Administrative difficulties are minimal. The exemption may aid administration and reduce competitive disturbance because a large portion of unprocessed food is sold by small vendors who cannot be brought within the scope of the tax. Furthermore, much unprocessed food is produced on a subsistence basis without sale; taxation of such food when purchased while that consumed by the producer is not taxable discourages the development of the commercial sector of the economy and discriminates against the urban poor, who are unable to produce their own food. Exemption of

3. For example, a 1962 study showed that in the lowest income groups in Accra, Ghana, food expenditures constituted 78 percent of total income. U.S. Department of Agriculture, *Ghana: Projected Level of Demand, Supply, and Imports of Agricultural Products in 1965, 1970, and 1975* (Washington, USDA, 1964).

food lessens the upward pressure on wages. There is only one major objection to the exemption: if food is scarce and the supply highly inelastic, the exemption may result in higher prices, with a consequent loss of benefit to the poor.

The case for exempting processed food is much weaker, apart from a few basic, widely consumed items such as powdered milk. The income elasticity of demand for processed food (often imported) is frequently high;[4] consumption, minimal in the lowest income groups, rises rapidly as income rises. Exemption seriously reduces the potential base of the tax, complicates administration, and does not improve the distribution of the burden. Discrimination against the processing of food may be regarded as undesirable but is not likely to have serious effects on development.

Exemption of basic clothing used by the poor is more difficult, since the items are less easily delimited and are frequently sold by vendors handling other commodities as well. Some countries have found it possible to exempt cheap forms of cloth without creating insurmountable problems. The importance of the exemption varies by country on the basis of climate and culture, which influence clothing needs in the lowest income groups. There are still some remote areas where the issue does not arise at all.

Exemption of several other types of goods and services may be justified both on grounds of equity and from the desire to stimulate certain types of expenditures. Drugs, medicines, and related items are examples, and exemption is strongly justifiable. The same reasoning applies to medical, dental, hospital, educational, and related services, which few countries regard as appropriate bases for taxation. Books, magazines, and newspapers are frequently exempted for educational reasons.

Exclusion of certain groups of products or services may also be justified on purely administrative grounds: the difficulty in reaching the particular type of vendor. This is true of small-scale noncommercial activity; personal servants, barbers (who in a developing economy typically have no fixed place of business), shoeshine boys. In particular countries other items, such as firewood, may be sold in similar fashion, and outright exemption becomes desirable.

Several types of services are rendered primarily to business firms with some incidental use by final consumers. If administrative considerations make taxation upon the basis of use impossible, as is often true, complete exclusion of the service from the tax is preferable. Freight transport and the services of bookkeeping and public accounting firms are examples.

It is often maintained—in developed as well as less developed economies—that for administrative reasons a sales tax should not apply to a commodity subject to a special excise or production tax. No general answer

4. For example, in Ghana the income elasticity of demand for imported food is estimated to be 1.6. *Ibid.,* p. 106.

to this question is possible. Exemption is not troublesome with a manufacturers sales tax. With a retail tax, if the product is sold at retail by many small, specialized vendors not selling other products, exemption may be preferable provided the commodity is clearly distinguishable from others. This may be true of cigarettes if sold primarily by peddlers a cigarette at a time, or of soft drinks. But if the commodities are widely sold by taxpaying vendors also selling taxable commodities, good administration requires that the sales tax apply despite the separate excise. To do otherwise complicates application and encourages evasion. If the combined burden is regarded as excessive, the excise can be reduced to give an acceptable overall figure. Application of two separate taxes may appear to be administratively wasteful but in fact may be more economical than freeing the commodities from the general tax. Exclusion of commodities subject to excises is particularly troublesome with a value-added tax.

Ease of Exemption

Several considerations influence the ability to exempt particular commodities or services. An important one is the degree of specialization of the sellers; if they typically sell only the goods exempted, few complications arise and overall administration is simplified. This is often the situation with service establishments, which frequently provide only one service, in contrast to sellers of commodities, who often handle a number of types. A second factor is the ease with which the commodity can be distinguished from taxable ones. Unprocessed food, for example, is a much more clearly definable category than is inexpensive clothing. Third, the nature of the tax influences the ability to exempt. On the whole, exemption is simplest with the manufacturers sales tax, since manufacturers are more specialized than wholesalers or retailers, are larger on the average (in most countries), and keep better records. Exemption is more difficult with the retail tax, even in highly developed countries, since retailers often carry a wide range of commodities and have less adequate record systems. In fact, exemption may become more difficult as development continues if retailers become less and less specialized with the growth of department stores and supermarkets. The value-added tax is the most troublesome form because of the multiple impact of the tax and the tax credit feature, but some exemptions, such as those of particular services and unprocessed food, are feasible.

The Approach to the Taxation of Services

There is no general justification for confining sales taxes to physical commodities, as noted above. But many services are not suitable for inclusion. One group of services is rendered primarily to business firms, and taxation of these is particularly objectionable, as we have seen. A second major set of services, in terms of total expenditure, is one that governments seek to encourage, the use in part being related to misfortune: medical, dental, hospital, and related activities. Legal services are rendered primarily to business firms and are related to the maintenance of justice. Educational services are clearly inappropriate for taxation in a developing economy. Another set is difficult to reach administratively: the work of personal servants, for example. Since many of these services are rendered by separate establishments, exclusion causes little administrative difficulty. Accordingly, the usual approach (except in Germany and some of the Latin American countries) is to tax only specified classes of services, typically those provided by commercial, as distinguished from professional, establishments and rendered primarily to individual consumers rather than business firms. Examples include repair services of all types, admissions and entertainment, hotels, laundry and dry cleaning, and barber and beauty parlor service. By contrast, all commodities are usually taxed except those specifically exempted.

Use of the value-added tax alters somewhat the optimal approach to the taxation of services provided to business firms. If these services are not taxed, sales of produced goods to these service establishments must be specifically exempted or a system of carry-through of estimated tax must be provided; otherwise, some tax will enter into the cost of the final product. Suppose, for example, that freight transport is not subject to tax, while equipment and supplies purchased by the transport firms are taxable, with no credit allowed to the users of the service. The result will be a tax element in the freight charge. But if a firm buys its own transport equipment and supplies, it will receive credit for the value-added tax paid on the purchases. Accordingly this action is encouraged, with discrimination against public transport. There are several possible solutions:

1. Apply the tax to the transport service and allow the users a credit for the tax as on other taxable goods and services purchased. A difficulty is that some of the services may be provided to nontaxpaying business users—farmers, for example.

2. Allow transport firms a tax credit on all purchases subject to tax. This approach is satisfactory for railroads and large motor transport firms and similar firms in other service fields. It is not satisfactory administratively with the numerous small transport operators found in many countries.

3. Allow the users of the service to deduct a specified percentage of the cost as constituting tax (as with purchases from farmers in the Netherlands). But this approach is arbitrary and is likely to discriminate among various types of service firms.

The choice rests between the first and second approaches on the basis of the particular circumstances.

DIFFERENTIATION OF RATES

Many developing countries regard the use of several tax rates instead of one as essential. Not infrequently three or four rates are employed: a reduced rate on seminecessities, the basic rate, and luxury and superluxury rates. Some of the states of India carry differentiation much further, with a large number of rates on various classes of goods.[5] The Chilean turnover tax has more than twenty rates.

Differentiation has two primary goals: to improve the equity of the tax and to discourage the consumption of luxury goods. Equity considerations have usually been dominant, the higher rates being designed to place a relatively greater burden on the upper income groups. The argument for such a policy is much stronger in developing economies than it is in more highly developed ones, which can rely on income taxation for distributional goals. Income taxes are often not highly effective in developing countries, partly for administrative reasons. They are particularly ineffective on wealthy landowners whose income is difficult to verify and whose consumption is high relative to money income. Only progressive consumption taxes may be effective in placing a more appropriate tax on such groups. Moreover, in many developing economies expenditure patterns are much more stratified by income group than they are in the developed countries, commodities used at the higher income levels not being consumed in the lower, and vice versa. Accordingly, rate differentiation produces much more satisfactory results in terms of the objectives in developing countries than in developed ones, with less discrimination on the basis of preference.

Nevertheless, on equity grounds, considerable doubt can be raised about the policy. A recent study in Chile concluded that differentiation contributed little to progressivity of the tax, although food exemption largely eliminated regressivity.[6] As shown in table 7–1, studies of distributional patterns in Colombia and the Philippines, despite sharp differentiation (especially in the latter), show little progressivity—although admittedly the distribution might have been worse without differentiation. Data of limited scope for India, related to expenditures, not income, show more progressivity (table 7–2). Studies of this type are of questionable significance even in the developed countries and have even less meaning in the less developed ones because of lack of adequate data of consumer spending and information about shifting.

In most countries differentiation has been introduced on the basis of estimates of "luxuriousness" of the various commodities without efforts to ascertain consumer expenditure patterns on the high-rate commodities at

5. There are 15 rates in Mysore, 11 in Andhra Pradesh, 8 in Madras. Only 4 states have fewer than 6 rates.
6. Gillis, "Sales Taxation," p. 112.

TABLE 7–1. SALES TAX AS PERCENTAGE OF INCOME AT VARIOUS INCOME LEVELS

Colombia		Philippines, 1960	
Monthly Income, Pesos	1965 Sales Tax as % of Average Income[1]	Annual Income Class, Pesos	Sales Tax as % of Income
100– 199	.91	Under 500	2.47
200– 299	.96	500 – 599	2.04
300– 399	.79	1,000–1,499	1.74
400– 499	.81	1,500–1,999	1.84
500– 599	.69	2,000–2,999	1.76
600– 699	.78	3,000–3,999	2.10
700– 799	.77	4,000–4,999	1.40
800– 899	.75	5,000–5,999	1.48
900– 999	.67	6,000–6,999	1.40
1,000–1,499	.60	7,000–7,999	1.36
1,500 and over	na	8,000–8,999	1.27
		9,000–9,999	1.68
		10,000 and over	.96
		Overall	1.73

Source: Colombia: J. Levin, "The Effects of Economic Development on the Base of a Sales Tax: A Case Study of Colombia," *International Monetary Fund Staff Papers*, 15 (March 1968), 30–99. Philippines: Joint Legislative-Executive Tax Commission, *Tax Burden by Income Class in the Philippines* (Manila, 1964), pp. 83, 89.

[1] Coverage of 1965 tax, based upon 1953 family expenditure data.

various income levels. An exception is the Philippines, where a *Survey of Essentiality of Commodities* resulted in a revision of classifications. While such studies produce limited data and observations, they are presumably better than pure guesswork.

While differentiation may be considered to improve overall distributional patterns, it inevitably creates discrimination on the basis of relative preferences as does any unequal treatment of consumer expenditures. The seriousness of this inequity must be balanced against the gains from the change in overall patterns.

The second goal is to discourage luxury consumption to free resources for economic development by lessening allocation to the production of luxury goods, and particularly to discourage consumption of imported goods or goods with a high import content. If persons continue to buy the taxed goods, substantial purchasing power is absorbed that they cannot use on other forms of consumer spending; if the taxes cause substitution of other goods for the taxed ones, there may be a net benefit if the substitutes (perhaps personal service) have less import content. If the taxes cause a substitution of savings for consumption, economic development is aided directly so long as there is adequate investment demand.

There are without doubt potential desirable effects along the lines indicated. But there are difficulties as well. Aggregate demand must be maintained or the additional savings will create unemployment rather than more rapid growth. Persons may continue to acquire as many luxury goods

TABLE 7–2. SALES TAX AS PERCENTAGE OF
CONSUMER EXPENDITURE, INDIA, 1958–59

Monthly Household Expenditures (Rupees)	Sales Tax as % of Consumer Expenditure
1– 50	.7
51–100	1.0
101–150	1.2
151–300	1.3
301 and above	2.0

Source: India Department of Economic Affairs, *Incidence of Indirect Taxation 1958/59* (New Delhi, 1961).

as before, curtailing saving or purchase of other goods. Or they may shift to untaxed substitutes that have as high an import content as those otherwise purchased—foreign travel, for example, which is difficult though not impossible to tax. In some countries stimulation of private savings is difficult because of the lack of suitable means of keeping the savings without having the value eroded by inflation.

Regardless of the motives for differentiation, there are certain to be administrative problems that will lessen the effectiveness of the operation of the tax. The problems are similar to those created by exemptions but will be quantitatively much more significant if the differentiation is extensive. Correct application of tax is made more difficult, an effect particularly serious in countries where clerks have only limited education. Record keeping becomes much more complex, as records of sales of various types of commodities are required. Endless questions will arise over the interpretation of the various rate categories. Commodities may be redesigned so that they will be classified in a lower rate group. Audit of records is made more difficult. Differentiation in itself paves the way for additional evasion by leading to misreporting the rate class, and the high luxury rates (for example, a top general rate of 50 percent in the Philippines) increase the pressure to evade. As some sellers evade, others must evade as well or be driven out of business. Pressure for smuggling is increased.

The administrative effects are not necessarily controlling, but they must be considered in establishing a rate differentiation policy. If they are ignored, the desired pattern of distribution will not be attained and the overall success of the tax will be reduced. Several policies are essential if differentiation is to be at all satisfactory:

1. The higher rates should be limited to commodities of high unit value, such as motor vehicles, to facilitate correct application of tax and effective control. This rule is imperative if differentiation is to be attempted at the retail level and is desirable at preretail levels.

2. Differentiation is facilitated if the vendors are relatively specialized firms. Various services, such as those of hotels and public utilities, can be subjected to higher rates with little administrative difficulty.

3. With commodities, differentiation is much easier at the manufacturing level than at the wholesale or retail levels because of better records and specialization.

4. The number of rate classes should be limited to a small number— two or three. Knowledge of expenditure patterns by commodity class is not adequate even in developed economies to permit precise refinements, and the greater the number of rates the greater the complications involved in the operation of the tax. Some governments, such as several of the Indian states, have carried differentiation to almost absurd degrees.

The value-added tax creates particular difficulties for differentiation because of the tax credit feature. This problem is sufficiently serious that with this form of tax, as with the retail tax, differentiation is likely to be more successful if it is provided by separate excise taxes at the manufacturing-importing level operated independently of the sales tax. Commodities so taxed must not be exempted from the value-added tax.

TAX TREATMENT OF IMPORTS AND EXPORTS

Under the theory that a sales tax is a consumption levy, the most commonly accepted approach to the foreign trade sector is to exclude exports from the tax, since they are consumed abroad, and to tax imported goods on the same basis as domestically produced goods. At given exchange rates, if exports are not freed of tax, domestic producers are placed at a disadvantage in foreign markets compared with firms in countries that do not impose equivalent taxes; and if imports are not taxed, foreign producers are given an artificial advantage over domestic producers. Were exchange rates free to move, the difference would not be nearly as great as might appear. If a country levied a sales tax that applied to exports and not to imported goods, the trade balance would become more unfavorable, the rate of exchange would fall, and equilibrium would be restored. But the introduction of artificial elements into import and export prices in the form of sales tax differentials may distort international economic activity generally, particularly when the tax components of prices vary among commodities. Therefore a convincing case can be made for the usual tax treatment.

Exclusion of exports creates no serious problems with a retail tax and a value-added tax through the retail level, since the tax applies to the final transaction. With the retail tax the taxable transaction is exempt, while with the value-added tax the exporter receives a refund of the cumulated amounts paid.[7] Exclusion is also possible with other single-stage taxes but with additional complications, since a good may be sold domestically on a taxable basis and later exported, making a refund necessary. Exclusion of correct amounts with a turnover tax is impossible. With any form of sales tax, failure to exclude all producers goods will leave some tax element in the export prices, to the disadvantage of exporters.

Retail sales taxes and value-added taxes through the retail level can be applied to most imported goods in the same fashion as to domestic goods. On imports by final consumers, the sales tax must be applied at importation, with some valuation problems but no serious issues of principle. With other single-stage taxes there is danger of nonuniform treatment, because the stage of importation in terms of functions performed may be different from that at which the tax applies on domestic goods and any adjustment may not be exact. The turnover tax inevitably favors imported over domestic goods since the latter pass through more taxable transactions.

A Common Market Area

So long as the sales taxes of the various countries in a common market area[8] (or states in a federal system) are compatible, no particular problems arise that differ from those with foreign trade generally, so long as customs frontiers are maintained. The destination principle can be utilized; exports to the other country or state are exempted and the tax is applied in the jurisdiction of final sale. Compatibility is greatest with value-added taxes through the retail level and with retail sales taxes; exports can be freed completely and the tax appropriately applied to imports. Manufacturers taxes and wholesale levies create more problems; the imported goods are likely to be overburdened when taxed at destination because some distribution margins will be included in the price, and administrative problems are troublesome. Turnover taxes are incompatible in a common market.

When fiscal frontiers are absent, as within a federal country and, perhaps ultimately, in common market areas, the destination principle is much more difficult to implement, even with retail taxes, since consumers are given an incentive to purchase from outside their state or country. Technically this problem can be solved by a use tax, making the purchaser liable for tax on out-of-jurisdiction purchases; but enforcement on many items is difficult, as experience in the United States has shown. Only by cooperation of the tax administrations of the various jurisdictions is enforcement pos-

---

7. Including the tax paid on producers goods, if the government so desires.

8. This question is examined in detail in Clara Sullivan, "Indirect Taxation and Goals of the European Economic Community," in C. S. Shoup, ed., *Fiscal Harmonization in Common Markets* (New York: Columbia University Press, 1967), 2, 1–102. See also Shoup, *Public Finance* (Chicago: Aldine, 1969), chaps. 8, 9.

sible, and even then at considerable cost. With preretail taxes the problem is much more troublesome, since a much larger percentage of the taxable transactions are interjurisdictional. Only a system of collection by the country of origin and transfer of revenue to the country of destination, as in the UDEAC countries of Africa, is workable. With retail levies, most interjurisdictional transactions are not taxable since the tax will apply at the final retail sale within the destination jurisdiction.

The fiscal frontier problem suggests the desirability of use of the origin principle in a common market, as is the ultimate goal in the European Economic Community and as is employed in part in India.[9] The tax would be collected by the country in which the vendor was located. With a retail tax the difference between the two principles would not be substantial. With value-added taxes the total revenue would be allocated automatically among the various jurisdictions in which the firms were located on the basis of respective values added. With manufacturers taxes and wholesale taxes the system would be less satisfactory, because the locations of the vendors differ so much from those of the final vendors and consumers. The areas in which manufacturing concentrates would receive such disproportionate amounts of the total revenue that in most common markets the rule would be intolerable. The origin principle also encounters difficulties when rates are different in the various jurisdictions. Manufacturers located in low-rate areas have an artificial advantage (unless the higher tax is offset by equivalent higher benefits to industry), causing industry and factors to migrate.

SHIFTING AND SEPARATE QUOTATION OF TAX

Sales taxes are usually designed to be consumption levies.[10] The actual distributional pattern depends, of course, on the extent to which they are reflected in higher prices of consumption goods relative to factor prices. Typically—except with the retail sales taxes in some of the states and the Canadian provinces—tax legislation is silent on the question of shifting, the presumption being that the taxes will be reflected in higher prices. Where price controls are in effect, the maximum prices are universally readjusted to reflect the taxes.

Governments differ in their attitude toward the concealment of the tax element in the price. Separate quotation of the tax is mandatory in the value-added tax with the usual tax credit form, except on the sale to the final consumer. Separate quotation is required in the Canadian provinces

9. Interstate sales are subject to a federal tax collected by the state of origin, which retains the revenue.

10. An exception has been the turnover tax in Ceylon; governmental instructions to vendors state that "the firms should not pass the tax on, as the rate is low." *Report of the Taxation Inquiry Committee* (Colombo, Ceylon: Government Press, 1968).

and in many states of the United States (and separate quotation is followed, although not mandatory, in the other states). It is also found in Honduras and Costa Rica, although exceptions are allowed, and with service elements of sales tax structures in Chile and some other countries. Still other countries using the retail tax either do not require separate quotation (and in practice it is rarely found in them, as in Ireland), or actually prohibit it (as does Norway). Separate quotation is neither required by law nor followed in practice with preretail sales taxes. Business firms strongly dislike separate quotation with these levies because it requires additional work and reveals distribution margins to customers.

With the forms of tax for which it is feasible, the question of separate identification of the tax from the price must be resolved on the basis of political philosophy. On the one hand, separate quotation emphasizes the tax payment, keeping persons aware of the taxes that they are paying, and thus has strong philosophical justification from the standpoint of democratic principles. Separate quotation also strengthens vendors' attitudes that they are tax collectors rather than taxpayers and may lessen evasion. From the standpoint of the intention to distribute the taxes in relation to consumer spending, separate quotation has the merit of facilitating uniform treatment of the tax by all competing vendors, a prime requirement for immediate and complete shifting. With concealment of the tax and readjustment of prices, a firm's adjustments are hidden from competitors and complete shifting is less likely.[11] In a developing economy strongly committed to speeding economic development and maintaining reasonable price stability, separate quotation of the tax may strengthen opposition to the tax and interfere with the attainment of the generally accepted goals. If the electorate can be kept fully informed of the merits of various alternatives in light of the objectives, separate quotation is obviously meritorious. When they cannot be, as in most developing economies, the justification for concealment is stronger though not necessarily conclusive.

EXACT MEASURE OF THE TAX

The measure of the tax should, in terms of the objectives, be the amount actually paid for the commodity or service by the purchaser. This rule, however, is not as clear-cut as it might appear to be.

1. The tax itself. Traditionally in parts of continental Europe, the amount collected to compensate for the tax is subject to tax; accordingly, with the assumption of shifting, a 10 percent tax actually constitutes a rate

---

11. Mandatory separate quotation was introduced in the United States primarily at the request of the retail vendors to lessen the danger of failure to shift. In Canada separate quotation is primarily the result of constitutional provisions.

of 11.1 percent of the price net of tax, for example.[12] There is nothing inherently objectionable about this rule, but it does complicate shifting of the tax and gives a somewhat misleading picture of the actual levy. All in all, application of the tax to sales net of the amount of the tax is simpler. If vendors keep records only of gross sales including tax they can easily factor out the tax element.

2. *Trade-in allowances.* Since the tax is designed to be distributed in relation to consumer expenditures, the price net of trade-ins is a more accurate measure than the gross price. But the base of the tax is larger if the gross price is used, much of the additional revenue comes from the higher income groups, and operation of the tax is simplified.

3. *Used goods.* One of the most troublesome questions relates to used goods, particularly with the value-added tax. A commodity is taxed and goes to a final user; it is then sold to a dealer, who resells it. Should the tax apply again? In terms of the objectives of the tax, if the price is higher than it would have been had the tax not applied to the original sale, there is justification for not taxing the good again. But excluding used goods is very troublesome administratively, since the vendor must distinguish between them and new goods and has an opportunity for evasion by reporting new goods as used goods. For this reason it is advisable to make used goods taxable as well as new ones. Equivalently, with the value-added tax, credit would not be given on the sale of used goods for tax paid on their purchase when new.

4. *Subsidiary services.* In virtually all countries, many services are not taxable when rendered separately. These same services, however, may be rendered in conjunction with the sale of a commodity, with a single price covering both elements. Freight is a primary example. Even when countries tax a number of services, freight is usually excluded, for reasons noted earlier in the chapter. Accordingly, freight should not be taxed when rendered in conjunction with the taxable sale of a good. Exclusion is not difficult if the freight is charged separately, but it is troublesome if a single charge is made. Accordingly the former rule is usual, even though it encourages the policy of separate charges. Exclusion of the freight charge does produce some distortions with the manufacturers levy and wholesale taxes. One of these is to encourage distribution from the factory instead of a warehouse closer to the consumer, since the freight from the factory to the warehouse becomes an element in the price but the freight on the shipment to the customer is not taxed. But no other rule is feasible. With a

12. Price before tax was $10. The firm raises the price to $11 to shift the tax forward. But the tax therefore becomes $1.10, not $1, as it applies to the entire gross price. The vendor may now add another 10 cents. With full shifting the tax will be $1.111111111 . . . ., or 11.1 percent of the original selling price of $10.

value-added tax and freight charges taxable and deductible, the freight charge can be included whether separately quoted or not.

5. *Customs duties and excises.* When tax is applied at time of importation, the duty-paid value is the appropriate basis and is almost universally used, for duty-paid figure is the measure of domestic expenditures on the good. The same is true of domestic excises; if the excise of a particular level is regarded as justifiable, there is no significant objection to applying a sales tax to the price that includes the excise, and the revenue is greater at a given rate.

8.

Administration

No tax can be successful in attaining the desired objectives unless it is collected with reasonable effectiveness. This rule is particularly true with sales, excise, and customs duties. Evasion or avoidance results not only in loss of revenue and inequity but also in serious competitive disturbances and interference with efficient organization of the economy. If some firms are able to evade the tax and others are not, the former receive an artificial advantage and, if the tax rate is high enough, may force the other firms out of business, even though the latter are more efficient. Firms that did not initially seek to evade are compelled to do so. This result is not encountered with income taxes, at least to the same degree, since competitive relationships are not so directly affected.

HAZARDS OF EVASION

In part as a result of this competitive pressure, unless some minimum level of compliance is attained there is danger of a gradual destruction of the revenue source. This level is difficult to define, but 80 percent may be regarded as an absolute minimum and 90 to 95 percent as a more reasonable one. As compliance falls to lower levels, more and more firms are forced to evade and officials are virtually compelled to tolerate this evasion. If most firms are underreporting sales by 50 percent, few inspectors would seek to compel one particular firm to report all of its sales. To do so is obviously unfair and will lead to strong complaints and possible liquidation of the firm. So the inspectors come to tolerate substantial understatement, and compliance levels off at perhaps 40 or 50 percent—a range widely quoted in India, the Philippines, and Chile, for example—and may fall still lower. But such general understatement prevents uniformity. Different inspectors will tolerate different figures, and some firms not checked for long periods will tend to reduce the percentage more and more, while others,

159

especially larger foreign-owned corporate enterprises, may be reluctant to underreport. The consequence is that these firms—probably the most efficient ones—are seriously hampered in growth and the smaller, inefficient firms are aided. A situation of general understatement encourages extortion, since an inspector can demand full compliance with the law unless a bribe is paid.

Since revenue is far below potential, the government must either use a higher rate or add other taxes. Thus the nominal rate may become extremely high, and the higher it goes the greater becomes the pressure, even necessity, of evading. Many governments have added more and more taxes instead of seeking to enforce effectively those they have; and the number of taxes acceptable under usual standards is, after all, rather limited. Thus less acceptable taxes are used, and compliance and administrative costs are increased. Some countries seek to tax every possible act or object to the detriment of effective operation of the overall structure.

The minimum standard of compliance must be obtained at a cost and use of resources regarded as tolerable. Administrative and accounting personnel are scarce in many developing economies; it is therefore necessary to hold their use for tax collection to an acceptable minimum. It is not possible to define maximum tolerable collection costs, but 2 percent of revenue may be used as a rough rule of thumb except perhaps in short periods for a strong drive to raise compliance standards drastically. Typical cost figures are included in table 8–1 at the end of this chapter. If reasonable compliance cannot be obtained at tolerable cost, the tax structure and administrative standards must be reconsidered.

SOURCES OF EVASION

Evasion of sales taxes arises through several routes:

1. Smuggling. In a developing country, a substantial portion of sales tax revenue may be collected at the time of importation. If the goods are smuggled into the country and do not subsequently pass through the hands of a registered vendor, sales taxes as well as customs duties are evaded.

2. Failure of firms to register and pay tax. This may be prevalent in a country with large numbers of small firms subject to tax, but it is relatively easy to detect with a strong effort.

3. Underreporting of gross sales. Vendors may not record all sales or any sales at all, or they may keep two sets of records, one for their own purposes and one for tax auditors.

4. Recording of taxable sales as exempt sales. This is a major source of evasion, and probably the chief type in more developed countries.

5. With differentiated rates, the misclassification of goods into lower rate classes.

6. Use for taxable purposes of goods purchased for exempt purposes, particularly purchases for resale. With a retail tax, this is a major source of assessment. The goods may be used for personal purposes or for taxable purposes by the firm.

Obstacles to Effective Administration

A serious obstacle to effective administration is the shortage of trained personnel. It is much more severe in some countries, such as those of tropical Africa, than in other areas, such as Latin America. Few skills are more scarce in tropical Africa than training in accountancy, and the university systems have not been designed to provide such training. The same situation is found with administrative personnel generally. Many countries find that tax administration, particularly of customs, excise, and sales taxes, is not particularly appealing. The opportunities for trained personnel are so great that it is difficult for the tax administration to obtain and retain first-rate personnel. As a consequence, such countries often must rely on expatriates for a period of years after independence.

The quality and contribution of expatriates vary greatly. Some have little knowledge of the country's conditions and seek to implement precisely the policies and procedures of their home country, with possible disastrous results. Others have had long experience in developing areas and are able to make significant contributions to effective tax operation as well as to train their successors in the standards of effective administration. But given their goals, these countries must give high priority to training personnel for the higher positions to replace the expatriates. The number of persons required is often small in terms of the government's overall need, but they may be of key importance in attaining development goals.

A related problem is the lack of trained accountants in business firms to keep satisfactory records of sales and purchases. Proprietors of smaller businesses not only are unfamiliar with record keeping but often are illiterate. It is difficult for them to ascertain their tax liability correctly even if they wish to do so, and auditing them is more complex. This problem can be exaggerated; often much of a country's total sales are made by large commercial firms, which are relatively easy to control. But the problem is nevertheless significant. It is complicated in some areas by nationality and language differences. The businessmen in a country may be of foreign origin and keep records in a language that auditors cannot read. Asian traders in various parts of Africa and Chinese in parts of Southeast Asia are examples.

A third obstacle is the tradition of tax evasion that has developed in many parts of the world, but apparently with particular severity in South and Southeast Asia. Business firms feel little responsibility for financing government, and the attitude of escaping as much tax as possible is wide-spread. This attitude is frequently associated with a tradition of passing money under the table to tax inspectors to sanction underpayment and with hostility between vendor and inspector.[1] These features are found to some extent in all countries, but they are particularly serious in many developing parts of the world. The attitudes are not confined to taxation alone but permeate all aspects of economic life. In some countries the attitude was fostered by a reaction to colonialism; the taxes were regarded as instruments of the colonial power and therefore a legitimate object of evasion. The attitude developed in other countries over long periods of dictatorship when taxes were obviously used primarily for the dictator's benefit.[2] The attitudes unfortunately carry on after independence and the restoration of democracy.

A final obstacle is the nature of governmental personnel policy in the field of tax administration. Employees may be selected on a political patronage basis rather than for their qualifications. Even more commonly, salaries are inadequate to attract and retain the type of personnel required. One consequence is moonlighting—inspectors serving as tax accountants for business firms during their off hours—with inevitable conflicts of interest. Low salaries may make bribery inevitable. The picture varies widely among the developing countries. Some of the British Commonwealth countries have sought to continue the high administrative standards that were established in colonial days, and some Latin American countries have greatly improved the quality of personnel, salaries, and the prestige of tax administration generally. But in many areas much remains to be done.

REQUIREMENTS FOR EFFECTIVE OPERATION

There are several major requirements for effective tax administration:

1. An effective staff of adequate size and qualifications, with suitable training programs and salary, adequate controls to ensure efficiency and prevent bribery, and development of a cooperative attitude between inspectors and vendors.

2. A suitable electronic data processing (EDP) system. Small countries do not require elaborate installations, but virtually any country today can advantageously make effective use of some type of EDP equipment, particularly for sales and income taxes. Despite the desire to avoid overly capital intensive methods in developing countries, the advantages of EDP are so great in the tax field that its use is clearly warranted. Specifically,

---

1. J. K. Godha, "The Working and Administration of Sales Tax in Bombay/Maharashtra State" (Ph.D. diss., University of Poona, 1969), pp. 847–48.

2. In the Philippines the attitude apparently developed as a reaction to Japanese occupation during World War II.

EDP equipment can be used to address returns, to record tax payments and provide internal balances, to check arithmetic, to ascertain delinquent accounts and address delinquency notices, and ultimately to aid in identifying accounts that are most likely to require audit.

3. Simplicity of tax structure, as stressed in earlier chapters. This requirement is frequently disregarded. Stress on other objectives, purely political influences, and lack of adequate understanding result in such features as numerous ill-defined exemptions and many different rates that preclude the possibility of effective administration. This is a major problem in India.

4. The establishment of simple, well-defined, effective procedures and suitable forms. The technique of assessment of tax by the revenue office after returns are filed in place of initial self-assessment is time-consuming and almost useless. Tax return forms should be as simple as possible, as should be the procedure for filing. Requirements for filing returns in person, for numerous copies, and for notarization create cost, nuisance, and irritation and interfere with effective operation of the taxes. So do refusal to accept bank checks in payment or to accept payment when returns are filed. In India, for example, payment must be made to specified banks and the receipt then filed with the return. Many of these procedures are obsolete carry-overs from the past. They are particularly objectionable in the sales tax field, in which the vendor is essentially a tax collector for the government. Another limitation in some countries is the inadequacy of the mail system.

5. An adequate yet equitable system of penalties that is used effectively. Low penalties are ineffective, while excessively high ones are rarely applied by administrators or courts and create ill will when they are.

6. Speedy and adequate control of delinquents.

7. An effective check upon the accuracy of returns through an audit program.

Several of the major questions require further attention.

Taxpayer Identification and Classification

With all sales and excise taxes, the initial step in operation is the registration of all vendors subject to the tax. Registration forms record the information necessary for effective administration. One important item is the nature of the business, which is required for classification by type of activity. This classification, in turn, serves as a basis for giving the firm information, selection for audit, and other purposes. Each firm must be issued a registration number, preferably the same one used for income tax and other purposes. Use of a single tax roll facilitates the comparison of data on different returns. With most forms of tax, initial checks must be made block by block to ensure that all firms are registered, and they must be repeated occasionally. With a retail sales tax, the vendor can be required to display his registration certificate in a conspicuous place so that registration can be checked quickly. At the same time care must be taken to avoid registering firms that should not be registered. These are likely to be ones with no tax liability, which often do not file returns and appear on delinquent lists. The registration may give them the privilege of buying tax free when they should not be doing so.

From the registration lists is prepared a master file of taxpayers, coded by type of business, location, and other relevant factors. The list must be continuously updated as new firms register and others are liquidated. Delinquency cannot be ascertained accurately without a correct master list. A major defect in some countries has been a failure to maintain any master roll of taxpayers.

THE SYSTEM OF RETURNS

Simplicity in return forms is essential in minimizing the cost and difficulty of compliance and in lessening delinquency. Many jurisdictions find data processing cards satisfactory and easy to sort and file; if the cards are prepunched they can be sorted and filed for storage by account number. If more information is required, paper returns may be necessary. The usual practice is to store paper returns by batch number after the information on them has been keypunched, but some jurisdictions prefer to store them in each vendor's file, which requires filing noncard returns by hand. This requires a substantial amount of effort and increases the danger of misfiling. Once the information from the returns is keypunched, the punch cards serve as the basic document for processing. With modern computers the information is transferred from cards to magnetic tape and then to memory cells to facilitate retrieval of information or is introduced directly into storage without the use of cards. Direct access systems are particularly advantageous because they allow immediate retrieval of all information on a given account, but they are more expensive than smaller jurisdictions may regard as necessary.

The optimal interval for tax returns is not easily defined. Monthly periods minimize the danger of loss of tax revenue if a business fails, avoid the accumulation of large tax liabilities that cannot be met, and speed the flow of revenue to the government. But this interval necessitates much more paper work than do longer periods; the problem is particularly serious for vendors who owe little tax. One solution is to place larger firms on a monthly basis to ensure revenue flow and the smaller firms on a quarterly interval, although the latter are the most likely to encounter difficulty from an accumulation of tax liability. A security bond system coupled with quarterly returns may prove most satisfactory. An alternative approach, used in some Latin American countries, is to require detailed returns only annually but payments monthly, based either on estimates of sales or upon the tax liability of the previous year. Any of these systems, if properly designed, can be made to function effectively, the choice depending on the circumstances in the particular country and the type of tax. If there are only a few large taxpayers, for example, a uniform monthly return system creates no particular hardship.

Periodic distribution of return forms to taxpayers is helpful in reducing delinquency, since they are a reminder that the time for filing is approaching, and the procedure avoids the nuisance of obtaining the forms by other means. Ideally, the forms should be addressed by EDP equipment and mailed to the vendors each month or other filing period. But the inadequacy of the postal systems in many countries makes this impossible, and other means of distribution, such as the issuance of the next month's form when that of the current month is filed, become necessary.

CONTROL OF DELINQUENCY

Failure to file returns and pay tax is a chronic problem with any sales tax and to a much less extent with the usual excise taxes. The percentage of vendors not filing on the due date ranges typically from 3 percent to as high as 15 percent in the states of the United States; the median figure is 7 percent.[3] The Canadian figures have been comparable in those provinces with effective delinquency control (Ontario, for example, shows 8 percent) but rise to 20 to 33 percent in the eastern provinces, which have not had effective control.[4] The Chilean turnover tax has a delinquency rate of nearly 25 percent. In all jurisdictions, most of the delinquents are small firms, and thus the lag in revenue from delinquency is much less than the figures suggest. A number of delinquent returns—often one-fourth or more—are received within two weeks of the due date, and first notices usually will bring in about half of those remaining. Investigations show that many delinquents owe no tax and have simply not bothered to file and that an additional number have gone out of business.

Delinquents are identified in each return interval by matching the returns against the master file. This is now typically done by EDP equipment. A card is punched for each return as it comes in and the data is transferred to magnetic tape, which is matched with the master tape to produce a delinquency tape. This tape is used to address the delinquency notices and

3. J. F. Due, *State Sales Tax Administration* (Chicago: Public Administration Service, 1963), p. 86, and "The New State Sales Taxes 1961–68," *National Tax Journal,* 21 (September 1968), 266–87.

4. J. F. Due, *Provinical Sales Taxes,* rev. ed. (Toronto: Canadian Tax Foundation, 1964), p. 138.

produce a printout of delinquents for control purposes. For the delinquency list to be accurate, the master tape must be kept current; failure to do so— as often occurs—results in the listing as delinquents of firms that have gone out of business.

Minimization of delinquency is facilitated by several procedures. One is careful screening of registrants to eliminate those that will owe little or no tax; such firms are likely to become delinquent, yet tracking them down produces no revenue. Some revision of the tax structure with exemption of very small firms may greatly reduce the number of delinquents. Firms that owe little tax but are financially responsible (for example, manufacturers under a retail sales tax with few taxable sales) may be placed on an annual return basis, perhaps with a security bond.

Effective control also requires rapid preparation of delinquency lists and contact of delinquents. The due date should be set at a reasonable interval after the end of the tax period—20 to 30 days, with the actual cut-off date a few days later. The common 15-day figure is inadequate for many firms. The delinquency lists should be prepared within 30 days after the filing date; some states are able to do so within 10 days. While transport conditions in many countries make this impossible, the six-month period sometimes encountered is far too long by any standard. Prompt action is necessary to discourage future delays in filing and to avoid losses in revenue owing to failure of the firms. Many of the firms not filing are those in financial difficulties, and if payment is not received quickly the government may not be able to collect.

The procedures for contact with delinquents vary.[5] A common method, widely used in the states, is to send an initial notice by mail, with a follow-up notice if payment is not received within two weeks. Alternatively, the first step may be a visit by a field inspector who seeks to ascertain why the payment has not been made and to collect. When an initial mail notice is employed, an inspector visits after one or two notices have failed to bring results. These letters and contacts usually bring payment or reveal that the firm owes no tax or is out of business. A hard core—often not more than 1 percent of the accounts, with frequent repeaters—remains.

Policies for dealing with these hard-core delinquents vary according to the legal traditions of the country and historical precedent. Legal action to enforce payment through seizure of property is common. Threat of revocation of registration certificates often proves to be an effective device, with actual revocation if necessary. If a firm continues to operate after revocation, criminal charges are filed. Some jurisdictions find that initial criminal prosecution is the most effective device, but others discover that public prosecutors and courts are often reluctant to become instruments of tax

5. Due, *Sales Tax Administration*, chap. 4.

enforcement except in the event of deliberate fraud. The exact method is less important than the prompt use of some technique that forces payment or liquidation of business by the chronic hard-core delinquent.

A significant element in the prevention of delinquency is the use of automatic penalties for failure to file on time, with application of interest to unpaid amounts. Such a penalty requires no court action but is automatically added to the amount of tax due if payment is not made on time. Ten percent is a common figure. Unfortunately many delinquents owe so little tax that a percentage penalty is not an adequate deterrent; accordingly a minimum cash penalty is highly important. An interest charge somewhat in excess of the market rate is also desirable to prevent firms from deliberately using tax collections as working capital, particularly in countries in which small firms find it difficult to obtain capital. Empowering the revenue department to waive penalties (but never interest) is also desirable to take care of hardship cases. If penalties are too high, administrators are reluctant to apply them and the system loses its effectiveness.

AUDIT

Checks on the accuracy of returns are essential for effective operation of any tax, direct or indirect, but are particularly significant for sales taxes, which vendors are presumably collecting from their customers. Vendors inevitably have an incentive to underreport total sales and overstate the portion consisting of exempt transactions. Unless they are checked periodically—and know that they will be checked—they will not only give themselves the benefit of the doubt on any question but will also become careless in recording information, and some will deliberately understate tax liability. Much of the gain from effective audit takes the form of more accurate subsequent reporting of tax, both by firms that have been audited and by those that have learned of audit assessments on other firms.

The first step is the selection of accounts for audit, particularly if all accounts are not to be checked in a given year. Selection is frequently based in part on type of business, since auditors learn that underreporting is much more common in some areas than in others. Office review of returns may suggest ones that are out of line with others in the same field, although few jurisdictions find it worthwhile to give all returns a close audit. Leads are frequently important. Auditors unearth information in one audit that suggests that other firms are incorrectly reporting tax. More and more jurisdictions are experimenting with EDP selection of audit prospects. Computers calculate norms from returns for typical gross sales, ratio of exempt to gross sales, and other features and compare them with the actual returns of each firm. This approach cannot yet make a perfect selection, but it calls attention to many returns that show good promise for audit.

Finally, a certain amount of well-publicized random selection is helpful in making firms more careful.

Audit procedures vary with the exact type of sales tax and the nature of the business. One step is to check the procedures for applying and recording the tax and to sample invoices, journals, and other records. Another is to examine sales records to make sure that the tax is being applied to all taxable sales and that taxable sales are not being recorded as exempt sales. One of the most significant comparisons is between reported sales and purchases adjusted by typical markups. With wholesale, retail, and value-added taxes, and even with a manufacturers tax, the keys to control are the records of purchases and the sales records of suppliers, to be checked if there is doubt about the completeness of purchase records. There are occasional problems with vendors who have no records at all or say they have none. The revenue department must be given the power to make assessments against such firms based on any reasonable criteria, such as size of establishment and number of employees. If these assessments are made relatively high, the vendor will often suddenly discover records that provide more accurate figures, or at least he will keep records in the future.

When audit assessments are made, review by senior auditors is necessary to ensure that the field auditors are not seeking to extort money from the vendors. Normally no penalties should be applied to audit assessments except upon evidence of fraud, but interest should be charged, since the firm has had use of the money.

The extent of audit coverage varies with the type of tax. With an excise levy of limited coverage, or with a manufacturers tax affecting a few hundred firms, an annual audit is feasible. Audits of these firms often require substantial time and effort, but nevertheless a relatively small staff can reach all the firms during a year. With this procedure, the problems of audit selection are avoided. But with retail, value-added, or turnover taxes, which affect many more vendors, governments rarely seek to audit each firm annually. A reasonable standard for such a tax is to audit each firm every three years. Many U.S. states and Canadian provinces do not approach this figure, some auditing fewer than 5 percent a year.[6] This coverage is far too low even in developed countries; it will allow mass evasion in less developed ones.

The potential audit coverage depends, of course, upon the number of auditors available. With a manufacturers tax, one auditor per 100 vendors may be regarded as a minimum; with a retail tax, involving a much less complex audit on the whole, one auditor per 300 accounts—given the need for good audit coverage in a developing economy—is reasonable, one per 500 a minimum.

6. *Ibid.*, chap. 5.

The general experience is that auditors—up to certain limits—will yield far more in direct additional tax revenue than they cost. In addition, there are significant indirect gains as a result of improved future compliance. The optimal expenditure on auditing is difficult to define precisely because of the indirect gains. Certainly it should be extended to and somewhat beyond the point at which the marginal direct revenue gain equals the direct marginal cost of the audit activity.

A major issue in many countries is the integration of sales and income tax audits. A single staff auditing both taxes at the same time would appear to offer significant economies, minimize the waste of time of the taxpaying firms, and facilitate cross checks of information reported on the two returns. But experience in various countries, for example Chile, has not been entirely happy with this form of integration. Auditors tend to stress the income tax rather than the sales tax, apparently in part because they find it more interesting and, in Chile, less complex. The stress in the audit of the two taxes is different, as are the criteria for selection of accounts to audit. If the audit is integrated, it is essential that the income tax not be allowed to dominate either the selection of accounts or procedures. Some auditors must be trained for specialized work with more complicated sales tax accounts. A separate sales tax audit staff, coordinating its work with that of the income tax unit, appears to be advantageous despite the apparent loss in efficiency.

The Forfait System

In France, Italy, and to some extent India and other countries, a *forfait* or *abonnement* system is employed for small firms—about a million in France under the value-added tax. These firms are not required to maintain detailed records. At the beginning of the year, by negotiation between the vendor and the inspector, a figure is agreed upon for taxable sales during the period and the tax is paid on this amount. The figure is determined on the basis of total purchases or (in Italy) an estimate of actual sales during the previous year. The system—largely forced on the governments by the recalcitrance of the politically powerful small retailers—simplifies the task for both vendor and government, but at the expense of any reasonable chance of payment of the correct amount. The system is particularly open to bribery, and there are many rumors in Italy that this is common. However poor actual assessment may be on some of the smaller vendors, any effort at assessment is to be preferred to the arbitrary charges of the *forfait* system—one particularly objectionable with the value-added tax.

SPECIAL DEVICES TO AID ENFORCEMENT

Various countries have considered and some have introduced special devices to aid enforcement, particularly of the portion of the tax at the retail level.

The Sorteo or Lottery System

The best known of these systems is the Chilean *sorteo,* also used in Bolivia. It is a type of lottery designed to increase the effectiveness of sales tax enforcement. The basic operation in Chile is as follows:

Each vendor is required to issue a receipt (in Spanish, *boleta*) to retail customers. Vendors must keep books of blank *boletas,* numbered consecutively and stamped with a pressure type of stamp by the local revenue office. The original of the *boleta* is issued to the customer, the duplicate is kept by the vendor.

On the eighth of each month, the lottery selects a thousand firms and a particular day of the preceding month as a basis for the drawing. The selected vendors are required to send their duplicate *boletas* for all sales of that day to the revenue service. Each of these boletas is numbered and the prize winners are selected by lottery. There are a number of small prizes and a few very large ones. To gain an award the customer must present his copy of the prize-winning *boleta.*

The intent is, of course, to ensure that vendors issue receipts on all transactions, and the receipts provide a basis for audit.

As this system now operates there are many undesirable features.[7] Retailers are put to substantial work to get their *boleta* pads stamped. There is no relation between the size of the purchase and the prize awarded. Failure to publicize the names of large winners lessens the effectiveness. There is also serious doubt that the system actually aids enforcement.[8] It works only if customers insist on receipts; many do not. On larger purchases customers are frequently offered the alternative of a lower price with no receipt. The percentage of prize money claimed is very low: only 7 percent in 1966, for example. The cost of administering the program and issuing prizes is substantial, 1 percent of the revenue being allocated for the purpose. Even if the customers do demand *boletas,* proper payment of the tax is not ensured. There is no assurance that the amounts written on the *boletas* are correct, and there is no easy way to check them. The mere issuance of receipts is not particularly important for successful sales tax operation.

Coupons or Stamps

The Chilean system could be improved, in the fashion outlined by A. G. Hart,[9] through sales tax coupons to be issued by the vendors in amounts related to the amounts of the purchases. These coupons would be

7. A. G. Hart, *An Integrated System of Tax Information* (New York: Columbia University School of International Affairs, 1967).

8. Chilean revenue officials regard the *sorteo* as an emergency substitute for an effective audit program and of limited value.

9. *Tax Information.*

TABLE 8–1. COSTS OF SALES TAX COLLECTION

India

State	Year	Type of Tax	Costs of Collection as % of Revenue
Maharashtra	1968–69	Collection at 3 stages	1.29
Gujarat	1966–67	Collection at 3 stages	1.5
West Bengal	1958–59	Primarily retail	1.3
Kerala	1958–59	Turnover	2.2
Orissa	1958–59	Retail	2.5
Mysore	1958–59	Turnover	2.8
Madras	1958–59	Turnover	3.45
Madhya Pradesh	1958–59	Primarily wholesale	4.3
Andhra Pradesh	1958–59	Turnover	4.5
Rajasthan	1967–68	Wholesale	2.9

Source: J. K. Godha, *The Working and Administration of Sales Tax in Bombay/Maharashtra State.*

United States (retail sales taxes)

State	Year	Costs of Administration as % of Revenue
Indiana	1967	0.77
Idaho	1966	1.2
California	1967–68	1.19
Illinois	1967	1.33
Michigan	1968	0.5
Tennessee	1969	1.13
Maryland	1969	.89
24-state average	1959–60	1.18

Source: State revenue department reports; J. F. Due, *State Sales Tax Administration* (Chicago: Public Administration Service, 1963).

Canada

Province	Year	Costs of Administration as % of Revenue
Federal (manufac- turers sales tax)	1966	.4
Provincial (retail sales taxes)		
British Columbia	1963	0.5
Newfoundland	1963	1.0
New Brunswick	1963	1.88
Nova Scotia	1963	1.5
Ontario	1963	1.7
Saskatchewan	1963	0.7

Source: J. F. Due, *Provincial Sales Taxes* (Toronto: Canadian Tax Foundation, 1964).

Chile (turnover tax)	1965	1.17
Norway (retail)	1954	0.5

THE REPUBLIC OF UGANDA.

TREASURY DEPARTMENT—MINISTRY OF FINANCE.

THE INTRODUCTION OF SALES TAX.

EXPLANATORY NOTES FOR THE GUIDANCE OF TAXPAYERS.

Notice to all Taxpayers.

The 1968 Finance Bill repealed the Consumer Goods Tax Act, 1965, as from midnight June 18th, 1968, and from the same date, there came into force a sales tax on certain goods and services.

2. These notes cover only the salient points of the Act and Regulations and are not intended to cover in detail the provisions of the law. For any additional detailed information as to how the tax affects your particular business you should refer to the Act and Regulations or seek guidance from the Treasury Department, Inland Revenue Division, P.O. Box 7023, Kampala. Telephone: Kampala 54857.

Imposition of Tax.

3. The tax is imposed at different rates on goods and services. In some cases the rates are specific and in other cases they are *ad valorem*. As a general rule a rate of 10 per cent has been imposed on prices of specified services and on the wholesale price of goods. However, on less luxurious items such as salt, hurricane lamps, bicycles, sewing machines, *etc.*, the rate applied will be 5 per cent *ad valorem*. Luxury goods such as private motor-cars, wines and spirits, beer, cigarettes, carpets, electric and gas domestic appliances, musical instruments and photographic equipment, *etc.*, will carry a rate higher than 10 per cent *ad valorem*. For example, wines and spirits and beers will be taxed the level of 20 per cent; cars will carry a rate ranging from 15 per cent to 40 per cent depending on engine capacity; electric and gas domestic appliances will be taxed at the rate of 15 per cent. Light diesel will carry a specific rate of 40cts. per gallon and kerosene of 15cts. per gallon, heavy diesel oil will be exempt.

4. As a general rule, to ensure control and facilitate collection of the tax, Government purchases of goods and services will not be exempt. In certain few cases, in order to avoid administration difficulties of collection from numerous small manufacturers, the tax will be collected on raw materials or components or semi-manufactured goods, such as leather, timber, flour, paper and cloth to avoid collection from shoe-makers, carpenters, bakeries, printers and book-binders and tailors. In such cases, in order to maintain the rate that would be applicable to the finished product, the applied rate is raised proportionately from say 10 per cent to 15 per cent or 20 per cent.

5. More details may be obtained from the Schedules Nos. 1 to 6 to the Act or from your nearest Customs and Excise Office or from the Inland Revenue Division, Treasury Department, P.O. Box 7023, Kampala. Telephone: Kampala 54857.

Basis for Tax.

6. Wherever the rate is an *ad valorem* rate, it is imposed on the wholesale price of the goods and will be computed as fixed by the Commissioner.

At present the wholesale price is to be taken as the manufacturers' price including excise or any other tax plus an uplift of 10 per cent. The tax on services is imposed on the price of such service in the normal run of business.

Marking of Goods.

7. All goods have to be marked. For goods in general the marking is by delivery note issued by the Inland Revenue Division, Treasury Department. Find enclosed a supply of twenty-five delivery notes receipt of which you are requested to confirm on attached Form ST 02. *All* goods leaving your premises have to be accompanied by a properly completed delivery note.

Any goods not accompanied by a delivery note(s) will be seized and are subject to forfeiture.

Returns and Payment of Tax.

8. Enclosed herewith is a supply of Sales Tax report forms. You are required to file monthly returns together with the remittance of tax due. If no sales of goods are made or services supplied during the month it is important that you file a report with the Inland Revenue Division for that particular month with the indication "No Tax Due" written across the face of the report, so as to avoid receipt of notice of default or estimated assessment for the month in question.

Remittance must be made by cheque made payable to Uganda Administration and crossed "A/c Payee Only—Not Negotiable".

Details of Enterprise.

9 (a) You are requested to supply all details relevant to your business (on Form ST 03 attached) by return mail and no later than the 10th of July, 1968.

(b) You are also requested to inform the Inland Revenue Division immediately of any new product or service you intend to supply on the same form.

Right of Appeal.

10. You have the right to appeal to the Appeals Tribunal whenever you feel aggrieved by any of the decisions of the Commissioner regarding classification or estimation of the tax due.

Exemptions.

11. Some transactions are exempt from tax such as sales to "Authorised Traders" and diplomats of foreign countries. Certain exemptions are provided for, for export transactions. For information and provisions relating to transactions exempt from tax, the procedure to be followed and the type of evidence required to support such exemptions consult the Inland Revenue Division Office at Udyam House Buildings (1st Floor), P.O., Box 7023, Kampala. Telephone: Kampala 54857.

Records.

12. Keep on file at your principal place of business duplicate copies of your returns, delivery notes, "Authorised Traders' " declarations (if your status is such) and accurate records and accounts of all transactions containing sufficient information to indicate whether the correct amount of tax has been computed and paid. Records and information in support of all exemptions and adjustments must also be kept. All records shall be maintained for a period of seven years from the date the tax was paid. Such records should be available for inspection and audit by inspectors of the Inland Revenue Division, Treasury Department.

numbered and used directly as a basis for the lottery, the prize being related to the size of the purchase. Under the old Ohio stamp system, comparable to the green stamp merchandising device used in the United States, customers were given stamps at the time of purchase with a face value equal to the amount of the tax. These were redeemable at a small fraction of their face value by charitable and religious organizations. There was no lottery feature, but one could easily have been included by numbering the stamps. This approach could presumably increase the appeal of the stamps to the customer, and if they were issued in correct denominations they would give an indication of total sales.[10]

While the Hart system would be greatly superior to the present Chilean *sorteo,* there is real doubt about the effectiveness or desirability of any such system. The Ohio technique proved to be expensive and ineffective and after long efforts by the state tax administration was finally eliminated by the legislature. Any such system involves considerable cost and nuisance to vendors in handling of stamps and, in the Chilean system, in stamping *boletas.* Many customers are not interested in coupons or receipts. More and more, even in the least developed countries, receipts are merely cash register slips, which are not useful for audit. The greatest danger of such a system is that it diverts attention from an effective audit program, which is the key to successful operation of the tax. A country comes to rely on a "gadget," while expenditure of equivalent money on tax auditors would produce far greater results. If the *sorteo* or coupon system could be used in conjunction with effective auditing, it would not be dangerous (merely costly) and might contribute some net gain.

INFORMATION AND INTERPRETATION

Regardless of the exact legal basis of sales and excise taxes, the vendors are in fact essentially tax collectors for the government. Accordingly, the government has a strong responsibility to provide adequate, understandable information to facilitate the vendors' task. The old legal doctrine that ignorance is no excuse does not justify a failure to provide adequate information. When a tax is introduced or changed, information should be widely disseminated through newspapers, trade associations, trade journals, and direct distribution of literature to the vendors—hand delivered if necessary. Informational visits by revenue personnel to places of business and local conferences for vendors are particularly helpful. Tax inspectors should also visit new vendors to give them adequate information. The bulletin issued when the Uganda sales tax was established is reproduced on p. 172.

10. The Ohio system also involved prepayment of tax: the vendors paid tax by purchasing the stamps.

Not only should information be readily available, but it should be in clearly understandable language, rather than obscure legal terminology. Some countries, including Canada, have been seriously deficient in this requirement.

If vendors are to understand the tax, the tax structure itself must be reasonably simple. The basic difficulty with the sales tax in many countries is complexity—numerous rate categories and special rules and exceptions. Providing simple information is impossible. The sales taxes of the Indian states are classic examples. There are numerous exemptions, a wide variety of rates, and many special rules for particular circumstances. Clear, simple information is difficult to provide. As a result, a profession of sales tax practitioners has developed. Now recognized by law and subjected to some regulation, they are hired by many vendors to fill out their sales tax returns. Sales Tax Practitioners Journals have been initiated in various states. With simple laws and clear information, such activity would be unnecessary.

Regardless of the adequacy and clarity of published material, questions of interpretation are certain to arise. A system for providing immediate and final answers to the vendors' questions is imperative, since if vendors fail to collect the tax properly, they will not be able to recoup any subsequent tax liability imposed upon them. The situation is thus completely different from that of income taxation.

COSTS OF COLLECTION

Data on costs of collecting sales taxes are not available for most countries, and where available they are not entirely comparable. Sales taxes are often collected in conjunction with other taxes, and the allocation of common costs is arbitrary. Governments differ in their allocation of general departmental overhead to particular taxes. Furthermore, the collection costs expressed as percentages of revenue depend in part on the tax rate; expenditures are not likely to rise in proportion to rate increases. A final note of warning is necessary: low cost may be evidence of inadequate administration rather than of efficiency. The figures in table 8–1 are given merely as samples of typical costs rather than as precise measures.

SUPPLEMENTARY REFERENCES

Centro Interamericano de Administradores Tributarios, Documentos y Actas de la Primera Asamblea General, 1967. (Cited throughout as *CIAT Papers*.) Buenos Aires: CIAT, 1968.

Due, J. F. *Provincial Sales Taxes*. Rev. ed. Toronto: Canadian Tax Foundation, 1964.

_____. *State Sales Tax Administration*. Chicago: Public Administration Service, 1963.

Godha, J. K. "The Working and Administration of Sales Tax in Bombay/ Maharashtra State." Ph.D. diss., University of Poona, 1969.

Gillis, S. M. "Sales Taxation in a Developing Economy: The Chilean Case." Ph.D. diss., University of Illinois, 1968.

Problems of Tax Administration in Latin America. Joint Tax Program, Organization of American States/International Development Bank/United Nations Economic Commission for Latin America. Baltimore: Johns Hopkins Press, 1965.

Singh, D. P. "Operation of the Sales Tax in Uttar Pradesh." Ph.D. diss., Benares Hindu University, 1964.

9.

Concluding Observations

The data of table 9–1, merged from earlier tables, summarize the major relationships in the use of indirect taxation:

1. Indirect taxes are major sources of revenue for the developing economies with very few exceptions[1] and with little decline in importance as per capita GNP rises, until it exceeds $500 per year. Application of the regression technique used by R. A. Musgrave in his *Fiscal Systems*[2] shows no significant correlation between GNP per capita and relative reliance on indirect taxation for countries below $500 GNP; even for the group under $850, correlation is not significant, though for the group between $500 and $850 as a whole, relative reliance is substantially less.[3]

The results of the analysis are as follows:

For countries with GNP under $850:

$$T_{id}/_T = e^{.03123} \quad Y_c^{-.1037} \qquad\qquad R^2: .08$$
$$(-2.247)$$

For countries with GNP under $500:

$$T_{id}/_T = e^{-.43545} \quad Y_c^{-.00410} \qquad\qquad R^2: .00$$
$$(-.08530)$$

T = tax revenue; T_{id} = indirect tax revenue (customs duties, excise taxes, sales taxes, miscellaneous, but not property taxes or export duties); Y_c = per capita GNP.

1. Of the 49 countries in the sample with GNP under $500, only Zambia obtains less than 40 percent of its revenue (21 percent) from indirect taxes, and only 1 of the 9 countries between $500 and $850 (Venezuela, 15 percent) receives less than 35 percent. These 2 countries obtain large revenues from mineral and oil production.
2. New Haven: Yale University Press, 1969.
3. Musgrave likewise found no correlation for the group under $600. He did find significant correlation for the entire group of countries including highly developed as well as developing.

TABLE 9-1. SUMMARY OF VARIOUS INDIRECT TAXES IN TAX STRUCTURES

Estimated Per Capita GNP, U.S. $	No. Countries Included	No. Countries Using Sales Tax	% Total Tax Revenue from:					% Total Indirect Taxes from:			
			All Indirect Taxes[2]	Customs Duties	Excise Taxes	Sales Taxes All	Sales Taxes Users	Customs Duties	Excises	Excises Plus Misc. Indirect Taxes	Sales Taxes
Under $101	20	13	68	35	15	14	21	52	24	28	20
$101–200	11	8	64	32	17	11	15	50	29	33	17
$201–500	19	9	64	33	20	8	16	51	29	36	13
$501–850	9	4	50	18	15	9	19	38	36	42	16
Over $850	15	14	32	4	15	13	14	12	47	(1)	41

Sources: Budget documents for the various countries; OECD, Border Tax Adjustments (Paris, 1968), for the over-$850 group.
[1] Miscellaneous included in other categories.
[2] Including miscellaneous indirect taxes.

For countries with GNP over $850, the relative reliance on indirect taxes is very much less.

2. Customs duties constitute the most important type of indirect tax in the developing countries, with no evident decline in importance until the $500 per capita GNP figure is reached. The high income countries show much less reliance on customs duties, with excise and sales taxes replacing customs as the major indirect sources.[4] For all countries of the group there is a significant correlation between the ratio of customs duties to total tax revenue and per capita GNP. There is no correlation for countries with GNP under $500.[5]

3. Excises yield roughly the same proportion of total tax revenues in both developing and highly developed countries (although rising with GNP as a percentage of indirect tax revenue).

4. Sales taxes have come to play a significant role at all levels of economic development:

a. They are now used in more than half the countries with GNP under $850, with no correlation of GNP and use, but with considerable variation in terms of colonial background. They are used, for example, in all former French West and Equatorial African countries but in only three British Commonwealth countries of Africa (Ghana, Uganda, and Tanzania).

b. They are used in all the highly developed countries except Japan.

c. They are a more important source of indirect tax revenue in the developed countries than in the developing, but they provide about the same percentage of total tax revenue of those countries that use the tax.[6] The higher contribution to indirect tax revenue is offset by the lower overall reliance on indirect taxation.

Use of sales taxes by the developing countries has been expanding rapidly, and the relative role is almost certain to grow.

4. Of the 15 countries in this group, only Switzerland obtains more than 20 percent of its indirect revenue from customs (30 percent), whereas of the 59 countries with GNP under $750, only Brazil receives less than 20 percent of its indirect tax revenues from customs.

5. See p. 55.

6. The Musgrave regression analysis shows no significant correlation between GNP and relative reliance on sales taxation:
Ratio of sales tax revenue to total tax revenue:
For all countries:

$$ST/T = e^{-2.283} \; Y_c^{.16820} \qquad\qquad R^2: .09$$
$$\phantom{ST/T = e^{-2.283} \; Y_c^{}} (2.016)$$

For countries with GNP under $500:

$$ST/T = e^{-2.1989} \; Y_c^{-.368} \qquad\qquad R^2: .07$$
$$\phantom{ST/T = e^{-2.1989} \; Y_c^{}} (1.416)$$

ST=sales tax revenue   T=total tax revenue.

OBJECTIVES OF INDIRECT TAXATION

The importance of indirect taxation generally in developing economies and the rapid growth of sales taxation suggest the need for careful framing of the levies in terms of the countries' goals, which typically are a rapid rate of increase in per capita real income, an acceptable pattern of income distribution, optimal use of resources, and price stability. Lack of an adequate general theory of economic development, of knowledge of the coefficients involved in the development process, and of required data for the solution of the model make it impossible to determine the optimal tax structure of any developing country precisely. But a general knowledge of the influences on and the requirements for development offer some general guidelines for examining particular structures.

More specifically, the indirect tax system offers possibilities for:

1. Increasing the rate of savings (S/Y) more than do other taxes.

2. Lessening the danger posed by other taxes of holding the rate of capital formation below its potential.

3. Reducing the incremental capital-output ratio (ICOR), increasing the rate of output obtainable from a given rate of capital formation. Indirect taxes increase the foreign exchange available for importation of capital goods and may be used to channel resources into domestic investment that is optimal in terms of development goals.

4. Reducing the resources, especially trained manpower, required for tax administration, freeing maximum resources for other uses.

5. Allowing greater total revenue to be collected by governments for developmental purposes. This is probably the most significant contribution.

6. Providing a distribution of the burden consistent with the attitudes of the contemporary society.

7. Altering consumption patterns to attain a pattern of resource allocation more satisfactory in light of development plans.

ATTAINMENT OF THE OBJECTIVES

Attainment of these objectives requires:

1. Relatively high taxes on goods regarded as luxuries and consumed primarily in the higher income levels. This requirement will increase the foreign exchange available for capital and other goods essential for development, since many of the goods are imported or have high import content. It may increase the S/Y ratio, and it will produce a more acceptable distributional pattern. Highly developed countries rely on direct taxes for distributional purposes; less developed countries must in part rely on indirect taxes for this purpose.

2. Avoidance of discrimination among individuals on the basis of their preferences except when warranted by other considerations.

3. Broad-based taxes on goods widely consumed, other than items essential for subsistence in the lower income levels and for health or other purposes necessary for development. Only such taxes will allow maximization of revenue from indirect taxes without adverse effects on development.

4. Avoidance of taxation of real investment spending, except possibly on a selective basis to discourage types of investment not regarded as significant for development or to prevent excessive capital intensivity created by artificial influences in the economy.

5. Establishment of the taxes in such a way as to minimize the resources required for compliance and administration yet provide reasonably complete collection. This rule requires that taxes be as simple as possible, that rate differentiation and exemptions be minimized subject to the need for fulfilling other requirements, that compliance with the taxes be made as easy as possible, and that the number of taxpayers be kept small.

6. Limitation of indirect tax rates to levels that will not interfere with incentives, or lead to political instability and rebellion.

7. Establishment of the tax structure in such a way as to avoid distorting effects—on the organization of production and on the choice of alternative inputs and methods of production—that will reduce efficiency in the use of resources. Decisions about the location of production and distribution functions at various levels of activity, relative labor and capital intensity, physical location of economic activity, and the like should not be altered by the tax structure except when specifically desired for development reasons. Taxes should not discourage imports and encourage import substitution except when this conforms with development goals, nor should they favor imports over domestic goods.

The requirements may be contradictory at times, and an optimal trade-off in terms of development goals should be sought.

OPTIMAL SYSTEMS

The system optimal for a particular country must conform with the objectives and circumstances of the country, that is, with an estimate of the coefficients of the relevant development model, and with the attitudes of the people toward various taxes. There is no universal indirect tax system optimal under all conditions. Nevertheless, certain generalizations are possible:

1. Customs duties

In the earliest years of development, with virtually no domestic production except subsistence agriculture and output of extractive industries for export, customs duties constitute the only suitable form of indirect taxation. Few countries in the world remain wholly in this situation today, but some have experienced so little development that duties appropriately remain the major type of indirect tax.

As domestic production develops, customs duties (but, initially, not necessarily collection of taxes at the time of importation) lose their advantages and their acceptability as the primary source of revenue. Import substitution reduces the revenue from the duties and their equity. At the same time duties artificially encourage import substitution beyond that desired for development. A failure to supplement or partly replace duties by domestic indirect taxes will not only sacrifice tax revenue but cause a serious decline in the efficiency of the use of resources, with inefficient small-scale enterprises developing in fields in which the country has a severe competitive disadvantage. Overlooking this danger has been a major error in fiscal planning in developing economies. This is not an argument against the use of tariffs for protection in conformity with the development plan; it is an argument against a revenue structure that leads to unwanted protection and import substitution.

2. Excises

A large portion of the customs revenue of developing countries is provided by three categories: tobacco products, alcoholic beverages, and motor fuel. Import substitution occurs with these commodities early in development, and excises provide a convenient, easily collectible means of preserving revenue from their consumption. Extension of excises much beyond these traditional items, however, quickly encounters problems of complexity of operation, discrimination on the basis of preferences, and potential excess burden. Excises also become progressively less effective in preventing unwanted import substitution created by the customs duties. They may, however, continue to serve a useful purpose in providing higher overall tax burden on selected commodities, especially consumer durables, more effectively than rate differentiation within a general levy.

3. Sales taxes

This type of tax offers the great advantage of blanket protection against undesired import substitution, since it typically applies equally to imported and domestic goods, with maximum revenue potential, yet much of the tax may be collected at customs on imported goods. The generality of the levy, applying to domestic as well as imported goods, prevents distorting effects. In addition, a sales tax is more productive of revenue at acceptable rates than excises and avoids their discrimination and possible excess burden. A sales tax is simpler and easier to operate than an extended system of excises. Properly designed in light of the circumstances, a sales tax can be introduced in relatively early years of economic development.

CHOICE OF FORM OF SALES TAX

X   The appropriate form and structure of a sales tax are of great importance for the attainment of the objectives. Because the tax is imposed directly upon business firms, it offers great potential for harm, particularly on efficiency in the use of resources, compared with taxes that are collected from individuals. Table 9–2 summarizes the relative merits of the various forms of sales taxes that were considered in previous chapters. The table is designed primarily to call attention to the various elements that must be considered in arriving at the most satisfactory answer in a particular situation.

As the table suggests, the optimal answer will depend upon the circumstances of the particular economy. Major determinants of the optimal choice include the following:

1. The importance of small noncommercial retailers. If these are very numerous and conduct most retailing activity, a retail tax or a value-added tax through the retail level is virtually impossible to operate. Even a retail tax with small retailers exempt is unsatisfactory, since the margins of so much retailing activity will escape the tax.

2. The number of small artisan producers and the nature of the channels for distributing their products. If artisans are numerous, a manufacturers sales tax is difficult to operate, with either substantial evasion or exemption of numerous firms and consequent discrimination. If the artisans sell directly to consumers or through equally small retailers, a substantial escape from a sales tax is inevitable regardless of the form of tax and the usefulness of a sales tax is reduced. But if most of the artisans' output passes through larger wholesalers or retailers, it will be reached by value-added, wholesale, or retail taxes.

3. The uniformity of wholesale channels. Extensive nonuniformity, particularly substantial backward integration by large retailers, complicates the operation of any preretail sales tax. This creates inequity, distortion of business methods, and the need for complex valuation adjustments.

4. The standards of education and record keeping at various levels of production and distribution.

5. The importance of imports in total consumption and the level of importing activity. Extensive importing makes the manufacturers tax relatively less satisfactory than it is in a country in which domestic manufacturing is more important, although a large portion of this tax can be collected at importation. If retailers carry on extensive importing, any preretail tax is less satisfactory than it is if most importing is carried on at the wholesale level.

6. Revenue to be collected. The larger the revenue, the greater are the advantages of the value-added tax, which spreads out the impact of the tax.

7. The desire for separate quotation of tax and price. This is feasible only with a retail tax or value-added tax carried through the retail level.

8. The importance attached to rate differentiation. Such differentiation is most difficult with the various retail taxes and the general value-added tax. If differentiation in the sales tax structure is regarded as imperative (because, for example, income taxes are not effectively progressive or the government wishes to discourage luxury consumption), it may be necessary to use a manufacturers tax either alone or as a part of a dual system. Alternatively, differentiation is possible if a retail tax is supplemented by excises at the import and production level.

9. The desire to exempt food. Unprocessed food can be exempted relatively easily under any tax; most of it will not be reached regardless of attempts to do so because it is sold through small outlets. Exemption of processed food and other consumption goods has the same significance as rate differentiation.

10. The desire to exclude producers goods. Any of the forms except the turnover tax can exempt major producers goods, but on the whole the value-added taxes provide the most suitable techniques for broader exclusion via the tax credit approach. Of the single-stage taxes, the ultimate use of goods is most easily determined at the retail level, but retailers are typically smaller and control of their correct application of the exclusion is more difficult.

11. Taxation of services. Since services are retail in nature, a retail tax, a dual system with a retail element, or a value-added tax through the retail level can incorporate services more easily than other forms, if this is desired.

12. Administrative competence. The quality of administrative personnel and procedures affects the degree of complexity possible in the sales tax structure. A value-added tax, for example, requires a larger number of trained personnel than a manufacturers tax.

13. Participation in a common market. Participation requires harmonization of sales taxes with those of the other countries. With the use of the destination principle, harmonization is possible with any levy except the turnover tax; with the origin principle a value-added tax is particularly advantageous.

14. Attitudes of various groups of taxpayers. If a particular group such as retailers is hostile and uncooperative toward a sales tax, it is important not to concentrate the burden upon it.

15. Federal system. In such a structure, it may be desirable for the central government to select a type that will allow use of another form by the subordinate units if they wish to employ it.

Selection of the optimal type and structure of a sales tax, therefore, requires the following information:

1. The revenue objectives.

2. The volume of imports of finished goods relative to the volume of domestic manufactures.

3. The typical conduct of importing—by manufacturer, wholesaler, or retailer.

4. The nature of domestic distribution channels: the importance of direct selling by manufacturers or importers; the relative importance of wholesalers.

5. The scale of manufacture: the relative importance of artisan versus large-scale manufacturing; the source of supply of artisans' materials; the distribution channels used by artisans.

6. The size of the typical wholesale establishment; the importance of dual wholesale-retail businesses.

7. The nature of retailing: the percentage of total business conducted by large-scale retailers; the nature of smaller establishments—the relative importance of shops, stalls, peddlers; family versus commercial operation of small businesses; the scale of operations of various types of service establishments.

8. The level of education and record keeping of artisans and small retailers.

9. The availability of audit personnel.

10. Consumption patterns by income group, particularly the patterns of the subsistence levels; the existence of commodities with high income elasticity of demand.

11. The existence or potential use of excise taxes primarily reaching the higher income groups; the effectiveness of the income tax in providing progressivity in the tax structure.

12. Attitudes of the public and business firms toward certain forms of sales taxes, where pronounced.

Complete data are not available even in developing economies on many of these items; all that can be hoped for is a reasonably accurate estimate.

GENERAL CONCLUSIONS ON FORM OF TAX

Analysis of various forms of sales tax and a review of experience with them suggests the following concluding observations relating to the form of sales tax in developing economies:

TABLE 9–2. EVALUATION OF

	1	2	3	4	5
Type of Tax	Number of Taxpayers	Required Tax Rate	Small Firms Problem	Problems of Determining Taxpaying Firms	Ease of Audit
Cascade C	Maximum (m+w+r)	Lowest	Largest number (with VA); X loses full tax	None, if universal and uniform	Poor on small firms
Value added through r level VA	Maximum (m+w+r)	Same as retail	Largest number (with C); X loses only margin	None, if uniform	Good cross check; tax paid by one firm is deduction for another
Value added through wholesale plus retail tax VA+R	Maximum (m+w+r)	Slightly lower than VA	Same as VA, C; X loses only margin	Must separate rs; problems with dual firms	Like VA except at r; audit of r difficult
Value added through wholesale VA-W	(m+w)	Same as W	Same as M, W	Must separate pre-r from r firms	Like M and W, plus cross-audit advantage
Manufacturers + retail M+R	Near maximum (m+r)	Less than VA; more than VA + R	Less of problem than M or R alone; lower rate; catch some at one or other	Must distinguish m and r	Records good at m level, poor at r
Manufacturers M	Least (m)	Highest	Depends on importance of artisans; high rate aggravates effect of X	Must separate m	Records of most firms good; little cross audit
Wholesale W	M + wholesalers (m+w)	M rate less effect of wholesale margins	Minimum, but some direct sales escape	Must separate w; dual firm problem, less serious than VA+R	Records better than R, probably poorer than M
Retail R	Near maximum (m+w+r)	W rate less effect of retail margins; lowest rate	Largest % of Tp small; X loses only margin	Must separate r; not serious	Many small accounts with poor records; cross check with suppliers possible
Retail on large rs, wholesale otherwise R−W	Less than R, more than W (m+w+(r−r_s))	Slightly higher than R	Small exempted, only margin lost; borderline firms	Must separate small and large r	Much easier than R; small firms exempt

cn = consumers   m = manufacturers   r = retailers   tp = taxpayers   w = wholesalers

VARIOUS FORMS OF SALES TAXES

6	7	8	9	10	11
Likelihood of Evasion	Distortion of Production and Distribution Organization	Ease of Adjustments in Prices to Avoid Distortion	Ease of Shifting	Likelihood of Pyramiding via Markups	Uniform Ratio of Tax to Consumer Spending
Much with small firms; many firms forced to evade as discriminated against	Maximum; integration in production and distribution	Impossible to adjust effectively	Difficult for small firms unable to integrate	Substantial from non-r portion	Maximum departure from uniformity as number of stages varies
Chief problem at r; high % of tax collected before r level; can collect part at importation	None, except if small r exempt; if so, as R tax	None needed	Should be complete unless firms consider net burden after tax credit	None if firms keep price separate from tax and don't apply markups to tax; otherwise some	Complete uniformity if shifting complete
Less than VA since less is collected at r level	Limited; m and w may try to push functions to r level; r may integrate back	Limited adjustments; uplift when r integrated back; discount on direct sales to cn	As VA, but more complete as more at r level	VA portion will be pyramided at r level; none on R portion	Uniformity high except from variation in r margins
Like W	Same as W	Same as W	As VA	Same as W	Same as W
Similar to VA + R tax; can collect portion at importation	m seek to push functions forward; less pressure than M tax as rate is lower	As with M tax but less urgent; lower rate	m portion like M tax, r complete; overall, better than M	On m portion; less than M tax since M rate lower	Partial loss on M portion through variation in w and r margins
Least, except for artisans and effects of high rate; can collect large portion at importation	Strong incentive to push functions to w level; check direct selling	Require discount on direct sales m to r or cn; may need uplift if functions to w	Should be complete except as uneven burden, and slippage at successive transfers	Maximum	High, except from variations in w and r margins
Probably more than M tax for small w; can collect large part at importation, more than M	r may seek to integrate back to m level	Uplift required when r buy from m at low price; uplift encounters strong resistance	As M tax; fewer transfers, less slippage	Somewhat less than M since only at r level; more than VA + R as whole tax at w level	More than M, less than VA + R
Maximum; can collect little at importation	None	None needed	Most likely to be complete	None	Complete uniformity
Less than R; collect little at importation	Exemption of small r favors them relative to large; not serious	None needed	Exemption of small firms may retard shifting somewhat	Very little	Uniform except less on purchases from small firms

X = exemption   Capital letter abbreviations = type of tax r_s = small retailers

TABLE 9–2

Type of Tax	12 Ability to Keep Tax Separate from Price	13 Ability to Exempt and Differentiate Rate	14 Ability to Exclude Producers Goods	15 Ability to Include Services	16 Uniformity of Tax on Domestic and Imported Goods
Cascade C	Difficult	Impossible to do effectively	Impossible by nature	Possible, but burden not uniform with goods	Nonuniformity; cannot compensate for tax; imports often favored
Value added through r level VA	Automatic if separation required at r level	Especially difficult at retail level	Easiest, as a tax credit system, except to nonregistered businesses	Satisfactory, but high rate on service firms, which are often small	Uniform
Value added through wholesale plus retail tax VA+R	Complete on R; Could do on VA but r would resist it	Relatively easy; confine to VA portion	Relatively easy at VA level, hard to exclude all from r tax	Easy, by including only in r tax	Uniform except minor problems on imports by r
Value added through wholesale VA-W	Same as W	Easier than VA, harder than W	Relatively easy except on sales to or by r	Requires separate tax	Same as W
Manufacturers + retail M+R	R portion no difficulty; resistance on M portion	Easy; do at M level, though results not exactly as desired	Like M (except lower rate) and R separately	Easy at r level	Same problems as M except rate lower
Manufacturers M	Difficult; w and r resist	Easiest since m are specialized, but results not as intended as margins vary	Can for major items, hard for minor items sold through r	Requires separate tax	Difficult, since manufacturing and import stages not identical; favors one or other
Wholesale W	Difficult but less than M; r resist	Easy but less so than M as less specialized	Somewhat easier than M since closer to actual use	Requires separate tax	Better than M as most goods taxed on sale instead of import
Retail R	No difficulty	Difficult; hard for r to apply various rates	Easier than M or W to determine use but hard to control on sales via r	Easy at r level	Uniform with minor problems on direct imports by cn, less than VA + R tax
Retail on large rs, wholesale otherwise R−W	No problem except on sales by small exempt firms	Same as R	Same as R	Same as R	Same as R

17	18	19	20	21	22
Ability to Exclude Tax from Exports	Compatibility with Common Market	Complexity to Taxpayers	General Acceptability	Experience Elsewhere	Significance for Inter-governmental Relations
Cannot do accurately as cannot ascertain tax paid	Incompatible, both imports and exports	Simple	None	Substantial, all bad	Nothing left for subordinate units
Complete; cumulated tax known	Complete	Somewhat complex at first	In many countries, partly as novelty	Little yet	Nothing for subordinate units
Complete as VA; minor problem if export follows sale to r	Complete	Much less than VA as r not covered; some problem in relation of two taxes	Likely better than VA, as not on r	Substantial in France, and R widespread	Can leave R to subordinate units
Same as W	Same as W	Easier than VA	Probably better than VA	Some	Leaves R for subordinate units
Satisfactory except same problems as M, but lower rate	Complete except M problem, but lower rate	Simple except for m price adjustments and relation of 2 taxes	Probably high	Substantial with each element	R left for subordinate units
Satisfactory; some refunds when goods sold by m, tax paid, and then exported	Satisfactory only if origin basis and uniform rates	Simple except for price adjustments	Usually is high; few taxpayers	Substantial not all entirely satisfactory	Leaves R to subordinate units but duplication
Satisfactory; easier than M because of fewer refunds	Complete; minor problem of M type but less	Simple except for uplift adjustment	Similar to M	Substantial, generally satisfactory	Leaves R to subordinate units but duplication
Complete	Complete under destination principle; shift revenue under origin principle	Simple	Often feared; many small r	Extensive in developed countries, some in others	Nothing for subordinate units; facilitate joint use; may fear high rate
Same as R	Same as R	Simpler than R; some problem for borderline r and w	Better than R	Considerable	Same as R

1. The turnover tax is so objectionable in so many ways and so hard to abandon once introduced that it should not be used under any circumstances.

2. The retail sales tax is the simplest and most satisfactory form of sales tax, in terms of economic effects, equity, and administration—if conditions of retailing permit its use. Unfortunately, they do not in a typical developing economy.

3. A retail sales tax with small retailers excluded, the tax applying on sales to them by their wholesale supplier, is almost as satisfactory as the general retail tax and is feasible in those developing countries in which a substantial portion of retailing is handled by commercial concerns.

4. A value-added tax extending through the retail level may be preferable to a retail tax when large revenues are to be collected, since the impact is not concentrated on retailers and the cross check in audit facilitates control. The tax shares the other advantages of the retail levy but is more complex.

5. If the retail tax can be used, it may be necessary to supplement it with a tax at the manufacturing level if differentiation of rates is regarded as imperative. Significant differentiation of rates at the retail level will make the tax almost unworkable.

6. When conditions in retailing prevent the levying of the tax at that level, the choice must be made among the manufacturers tax, wholesale tax, and value-added tax through the wholesale level. All have certain difficulties; all will function. The choice must be made in terms of the exact circums'ances.

STRUCTURAL AND ADMINISTRATIVE ASPECTS

Regardless of the exact form chosen, the precise structure and administrative organization are significant for the attainment of the objectives. A few major generalizations are summarized below:

1. Simplicity in the tax structure is all-important for effective operation in developing economies.

2. Exemption of producers goods—inputs of production units—is highly desirable as far as feasible, with a very few exceptions.

3. Exemption of consumption goods must be confined to a minimum number of clearly definable items used primarily in the lower income groups—unprocessed foods, drugs and medicines, and perhaps a few other items—if revenue is to be maximized, operation of the tax kept feasible, and undesirable effects of differential tax treatment avoided.

4. Rate differentiation, if provided within the sales tax structure, must be restricted to a few well-defined groups of commodities selected on the basis of a study of consumer expenditure patterns; goods with a high unit

value are preferable for the higher rates. The use of many rates has no justification in terms of goals and destroys the possibility of effective enforcement.

5. Consumer services provided by commercial establishments are suitable for inclusion within the tax base. Many services are not usually regarded as suitable for taxation.

6. Imported goods should be taxed on the same basis as domestic goods.

7. An effective administrative structure, with adequate personnel and salaries and adequate programs for identification and registry of taxpayers, control of delinquents, and effective audit, are essential if the tax is to attain its objectives.

8. An adequate system for informing vendors about the tax, and simplification of the tasks of collection and compliance, are important.

SUPPLEMENTARY REFERENCES

Due, J. F. *Sales Taxation.* London: Routledge & Kegan Paul, 1957.
Masoin, M., and Morselli, E., eds. *Impôts sur Transactions Transmissions et Chiffre D'Affaires.* Archives Internationales de Finances Publiques. Padua, CEDAM, 1959.
Report of the Taxation Enquiry Committee, vol. 3. New Delhi: Ministry of Finance, 1955.

Appendix

SOURCES OF DATA

Table A–1 provides data on various forms of indirect taxation by country, the data for the developing economies being taken from the latest available budget documents of the respective countries. As a consequence, the years are not identical. This disadvantage was regarded as more than offset by the advantages of placing the data on as current a basis as possible, particularly in view of the recent growth in sales taxes in a number of countries.

Data for approximately half the countries are for the fiscal year ending in 1968. For six (Liberia, Malawi, Lesotho, Sierra Leone, Brazil, and Ecuador) budget estimates for the 1969 fiscal year are used. Data for 1967 are used for Congo (Brazzaville), Chad, Togo, Cameroon, Rwanda, Iran, Paraguay, Honduras, Panama, the Dominican Republic, and Jamaica; 1966 data for Congo (Kinshasa), Niger, the Central African Republic, Gabon, Burundi, Surinam, Trinidad and Tobago, and Argentina; 1965 data appear for Greece, Spain, and Dahomey.

For the developed countries, the tabulation prepared by the Organization for Economic Cooperation and Development in the volume *Border Tax Adjustments and Tax Structures* (Paris, 1968), which uses 1965 data, was employed since for them there is relatively little change from year to year. Data for Canada, defective in the OECD volume, were corrected from Canadian Tax Foundation sources.

In the preparation of the percentages of tax revenue from various sources, an attempt was made to exclude nontax revenue from the total, although in some countries this is difficult to do with accuracy. Royalty from mining corporations was included in the total because these payments are so closely linked with taxes on the mining companies. Export and property taxes were not included in the category of indirect taxes.

Countries were classified on the basis of World Bank estimates of per capita GNP. The inadequacies in these figures are obvious, especially for countries with large subsistence sectors, but no alternative appeared to be better.

TABLE A–1. RELIANCE ON INDIRECT TAXATION BY COUNTRY

Country	Estimated Per Capita GNP, U.S.$	Percentage of Total Tax Revenue from				
		All Indirect Taxes	Customs Duties	Excise Taxes	Excise and Misc. Indirect Taxes	Sales Taxes
GNP $100 or less						
Rwanda	40	48	29	16	19	0
Burundi	50	57	31	16	22	4
Somalia	50	79	46	27	33	0
Upper Volta	50	67	22	11	12	33
Malawi	50	55	43	7	12	0
Congo (K)	60	55	15	19	21	19
Lesotho	60	60	52	8	8	0
Mali	60	68	15 (38)	7	8	45
Chad	70	55	21	..	20	14
Nepal	70	62	39	8	18	5
Dahomey	80	84	60	..	6	18
Niger	80	56	19 (40)	7	10	27
Tanzania	80	66	..	..	..	0
Kenya	90	60	36	17	24	0
Malagasy Rep.	90	76	29 (33)	13	26	21
Gambia	90	88	79	1	9	0
India	90	72	15	37	44	13
Pakistan	90	81	29	31	31	21
Uganda	100	58	34	20	23	1
Togo	100	85	35 (78)	..	..	50
Average		68	35	15	19	14 [21]
GNP $101–200						
Cameroons	110	67	.. (51)	..	5	11
Central African Rep.	110	63	.. (43)	..	4	16
Congo (B)	120	80	32 (43)	3	17	31
Mauretania	130	54	30 (39)	8	8	16
Sierra Leone	150	59	52	7	7	0
Ceylon	150	70	34	25	32	4
Philippines	160	76	25 (43)	16	20	31
Morocco	170	68	26	42	42	0
Zambia	180	21	8	11	13	0
Ecuador	190	76	59	10	16	1
Paraguay	200	75	21	34	44	10
Average		64	32	17	21	11 [15]
GNP $201–500						
Liberia	210	40	34	2	6	0
Senegal	210	69	34 (47)	14	15	20
Honduras	220	69	35	16	20	14
Ivory Coast	220	54	29 (41)		3	22
Ghana	230	49	24	11	14	10
Brazil	240	73	7	20	20	46
Dominican Rep.	250	79	50	25	29	0
Iran	250	73	46	27	27	0
Malaysia	280	56	45	11	11	0
Colombia	280	67	28	22	28	11
Guyana	300	59	40	13	19	0
Peru	320	63	29	..	..	..
Guatemala	320	80	21	44	59	0

TABLE A–1 (*continued*)

Country	Estimated Per Capita GNP, U.S.$	Percentage of Total Tax Revenue from				
		All Indirect Taxes	Customs Duties	Excise Taxes	Excise and Misc. Indirect Taxes	Sales Taxes
GNP $201-500 *cont.*						
Nicaragua	330	75	30	35	38	7
Surinam	360	67	47	11	20	0
Costa Rica	400	75	37	28	33	5
Gabon	400	61	48	..	4	9
Jamaica	460	62	29	26	33	0
Panama	500	54	21	18	33	0
Average		64	33	20	23	8 [16]
GNP $501–850						
Chile	510	54	13	6	11	30
South Africa	550	38	15	21	23	0
Singapore	570	65	36	24	29	0
Uruguay	570	83	..	..	..	..
Trinidad & Tobago	630	51	29	13	22	0
Spain	640	45	14	13	13	18
Greece	660	35	10	17	19	7
Argentina	780	65	21	20	26	19
Venezuela	850	15	6	8	9	0
Average		50	18	15	20	9 [19]
GNP over $850						
Japan	860	24	4	20	..	0
Italy	1,030	33	2	19	..	12
Austria	1,150	38	6	10	..	22
Netherlands	1,420	24	3	8	..	13
United Kingdom	1,620	35	2	27	..	6
Belgium	1,630	36	4	9	..	23
Germany	1,700	30	2	11	..	17
Norway	1,710	41	3	17	..	21
France	1,730	34	2	10	..	22
Denmark	1,830	45	3	32	..	10
Luxembourg	1,920	22	4	7	..	11
Canada	2,240	30	5	9	..	16
Switzerland	2,250	33	10	12	..	11
Sweden	2,270	31	3	17	..	11
United States	3,520	21	2	14	..	5
Average		32	4	15		13 [14]

Source: Budget documents for the various countries, except for GNP-over-$850 group, from Organization for Economic Cooperation and Development, *Border Tax Adjustments and Tax Structures in OECD Member Countries* (Paris: 1968). Figures are for latest year available 1965–69; 1968 in most instances.

Figures in parentheses in the Customs Duties column include both customs duties and sales taxes collected at customs.

Figures in brackets in the Sales Taxes column indicate the average for those countries using the tax.

Data for federal countries include both national and state governments.

Domestic indirect tax data for Peru and Uruguay are not segregated by type of tax.

.. indicates no separate data available; figures are included in those of another column.

Index